Mark Hodgkinson, the founder and editor of thetennis-space.com, first met Andy Murray when the Scot, then aged 17, was living in a bungalow at an academy outside Barcelona. A former tennis correspondent for the *Daily Telegraph*, Hodgkinson has written a short television feature about Wimbledon for the BBC, contributes to British *GQ*, and wrote the tennis features in the official programme for the London 2012 Olympics. During his time at the *Daily Telegraph*, he helped Judy Murray with the articles and columns which appeared under her name, in addition to his other role at the paper as Boris Becker's 'ghost'. Hodgkinson lives in south-west London with Amy and their daughters Molly and Rosie.

D0784220

Andy Murray

WIMBLEDON CHAMPION

MARK HODGKINSON

SIMON &
SCHUSTER

London · New York · Sydney · Toronto · New Delhi

A CBS COMPANY

First published in Great Britain by Simon & Schuster UK Ltd, 2012
This paperback edition published by Simon & Schuster UK Ltd, 2013
This revised paperback edition published by Simon & Schuster UK Ltd, 2013
A CBS COMPANY

Copyright © 2012, 2013 by Mark Hodgkinson

3 5 7 9 10 8 6 4

Simon & Schuster UK Ltd
1st Floor
222 Gray's Inn Road
London
WC1X 8HB

www.simonandschuster.co.uk

Simon & Schuster Australia, Sydney
Simon & Schuster India, New Delhi

A CIP catalogue for this book is available
from the British Library.

ISBN: 978-1-47113-274-2
Ebook ISBN: 978-1-47113-275-9

Typeset in the UK by M Rules
Printed and bound by CPI Group (UK) Ltd, Croydon, CR0 4YY

For Amy, Molly and Rosie

Contents

Boris Becker interview

'The day that Andy Murray won Wimbledon was the day he changed his life forever, and the day I thought, "It's not going to be long before we're calling him Sir Andy." Murray is on a different level now.

'It's a special moment for a player of any nationality to become Wimbledon champion, but even more so when you're competing on home soil and you're the first British man to hold that trophy for 77 years. Britain had been waiting a long time for this. In the minutes, hours and days after the final, I'm sure he was thinking "Wow!", but I believe it could take him a while to fully appreciate what he did on Centre Court. There will be a moment, maybe months later, when it hits him – perhaps that won't come until he returns to the All England Club in 2014 for the defending champion's privilege of opening the tournament by playing the first match on Centre Court. That's going to be a special time for Murray, returning as Wimbledon champion, the sort of moment that he's going to want to tell his children and grandchildren about.

'I was on Centre Court and I can tell you it was emotional

and it was incredibly tense. The atmosphere was electric. I was on court before the match started, and even then it was so loud that you could hardly hear yourself speak, and the crowd just got noisier as the match went on. Murray is the only one of the Big Four who has a home grand slam – Novak Djokovic, Rafa Nadal and Roger Federer don't – and in my opinion that's to Murray's advantage. Yes, Murray is under great pressure when competing at Wimbledon, but if you look at the tennis he has produced, he thrives under that pressure. If you ask any of the players in the locker-room, Wimbledon is the number one grand slam, the major they really want to win. There are many reasons for that – the history, the heritage, the Royal Box, the fact it's played on grass, and that the tournament has been in the same place for so long. For any tennis player, winning Wimbledon is the ultimate, and now Murray has joined the elite group of players who have got their names on that trophy.

'What would have happened if Murray had been broken as he served for his first Wimbledon title? That's a question we probably don't want to think about. Murray was facing a very strong Djokovic at that moment. But Murray got through that game – though, as he said afterwards in an interview on the court with Sue Barker, he couldn't quite remember that the final point ended with Djokovic hitting a backhand into the net. Murray demonstrated great mental and physical strength in those final moments, and it was a reward for all the hard work he had put in, including all those boot camps in Miami. It was a draining match – it was a straight-setter but it would have felt like a five-setter – and I'm sure Murray would have been very glad to have finished the match when he did. It was a historic moment when Murray won that final point, and I'm sure all of us who were there on Centre Court are pleased that we can look back on that day and say, "I was there."'

Prologue

So we were watching the final reel of what American commentators had been styling 'Wimble-geddon' – pretty much all fortnight, they had spoken as if this wasn't so much a tennis tournament as a big-budget grass-court disaster movie. The standard Hollywood apocalypse, just with the protagonists dressed all in white, and towelling themselves down every couple of minutes. On Centre Court, Andy Murray was serving to become – this is what it says on the trophy – The All England Lawn Tennis Club Single-Handed Champion of the World, and the spire of St Mary's Church in Wimbledon Village wasn't on fire, but perhaps it should have been. This was lawn tennis as re-imagined by James Cameron.

This had already been the most unpredictable of fortnights – Rafa Nadal had lost on day one, Roger Federer and Maria Sharapova had been eliminated on day three, and Serena Williams hadn't made it through to the business end of the tournament – and the 2013 Championships were to end with chaos and crisis in the mind of Andrew Barron Murray. When Murray, serving with a two-set and 5-4 lead, had reached 40-0 to give himself three championship points, there had been a voice in his head telling him, 'Andy, you're about to win Wimbledon. You're about to become the first British champion wearing short trousers, the first British man to lift the cup since Fred Perry's Dinosaur-Ball Age.' After all, that voice was saying to him, who loses their serve on grass from 40-0 up? Really, who would be so foolish as to do that?

The truth is, a grass-court disaster movie did not represent a new genre; every summer, the tournament is much more a 'Wimble-geddon' than it is garden-party tennis, which is how the Club sees it. This faux-Victorian idyll is more than capable of putting great rips and tears in a player's psyche; it's a place of hanging baskets, strawberries and panic-attacks. You only had to have been on Centre Court for the women's final, played a day earlier, to have had that confirmed as Germany's Sabine Lisicki, the 'Doris Becker' who had smiled all the way through the draw, wept at the baseline between serves. In a search for some inner peace on court, Novak Djokovic had been visiting a Buddhist temple on his days off during the tournament, and the Tennis Buddha saved the first of Murray's match points with a volley winner, and the second by ripping a backhand return beyond the Scot. For the third time, Murray was just a point away from winning the 'pinnacle of tennis'; he fired a backhand long – deuce. Then suddenly, after Murray's forehand landed in the net, advantage Djokovic, and no one, not even that voice in Murray's head, could be sure who would be going to the Champions' Dinner that evening.

Sure, Murray was two sets up. 'But Novak isn't buried until he's buried,' thought Murray's mother, Judy, and even then you wouldn't have known whether there was any more life left in the world number one. Djokovic had a reputation for being the zombie of the sport, someone who often produced his finest tennis when it looked as though he was beaten. A BBC montage had described the former champion as 'part man, part supreme being', as 'the man of steel', while Tomas Berdych, who had lost to Djokovic in the quarter-finals, wondered on Twitter whether the Serbian had 'DNA from space – a spaceman, congrats'. Murray knew from his own past experience what his rival was capable of; in the 2012 US Open final, the Serbian had come from two sets down to take the match to a fifth-set shoot-out.

And if Murray, having been so close to victory here at Wimbledon, were to lose his serve, there was a chance that he would never regain the poise and composure needed to win the match. There were 15,000 people watching Murray's every move in the broiling heat of Centre Court – Prime Minister David Cameron was in shirtsleeves on the front row of the Royal Box – and there wasn't a spare patch of grass to be had in front of the big screen on Henman Hill. Another 17 million had tuned in to BBC One; most were aware that Murray's entire Wimbledon career hung on the tenth game of the third set. Murray was stressed, he was panicked and he was excited, and he could hardly breathe. He was suffering like he had never suffered on a tennis court before (his coach, Ivan Lendl, had been wrong when he had suggested after the 2012

Wimbledon final that the Scot would never experience that sort of pressure again).

Murray's head was everywhere. Perhaps that was why, when Murray looked back on that sunny Sunday, he wouldn't have any clear memories of what had happened in that service game; it would just be a 12-minute, 14-point blur. So Murray was already the Olympic and US Open champion. But so what? That wasn't much help here. Neither was his sports psychologist. Nothing could have prepared him for this, a Djokovic breakpoint. They say that winning your first slam makes the rest of your tennis life much easier. Try telling that to Murray as he served for history.

No one loves discussing the psycho-soap-opera and life-lessons of a tennis match more than Boris Becker does, and the German thought Murray was showing his 'heart and soul' in the white heat of Centre Court. Another former Wimbledon champion, Dutchman Richard Krajicek, felt that, with the tenth game 'going back and forth, you just didn't know who was going to win the match, even though Andy was two sets up'. By his standards, Lendl had looked animated and agitated all afternoon – he was tense and fidgety, repeatedly up and out of his seat trying to shake the tension from his legs.

There were two possible endings to this disaster movie. One was that on the seventh day of the seventh month, Murray would become the first British male to win Wimbledon for 77 years, so ending the wait since Perry's victory in 1936. Murray has never been a superstitious sort, but there was no avoiding the sevens; he was making his seventh appearance in a grand slam final; he was hoping to prevent Djokovic from winning what would be his seventh major; and he wanted to become Britain's first singles champion of either sex since Virginia Wade won the ladies' title in 1977. Murray's first break of the match had come on his seventh breakpoint. There was another possible ending – a nasty one, this – that Murray would become known as The Nearly-Man Who Couldn't Convert Three Championship Points.

As someone had observed during the tournament, Centre Court is 'a nice place where horrible things happen'. Here is a Club fuelled on fear and adrenaline, not barley water and tea-cakes. The players would have passed a quote from Rudyard Kipling's 'If' as they walked into the court – 'If you can meet with triumph and disaster/And treat those two imposters just the same'. In the circumstances, the poem was laughable.

1

The Worst Tennis Nation on Earth

Jane Henman, as far as anyone has ever established, never received hate mail. Judy Murray's greatest crime, it is sometimes said, is that she is not Tim Henman's mother – prim, still, silent, and in the background. That she is not a Home Counties tennis mum, cloaked in Laura Ashley and upper-middle-class discretion. That she doesn't follow dress codes.

You occasionally still hear people talking about the incident, during the 2006 Wimbledon Championships, when Mrs Murray had difficulty gaining access to the Members' Enclosure at the All England Club because she was wearing jeans. Andy Murray had just won a third-round match against Andy Roddick, for what was then the biggest win of his career at the grand slams, but this, alas, was a breach of the no-denim rule. A couple of days later, Judy wrote a newspaper column about how Wimbledon was 'a bit too formal for me – I am not the floral dress type.'

When Jane Henman gave rare interviews to promote the range of ladies' tennis wear she had designed, she would decline to discuss her son's career – for the journalist getting her to acknowledge that Tim was actually her child, it must have felt like a significant victory. As much as she could, Jane Henman withdrew from Tim's story. However, there is no doubt that tennis parents are more visible than any other athletes' mothers and fathers; the television director knows where to find them, in their offspring's guest box beside the court, going through what Judy Murray has called a cross between seasickness and heart attack.

And Judy has never been one to sit on her hands or on her voice. There have been times when Murray has been playing in front of 15,000 spectators on Wimbledon's Centre Court and it has been possible for someone sitting on the other side of the grass to have heard his mother above the rest of the crowd. Ivan Lendl pleaded with her once: 'If you're going to sit behind me again, you're going to have to bring me ear-plugs.'

Judy Murray has been called the Tiger Mum of British tennis. She has also been called far worse. Opening the morning post is sometimes to wonder what vitriol the Royal Mail has delivered today, whether there will be another letter telling her what a bad mother she is. How awful she is. That they find her cries of 'C'monnnnn', or how she bares her teeth, shakes her fist or otherwise encourages her younger son when he is playing tennis matches, nothing less than repellent. This being tennis, the poison had often been typed up and printed out from the home computer (presumably after being spell-checked), or written carefully by hand; somehow the idea of hate mail on Smythson stationery seems more calculated and more offensive.

'I used to dread the letters. A lot of my self-image, like most mothers, is bound up in being a good parent. It was incredibly hurtful to get letters from people I didn't know – and who didn't know me – telling me that I was harming my kids,' Judy said in an interview with *The Times* during the Wimbledon fortnight. 'It shook my confidence. For a while, I tried to change. People seemed to be offended by my fist pumping when I watched Andy from the stands. So I became more demure, but it didn't feel natural. A friend said to me, "Why are you being so quiet?" So I went back to the way I was. It feels much better. I just hope people can accept me for who I am.'

It is not as if tennis had never seen a strong mother before. Gloria Connors would urge little Jimmy 'to play like a crazed animal', and 'to knock the ball down my throat, and he learned to do this because he found out that if I had the chance I would knock it down his'. Ivan Lendl's mother, Olga, was fierce. When Ivan was a boy, the story goes that Olga would strike him with her left hand if he talked back, until she broke her wristwatch with one of the blows, and she then had to remember to hit him with her right. An old issue of *Sports Illustrated* magazine tells the tale of Ivan's initial refusal to eat his carrots and peas; Olga set a timer for ten minutes and left the room – he knew then to clear his plate.

Those two were truly tennis matriarchs. And yet it can sometimes feel as though Judy Murray, who never tried to turn Murray into a street-hustler of a tennis player, and who certainly never struck her son, has become the most controversial mother in the sport's history. Perhaps that is because Connors and Lendl were playing in a gentler age, before the invention of 'trolls' and the internet message-board. To scroll through the comments beneath an article about Judy is to be shocked by the anger. 'I know I'm not hugely popular,' she has said. You would think, from the reaction she gets, that she was in the same nightmare parenting premier league as Jelena Dokic's father, Damir, who once threatened to assassinate the Australian ambassador to Serbia with a grenade-launcher. Or Jim Pierce, Mary's father, whose rap-sheet included calling out during one of her matches, 'Go on, Mary, kill the bitch,' and punching her bodyguard. Ever since ladies started flashing their ankles at Victorian garden parties, British tennis has had its scandals and its controversies, but Andy Murray is surely the first player on the main tour to have found himself defending his mother from an opponent's verbal attack.

On one of the rare occasions that Murray spent a 90-second change of ends trash-talking with an opponent, it was because Juan Martin Del Potro, who was a year and a bit off winning the US Open, had brought Judy into the argument. Murray and the Argentine were playing a night match at the clay-court Rome Masters in 2008, and Murray was unhappy with Del Potro for not apologising after appearing to deliberately aim the ball at his head. Del Potro's response was to say that

Murray and his mother had not changed from the junior days, 'were always the same'; the South American seemed to be implying that he was still hearing too much of Judy.

Tennis does seated arguments better than any other sport, and the two young men sat there on their chairs, raging for a minute and a half. No one could recall Murray previously looking so angry on a tennis court, and the umpire asked him to calm down. 'I've had a lot of bad things said about me before, and that didn't really bother me. But I think when people start talking about your family, you're naturally not going to take that well. Someone saying something about your mother who is one of the nicest ladies you're ever going to meet? I don't think that's cool.'

Once Scotland's national coach, and now Britain's Fed Cup captain (the women's team competition), Judy has wondered whether there is sexism at play across the international tennis world. Richard Williams started plotting Venus and Serena's tennis lives before they were born – his wife was not sure whether she wanted any more children, but he, hoping to raise tennis champions, hid her birth-control pills. He taught them how to play the game, and he is still on the scene. People don't tell him to back off. Rafa Nadal has had only one coach, his uncle Toni, and the family is celebrated for its closeness ('Sicilian, just without the malice or guns,' said the writer who collaborated with him on his memoirs). Novak Djokovic's father, Srdjan, turned up at the US Open one year wearing a T-shirt with a large image of his son's face on the front, and he just about got away with it; had Judy tried the same trick, there would have been letters. Lots of neatly written, poisonous letters.

Does modern tennis have one rule for the males in players' families and another for the females? 'I think a lot of the problems were to do with my gender,' she has said. 'People seemed to have a problem with a mother pushing her sons. If I was a man, nobody would have batted an eyelid.'

It has never been properly explained how Judy is supposed to have pulled off this 'control freakery', what with her living in Scotland, her other commitments, and travelling to only a small number of tournaments a year. And with Murray living in England and spending most of the year out on the tennis road, either playing events or killing his lungs during training blocks in Miami. While Judy and Murray naturally still talk to each other about tennis, much of the time they have the conversations you would expect any mother and son to have. There are paparazzi shots on file of Judy shopping with Murray, with the pair carrying loo roll and a new ironing board; you can bet that they didn't fill the silences by breaking down Roger Federer's backhand.

Throughout the 2013 Championships, Judy stayed in one of the guest-rooms in her son's home in Oxshott in Surrey commuter-land; she had done the same during previous Wimbledons, believing that she could offer him some extra emotional support. That is not to say that Judy was in control-freak mode. 'The apron-strings stuff was always overdone. I was very involved in his tennis when he was young, but the idea that I spend my time ordering him around today is ridiculous. He is his own man. But he likes to have emotional support when the pressure is intense. He has a big team, but they are all employed by him,' she told *The Times*. 'It is sometimes easier to talk about your feelings and fears to your girlfriend or family than your coaching team, who are much older, and all male.'

Still, it would be wrong to imagine that their conversations were dominated by tennis; they were just as likely, if not more likely, to have been discussing *The Apprentice* as analysing first-serve percentages. Judy was also lending her support as a dog-walker; every morning after she, Murray and his girlfriend Kim Sears had had breakfast together, she would take the two Border Terriers, Maggie May and Rusty, out for a stroll. That allowed Murray to 'get his head together'.

The criticism has been wounding, no doubt, even though Judy, as a former tennis columnist for Scottish broadsheet the *Herald*, knows how the media game works. She was understandably unhappy when, during Wimbledon one summer, she picked up the newspaper she was writing for at the time, and saw that the front page was puffing a debate on the features pages about whether she was too pushy for her son's own good, how her tennis elbows were sharpened to a point that could take his opponents' eyes out. She didn't contribute many more columns for the paper after that.

When the former Wimbledon champion Boris Becker accused Judy of smothering Murray to the extent that she was potentially harming his chances of winning a grand slam title – in some quarters, this was reported as Becker calling him 'a mummy's boy' – she retorted that the German knew nothing about her family.

There is only one person who has divided opinion more sharply in British tennis than Andy Murray and that's his mother. For years, her critics have shouted so loudly that it has been tricky to hear much recognition and praise for the positive role she has played in British tennis. Of how she raised two boys from Dunblane in Stirlingshire – a part of the world where the climate is not conducive to playing tennis – who have gone on to play the sport at the highest level. You have Judy's permission to call her a pushy tennis mother, she once said, but only if you mean that she pushed for Andy and Jamie to have the best opportunities to further their tennis. Not if you mean that she forced them into playing a sport they did not love. Because she didn't.

There was the sense at the 2013 Wimbledon Championships, her son's eighth, that the British tennis public were starting to look at Judy a little differently, and that wasn't just because she had dyed her hair 'white-hot blonde'. Of course, there were still a few haters and letter-writers – you're never going to win everyone over – but her mail-bag was no longer as nasty as it had once been, and it felt as though most tennis-watchers had come to acknowledge that she had been a force for good in Andy and Jamie's lives.

One of the great pleasures Murray took from winning the Olympics and the 2012 US Open was that it gave him the opportunity to explain to his mother, and to every other important figure in his life, how grateful he was for everything they had done for him throughout his tennis life: 'A lot of my drive comes from wanting to repay those close to me.' Murray once said that his mother is the only person who 'gets' him. One Christmas, he gave Judy a card in which he thanked her for 'always believing in me, always supporting me, always letting me make my own decisions. But, most of all, I want to thank you for being the best Mum in the world.' There were tears. Murray affectionately scolded her: 'What are you crying for, stupid woman?'

Only two subjects were being discussed in the days leading into the Wimbledon fortnight. Firstly, and this was no small matter, where did you stand on the Great Serena–Maria Ding-Dong, Serena Williams having been quoted in *Rolling Stone* magazine as describing Grigor Dimitrov, Maria Sharapova's boyfriend and one of the American's exes, as 'the guy with a black heart'?

Had Sharapova relinquished the moral high ground – the Henman Hill of off-court ethics? – when, in her pre-tournament press conference, she had argued that Williams shouldn't be discussing other players' love lives when her own boyfriend 'was married and had kids, and is getting divorced'? That was debated at length; Wimbledon cares more for soap-opera than it does for the technical proficiencies of the competitors, and the bitching meant that Andy Murray had a slightly quieter build-up than he would otherwise have done.

The other parlour discussion, and this wasn't one you hear every summer, was chewing over all the possibilities before the draw was made; it was a long time since there had been such interest in who was going to land where on the draw-sheet. There was one reason for that, and that reason was Rafa Nadal – he was seeded fifth and so there was a chance, if the draw worked out that way, that he could be projected to play Murray as early as the quarter-finals. Less than a fort-night had passed since Nadal had scored yet another title at Roland Garros to become the first man in history to win the same grand slam eight times, and yet, as the Majorcan had missed seven of the previous 12 months because of his recurring knee problems, he was outside the top four. The All England Club's grass-court formula, which takes into account past performance on the surface, wasn't going to bump him up the seedings; David Ferrer would be the fourth seed, and Nadal fifth. So, if the draw-computer was rough on Murray, the Briton would have to beat all three of his biggest rivals to win Wimbledon – there was a scenario in which he would have to play Nadal in the quarter-finals, Roger Federer in the semi-finals, and then Novak Djokovic for the title.

Murray's absence from Roland Garros because of back pain – it was the first slam he had missed since with-drawing from the 2007 French Open and Wimbledon Championships after damaging his wrist – only heightened the interest in his potential route through the 128-player jungle.

Of the four big beasts of men's tennis – Ferrer, nicknamed The Little Beast, wasn't part of that herd – Murray had had the best preparation for Wimbledon. The hardest transition for professional tennis players is when they go from the clay to grass; after months of high, looping bounces, they are suddenly trying to deal with low, shooting balls, and the daisy-cutter slices. Your glutes are trying to remember that you need to be as low to the ground as possible. And, unless you have Djokovic's flexibility, sliding on a grass court, just as you would on clay, is not to be recommended; unless, of course, you fancy a couple of broken ankles. And there is so little time to adjust to this change from red to green, with just a fortnight between the French Open and Wimbledon.

Missing the French Open meant that Murray had had extra days on the grass; from almost the first point he played at the pre-Wimbledon tournament at Queen's Club, he looked to be at ease on the lawns, and he would win the title by beating Croatia's Marin Cilic, the defending champion, in the final. That same afternoon, Federer won a pre-Wimbledon title with victory in Halle, Germany, but it was Murray who had played the sweetest tennis of the week. Djokovic and Nadal had both decided against playing a tournament.

There are generally only two ways that Murray's draws are presented in the press; 'Lucky Murray has an easy ride through the tournament' or 'Murray has the draw from Hades', with no inbetween. But this was genuinely one of the inbetweeners. It could have been better and it could have been worse. Djokovic had had the best of it, with the top seed projected to encounter Ferrer in the semi-finals, while the bottom half was loaded with talent, containing all three of Murray, Nadal and

Federer. But Murray wasn't projected to meet Nadal in the last eight; that was Federer's misfortune, and already racket-heads were fantasising about the possibility of the Swiss and Spaniard, who had played that near-mythical final in 2008, producing The Greatest Quarter-Final of All Time. If the draw went with the seedings, Murray would play the winner of Nadal and Federer's match.

Still, you won't hear players looking that far into the future. For now, Murray was concerned only with his first-round opponent, a B. Becker from Germany. Boris hadn't been kept cryogenically frozen since the 1980s, to reappear in the 21st century to torment another generation; this was Benjamin, no relation, whose greatest claim to fame was that he had sent Andre Agassi into retirement by beating him at the 2006 US Open.

Heritage matters to the Wimbledon crowd. You could mount a serious argument that Boris Becker did more for post-war Anglo-German relations than any grey man in a suit. Certainly, you will not find a more popular German in Britain than the former boy-wonder, who in middle age had made Wimbledon Village his home. The way that Becker sometimes speaks about tennis and Wimbledon, using 'we' when a German should really be saying 'you, the British', you do wonder whether he should just be done with it and upgrade from being merely a honorary Brit by officially applying for citizenship.

There had never been any confusion over Murray's nationality, where he came from, or who he would be playing for in years to come. Once in a while at Wimbledon, a player beats someone they are not supposed to, goes deeper still into the draw, has a career breakthrough, and then the full story emerges of how he or she made it from whatever tennis 'backwater' they are from, all the way to the wrought-iron gates of the All England Club.

But it is no less remarkable for the small city of Dunblane, just off the M9 motorway heading to the Scottish Highlands, and a few hundred miles north of Wimbledon's Centre Court, to have produced a player of great international standing. World-class British tennis players are rare enough. However, Scotland had never previously had a man in the world's tennis elite. The world was cruel and it laughed at British tennis, at how Britain had failed to produce a male Wimbledon singles champion since Perry was in flannels and Brylcreem. And Scottish tennis was even taking hits from *Monty Python's Flying Circus*; there is a sketch about a tennis-playing blancmange which comes close to winning Wimbledon by ensuring its opponents are from Scotland, 'well known as the worst tennis nation on earth'.

The Scottish climate is not the weather you need for producing tennis players. Plus, as Judy once noted, Scottish children have been deep-frying their bodies in chip fat. It is a short drive from Dunblane to the William Wallace monument in Stirling. And, for kids from that part of the world, William Wallace probably has as much relevance to their daily lives as another man immortalised by a statue, Fred Perry. You don't expect tennis players who know the words to 'Flower of Scotland'. One of the first reports of a Murray victory was a report in the *Scotsman* in 2000 headlined 'British Player Wins Tournament Shock', and which began: 'Wee Andy Murray ...'

About the only family north of Hadrian's Wall with any great tennis pedigree were the Erskines. Judy Erskine's parents, Roy and Shirley, enjoyed their tennis. Roy, who had played football for Hibernian, Stirling Albion and Cowdenbeath, was a half-decent tennis player and, to this day, he still thinks he invented topspin. Watching his grandson's matches when he is at home in Dunblane, Roy can find himself shouting at the television screen, imploring Murray: 'You shouldn't be playing like that.' But he knows that, when they go to watch Murray play live, he has to control himself.

Judy was the dominant force of Scottish women's tennis – the tartan Chris Evert, if you like – winning 64 Scottish girls' and ladies' titles. But life was not so easy when she left Scotland to scuffle around the lower levels of the international tennis circuit. The tent she was sleeping in at a French camp-site, where she was staying for a tournament nearby, collapsed around her during a thunder-storm. Even with the money her parents were wiring her from Scotland, which she picked up from post offices, she often did not have the funds to fly between tournaments, and so bought bus tickets instead. This was a backpacker's tour of Europe, just with tennis skirts and rackets stuffed into her bag. Judy was a good sport – she once lost in the first round of a tournament to Mariana Simionescu, and then stayed in the locker room to provide cover so the

Romanian could enjoy a cigarette without having to deal with her boyfriend Bjorn Borg's disapproval.

The day that Judy's playing career effectively ended was when the teenager had her purse pinched while riding a bus in Barcelona. Inside the purse had been her passport, some money which her parents had just wired to her, and her airline tickets. On her return to Scotland, her father told her she should think seriously whether it was wise to continue. He was concerned for her safety, and also wondered whether this was really heading anywhere. So she learnt some shorthand and typing, and found secretarial work, first in a glass factory and then for an insurance firm. A job as a trainee manager at a department store followed, before she worked for a while as a travelling saleswoman for a firm which made sweets and chocolates. She studied French and business at Edinburgh University, and met and married Willie Murray, a retail manager.

Such was the pain that Judy experienced when she gave birth to a son, Jamie, on 13 February 1986 ('He was a very big baby with a very big head, it was horrendous and I thought, "Oh, I'll never do that again,"' she is quoted as telling the *Los Angeles Times*), that there was some doubt whether she and Willie would ever have a second child. But she must have quickly changed her mind, as Andy arrived just 15 months later, born on 15 May 1987 in Queen Mother's Hospital in Glasgow.

Years later, Stephen Bierley, then the tennis correspondent for the *Guardian*, wrote that Judy 'should be held personally responsible for the ills of British tennis; she stopped producing children after she had Andy'.

With the two young boys she had 'produced', she sometimes struggled with what she called 'the frustration of an active person suddenly surrounded by mashed vegetables'. As the boys grew, she found that tennis – or at least a version of it – would burn off some of their energy. Murray's tennis life began when he was a toddler; he started by hitting balloons and sponge balls around the house and the garden.

Judy wasn't starting the long march to Wimbledon's Centre Court or to the US Open's Arthur Ashe Stadium; she was just trying to improve their co-ordination and movement so they would get the most out of any sport they played (as the years have passed, she became so convinced that the games she devised for her sons had helped them, and also convinced they could benefit others, that she pulled them all together and put them on an iPad app).

The boys graduated to swingball, which involved striking a small ball that was attached to a string on a pole in the back yard. Judy still remembers Andy's first racket – a 16-inch psychedelic Slazenger which had a bright metallic frame and multi-coloured strings. Initially, Judy thought that Murray had poor hand-to-eye co-ordination. 'My mum, my first tennis coach, will tell you that when I started playing tennis she thought I was useless. Mum used to spend hours throwing balls for me to hit. She says I kept missing whereas my brother, Jamie, could do it right away. It wasn't until I was about seven that I started to become noticeably better. I had bad concentration, bad co-ordination and a temper. It was not a good combination,' Murray recalled in his 2008 autobiography, *Hitting Back*.

An explanation for Murray's high tennis IQ, for his understanding of strategies and how to construct a point, and for the variety in his game, can be found in his tennis upbringing, which was in contrast to how his idol Andre Agassi had been introduced to the sport. Murray loved Agassi when he was a tennis punk. He forgave him his sins (eyeliner, shaving his legs, Barbra Streisand). And Murray kept on loving Agassi as he transformed himself into a tennis gentleman who finished matches by bowing to all sides of the stadium, and became, at least in Streisand's head, a Zen master. To Murray's mind, Agassi was the first tennis player to have become a worldwide icon. John McEnroe, Murray thought, had been popular in America and in Europe, but not so much in Asia. Agassi's name meant something in every country of the world.

Murray's adoration was such that, to watch the Las Vegan win his first US Open title in 1994, the seven-year-old sat in front of the television wearing Agassi's signature 'hot lava' look – cut-off denim shorts, neon pink and purple cycling shorts and a baseball cap with a long blond ponytail clipped on to the back (it was only years later, with the publication of his book, that we discovered Agassi's hair had been fake). The outfit, which had cost Murray eight pounds at a local market, was several sizes too big for him, and his mother remembers how ridiculous he looked.

On his first trip to Wimbledon, earlier that year, Murray had been less interested in using a ticket to a show court than in stalking out the practice courts for three days in the hope of getting Agassi's autograph; the disappointment he felt when he went home with a blank pad – he was too small for his hero to have noticed him – is the reason that he now tries to sign as many programmes, body parts and giant tennis balls as he can. The young Murray copied what he could from Agassi's game, and years later one could detect certain similarities in the way that both hit their double-handed backhands or prepared for their forehands. The pair are two of the best returners of serve that the sport has ever seen.

Even when the adult Murray joined the main tour, and had the chance to meet Agassi for the first time at the pre-Wimbledon tournament at Queen's Club in 2006, he still felt a bit like the little boy dressed from head to toe in Nike; for the first time in his life he was nervous before a practice session, and, palms sweating, he forgot his water bottle. Perhaps Murray saw something of himself in Agassi. Judy has noted that both her son and Agassi are Taureans, 'so stubborn and perfectionists, and both have had dodgy mullets'.

For all that, Murray and Agassi could hardly have had more different starts to tennis. Agassi's early tennis life centred around a ball machine which became known as 'the dragon'; his father Mike, a former boxer who carried salt and pepper in his trouser pockets in case he needed to temporarily blind someone in a fight outside a Las Vegas casino, would have Andre in front of that machine, hitting balls, for hours. Murray, though, learnt the game through regularly playing points and then matches, not through drills.

It was Murray who decided that he should start competing. Murray was born, to borrow the phrase Ivan Lendl once used about himself, a competitive bastard. He was nicknamed Bamm-Bamm, after the character from *The Flintstones* who loved to smash things. And he would fling a Monopoly board in the air if he landed on Park Lane – to keep the peace, he was sometimes allowed to win. Murray was five, so not much bigger than his mid-sized racket, when he announced to his mother that he wanted to play, and she can recall his exact words: 'a proper match in a proper tournament'. Since he could already serve over-arm, keep score, hit double-handed ground-strokes and use topspin and slice, she could see no harm in it.

Within three years – so when he was eight – Murray was playing in the Dunblane third team in the local league, when everyone else was at least a half-century older than him, though that did not stop him from sidling up to his doubles partner, a respected architect, to say: 'You're standing a bit close to the net – you should stand back a bit as you might get lobbed if I decide to serve and volley.' A number of other players in the Central District League did not like playing against an eight-year-old and proposed the introduction of a minimum age – effectively a ban on Andy Murray – but the motion did not pass.

Whenever Judy passes the artificial grass courts at Dunblane Sports Club, she thinks to herself, 'Here we go, where we started.' 'Looking at what Andy has done since, you sometimes have to pinch yourself,' she has said. Recalling all those hours they played on those courts, just a couple of hundred yards from what was then the family home, Judy believes she gave Murray a tactical rather than a technical base. There was no scheming on her part; it was just Murray trying to get the better of his mother and to do that he had to be clever. From an early age, Murray would analyse other players' games – opponents he might never encounter, but who just happened to be on court at the club or at a tournament – and work out in his mind how he would go about beating them.

Judy kept on taking her boys to the tennis courts because they enjoyed it, but also because she often did not have the money for a babysitter. When Judy could not take them with her, the boys' grandmother Shirley allowed Jamie and Andy to play with foam balls in her house, once she had removed all ornaments from the sitting-room. They praised Shirley for the shortbread she baked, and teased her about her slow driving when she ferried them to training at the indoor tennis centre on campus at the University of Stirling.

The Murray brothers were extremely fortunate, considering how many indoor courts there were in Scotland, to be able to spend ten minutes in the car – or 15 if Gran was driving – and to find themselves at a facility where they could practise with a roof over their heads. All that tennis in the Stirling hall helped Murray in future years – he is behind only Roger Federer on the list of the best indoor players of his generation.

Funny to think that, in his early years on the tour, Murray would be likened to Kevin the Teenager, the character created by comedian Harry Enfield which brilliantly captured adolescent angst. When he was at home with his mother, he rarely, if ever, went into angry Kevin mode. He cannot recall ever slamming a door in her face. Not once did Murray tell his mother: 'I hate you.' Perhaps, though, some of the blame for his fruity on-court language is hers. When they played doubles together, she would occasionally curse under her breath at a biffed shot (or so he has recalled). And, on long journeys travelling back and forth between home and tournaments, they would listen to cassettes of Billy Connolly, a Scottish comic who, to use the American tennis vernacular, is forever 'dropping f-bombs'.

For all the help that Judy gave her son, what she refused to do was to intervene in any of his tennis squabbles. That would have been the behaviour of a pushy tennis parent. Judy has some horror stories to tell of her days taking her sons to junior tennis tournaments. Junior tennis often isn't for the faint-hearted parent. There was the time she saw a father outside an indoor tennis hall, with his hands around his 12-year-old daughter's throat. She had just lost. Or the parents spewing at, or ignoring, their children after defeats. There were parents who tried to intimidate or distract their children's opponents, with tricks including cheering when the other child makes a mistake, calling balls out from the sidelines, or clapping when a shot landed close to the lines so that the opponent would be too scared to disagree.

Murray soon learnt that he was going to have to fight his own tennis battles. Judy remembers the day when a six-year-old Murray was playing in Wrexham – it was his first tournament outside Scotland – and on match point, when a drop-shot bounced three times on his opponent's side of the court, the young Scot walked to the net to shake hands. But, without an umpire and with no one watching, Murray's opponent was able to run in and hit a winner into the undefended court. Murray was so shocked that he did not win another point. The match had been an education.

Judy has a good recall of an under-12 doubles match that Murray was playing, when the father of one of the opponents was applauding Murray's double-faults. 'Andy ended up hitting a ball towards him, as if to say, "Will you just shut up?" I've never got into arguments with other parents. It's not worth it. Some parents send on bottles of water with notes taped to the side saying things like, "hit it to the backhand". I've seen parents reading newspapers from behind the court during matches, with instructions written in big bold letters on the back pages. There are parents who have devised coded signals, so if they scratch their right ear that means serve to the forehand, and if they scratch their left ear that means serving to the backhand.'

Judy has never been one of those tennis parents – they can be even worse than stage mums in this regard – who lives vicariously through their children; she had not achieved everything she wanted as a tennis player, but that was not why her sons had ended up in the sport. 'It's important to know why the child is playing, as it has to be because they love tennis. Sadly, you do get instances of parents who are living their dreams through their children. The parents didn't get as far as they wanted when they were playing, so they will try to get the kids to win the tournaments for them. I'm always getting asked if I was a pushy parent. I'll admit I often had to push to make things happen, but I never had to push my kids because they always wanted to play,' Judy once said in an interview with the *Daily Telegraph*.

Perhaps because her own father had always waved her out of the door with the words 'see and win', encouragement which inadvertently made her more fearful of losing, she has always tried to keep it light with her sons. As light as the best sponge-cake. If the uninitiated were to read the timeline for her personal Twitter account – she reports back on every profiterole, Battenburg or Death By Chocolate that crosses her plate – they might guess that she was a professional cake tester and not the mother of two tennis players. She has never wanted to control her sons' lives, the thinking being that if they don't take their own decisions, and don't take responsibility for the mistakes they make, they will never learn.

One thing that Judy pushed for, and made happen, was the chance to play against other talented juniors from across Britain. For her sons, and the other Scottish juniors, to test themselves, they had to leave Scotland, and travel south to play in English tournaments. Almost every weekend Judy was at the wheel, taking her troupe around the country. Turning up to these tournaments full of English boys, Andy and Jamie would have been forgiven for feeling like outsiders; the Scots, who had come in a mini-bus decorated with Saltires, were on cross-border tennis raids. Judy got to know Britain's motorways better than she could ever had imagined she would. Soon, the Murrays would grow out of taking on only the English.

There is a point in any tennis parent's life – well, in most, anyway – when they realise they have taken their child as far as they can. Or that they have become an embarrassment. When Andy was 11, Judy realised her son was reaching the age when being coached by your mother would not be considered 'cool' (her word, or possibly his).

Initially, Judy asked Leon Smith to have a couple of hits with her son. Many years later, Smith would go on to become the head of both men's and women's tennis at the Lawn Tennis Association. Back then, Smith was in his early twenties, and had an ear-ring and a sense of fun. Murray immediately took to him and it developed into a six-year relationship.

The first trip Smith and Murray took together was to Florida, when he played in the 12-and-under singles competition at the Orange Bowl in Florida, which is regarded as the unofficial world championships. Smith watched Murray use lobs and drop-shots to win the final, and then sat on the plane home thinking, 'We're dealing with one of the world's best talents.' That same season, Murray also won the British 14-and-under championships (when he still had two years left in that age group), and that was the time when Judy first thought that her son might have something special.

Murray never did have the opportunity to win the club championships at Dunblane Sports Club. Judy had given her son the best possible start in tennis. Murray had the option of trying to make a life for himself in football, just as his maternal grandfather had done, but he declined the offer of a six-week trial with the Glasgow Rangers School of Excellence for young players. He chose tennis. 'Bats above boots,' Mum said.

On the opening page of Agassi's book, *Open*, he writes that he 'hated tennis with a dark and secret passion'. Not once has Murray ever come close to echoing his idol's thoughts and that, surely, is Judy's greatest achievement.

Like all brothers, the Murrays have fallen out, with arguments settled either verbally or, sometimes during their childhood, with Chinese burns and clenched fists. The only difference is that Andy and Jamie have sometimes got into their tangles in public, with the cameras and the tape-recorders rolling.

There was the occasion when Jamie travelled with Britain's Davis Cup team to Buenos Aires for a tie against Argentina. If Andy had made the trip to South America in 2008, Jamie felt that Britain would have had half a chance on a clay court against Argentina. But Andy had withdrawn from the tie just days before, as a prevention against injury, and in a press conference Jamie spoke of his anger and disaffection: 'It kind of affects the way I feel about him.' Or there was the time when Andy and Jamie lost in the second round of the doubles competition at the 2008 Beijing Olympics, and Jamie bolted so quickly that he left his rackets and the rest of his kit on the court.

If Andy ever wants a reminder of the intensity of his childhood rivalry with his brother, he only has to look at the fingernail, which has never grown back properly after being thumped by Jamie. Andy, aged ten, had just beaten Jamie for the first time, in the final of an under-12s tournament in Solihull, and throughout the long mini-bus journey back to Dunblane, he kept on taunting his sibling. Jamie, an easy-going boy who was usually slow to anger, had heard enough and brought his fist crashing down on the ring finger of Andy's left hand. Judy, who had been at the wheel, had to stop the bus. She cleaned up the bus and carried on up the motorway, but the next morning she was on the phone making an emergency doctor's appointment as Andy's finger had swollen up with pus, and the nail was about to drop off. Someone who has closely examined the nail has described it as looking indented, purple and stunted.

The impression should not be formed, though, that brotherly love has always been in short supply. As grown men playing for prize-money, ranking points and glory, Andy has often felt more nervous partnering Jamie on a doubles court than he has when playing singles, as he puts extra pressure on himself to help his brother succeed. And he took as much pleasure from watching his brother flirt his way to the mixed doubles title with Serbia's Jelena Jankovic at the 2007 Wimbledon Championships as he has from any of his own triumphs. Andy cried that day, and took offence when someone asked him on live radio whether he was jealous that his brother had gained an invite to Wimbledon's Champions' Dinner before he had.

Andy found himself 'welling up big time' after he and Jamie

won their first doubles title together on the main tour, at a tournament in Valencia in the autumn of 2010. When Andy sobbed after the 2012 Wimbledon final, Jamie was on Twitter playing the part of proud older brother: 'My brother is a champion. He may not have won. But he is a champion.'

As they grew older, and started to play professional tennis, it was undoubtedly a blessing that right-handed Andy was making a career in singles and lefty Jamie in doubles. Andy and Jamie have never had to go through what Serena and Venus Williams have throughout their careers – chatting over breakfast bowls of Cheerios and then, later that day, slugging it out against each other on a tennis court while the world is watching. While Andy and Jamie have played the same tournaments, they have been on different draw sheets. If Andy and Jamie clash on the schedules at grand slams, when Andy is playing singles and Jamie doubles at the same time, Judy does not prioritise her more famous son over the other; she tries to watch the same number of their matches.

As young boys, and then as young teens, they were constantly trying to outdo each other. That was the making of Murray. Without Jamie, Andy may never have had a future in tennis. Andy was always a competitive boy. But Jamie made Andy even more determined to succeed on the tennis court. Whatever Jamie was doing, Andy wanted to do, and he wanted to do it better. Andy remembers that Jamie was more intelligent and better academically than he was. Jamie was also faster around a running track. Judy's friends would tell her that Jamie was the better looking of the boys. 'Was Jamie nicer than you?' the *Guardian* once asked Andy, to which he replied: 'Probably, yeah. Yeah.' But Andy thought he could beat Jamie on the tennis court. That was where he would compete against his brother. Andy did not just want to beat Jamie, who at one stage was the second best junior player in the world; he wanted to crush him.

'I think Andy has a lot to thank Jamie for. Jamie was just a bit older, and a bit better, and Andy was always striving to keep up,' Judy has said. Even when the brothers did not play against each other, Andy never missed an opportunity to score points against Jamie. The first overseas tournament Andy went to, he was nine and Jamie went as well. It was an under-11 tournament in France, and Andy got to the semi-final and lost in three long sets to Gael Monfils (who would go on to become an elite player in the senior game), and Jamie got to the final and beat Monfils, one and love. 'And the whole way back home, Andy was saying, "You only won because I tired him out for you,"' Judy recalled in an interview with the *New York Times*. 'It was hilarious.'

The non-aficionados of men's tennis would not recognise Willie Murray if he was sitting having a pint on the next table of the Dog and Fox in Wimbledon Village. 'People don't see my dad as much, but that doesn't mean that he's not a big part of my life,' Murray has said. As the area manager of a chain of shops in Scotland, Andy and Jamie's father has not always found it easy to take the time off to watch his sons play international tennis tournaments, though on occasion his younger son has paid for him to travel to the grand slams. Judy, as the boys' first coach, and with her experience in the sport, has been much more closely involved with their tennis. And when Willie does come to watch Murray playing tennis, he tends to sit on the back row of the box, and he looks calm on the outside, so the television networks are not as interested in him. Inside, though, he will be experiencing the same as his ex-wife: nausea and heart-attack. 'I'm like a swan. I'll appear calm on top, but underneath my legs will be going like the clappers. Emotion takes over when I see Andy walk out to play really big matches,' he once told the *Mail on Sunday*. 'I well up.'

Judy's long and often unsociable hours in her job as Scotland's national coach – she worked most weekends – had an impact on her marriage. 'I was away a lot and then obviously you're coaching until quite late into the evening. Your domestic life gets hit for six. You're not eating at the same times, holidays become difficult.'

Willie has spoken endearingly of Andy and Jamie as 'two little guys from Dunblane' who took on the tennis world. One of the hardest things he ever did was telling his sons, still very young, that Judy was leaving home (they were separated for a few years before divorcing when Andy and Jamie were in their teens). 'It ripped me apart to have to hurt them by telling them what I did,' Willie has said of the initial break-up. 'They were distraught. They are very different personalities, but they took the news in much the same way, and I remember they were very upset. I worked full-time, but I cooked when they came home from school. I did the washing and ironing. I wouldn't say I was a single parent, because Judy stayed in Dunblane and she was around. She still took them to tennis, but I was the one in the family home with the boys.'

Murray has recalled being caught in the middle of his parents' arguments: 'My parents didn't speak too much and they didn't get on too well together. They are just two different people. I stayed with my mother for two nights, then I felt as though I should stay with my father for two nights. At Christmas, I didn't know how long to spend with each of them. I would get stuck in the middle of their arguments. I would get really upset, and one of the things I would have loved to have more than anything was a family that worked better together, although I love my mother and father to bits.'

Armchair psychologists have often speculated whether Murray's anger on a tennis court has something to do with his parents' divorce. 'It could be,' he has said of that theory. 'When I was younger and went on court, and was away from the arguments my parents were having, I could just go out and play.'

Divorce or not, one suspects that Andy Murray would always have been a cussed, emotional character on a tennis court, unlike Jamie, who everyone always felt was a little too nice for tennis. One lesson that Willie wanted to instil in Murray – whose middle name Barron translates from the old English as 'young warrior' – was to never allow anyone, whatever their age or position, to take advantage of him. 'He was always strict with me. If someone was trying to wind you up or take the mickey out of you, he told me to give them some stick back. If they were going to do it, you were going to come back with something. I played football a lot with his friends, five-a-side and seven-a-side, and playing football with forty-year-old men, although they're not the fittest, they'll kick you a little bit and try to sort you out.'

Willie tells the story of the time they went on holiday, to a place where there was always a tennis tournament on, and Murray started beating a boy some six years older, and a foot taller. When the older boy tried to preserve his dignity by cheating over the line-calls, Murray got angry, and, if Willie's memory serves him right, 'then it all kicked off'. 'That was an early indicator of Andy's competitive will to win,' Willie told the *Mail on Sunday*. 'He wouldn't let anyone climb all over him, and he wasn't afraid of any reputation – and he carried that with him into professional tennis.'

The worst day of Judy Murray's life was 13 March 1996. Everyone else in Dunblane, if asked, would give the same date; they'll know someone who had a son or daughter in the primary school that day.

When Judy heard there had been a shooting – it was only later that the full story emerged, of how Thomas Hamilton had killed 16 children and a teacher, Gwen Mayor, before turning a handgun on himself – she jumped into her car and sped towards the school. 'I can remember slamming on my horn and swearing at the top of my voice while shouting, "Get out of the way." Eventually I had to stop the car and pull over. You couldn't get near the school for all the police vehicles and other cars that lined the road. I ran towards the school gates. You couldn't get near those either,' Judy wrote in Murray's autobiography.

That was one of the rare occasions that Judy or her sons have spoken or written about the mass murder, mostly because they do not want to dwell on the events that day, but also because, you would imagine, they do not want to take ownership of a tragedy that affected the whole cathedral town. Another occasion was in the BBC's excellent documentary, *The Man Behind The Racket*, which was broadcast the evening before Murray played Benjamin Becker. 'I haven't spoken about it ever since going on the tour. At the time, you have no idea how tough something like that is, but then as you get older you start to realise. It wasn't until a few years ago that I started to research it and to look into it, as before I didn't really want to know,' said Murray, who broke down during the interview.

Perhaps the only time he has volunteered to speak publicly about the tragedy – on all other occasions, his comments were prompted by an interviewer or a ghost-writer – was after he won the junior US Open, and he dedicated his victory to the victims and to the people of Dunblane, as well as to the victims of the terrorist attack on a school in Beslan in Russia in 2004: 'I found it hard to watch those children coming out of the Russian school. I watched it on television and felt so much sorrow for them.'

Judy waited outside the gates of Dunblane Primary School with the other mothers and fathers. When the parents of Mrs

Mayor's class were asked to come forward, Judy felt such a surge of relief that she almost collapsed on to the tarmac. Almost immediately, she felt guilty as one of the women she had been talking to had a daughter in that class.

When Hamilton had opened fire, eight-year-old Andy and ten-year-old Jamie had been walking towards the school gymnasium for a PE lesson. They diverted to the headteacher's office, where they hid under the desk. Andy does not have a clear memory, only what he calls 'patchy impressions'; what he does remember is, in the hours after the massacre, sitting in a classroom singing songs. 'The weirdest thing was that we knew the guy,' Andy has written. 'He had been in my mum's car. It's obviously weird to think you had a murderer in your car, sitting next to your mum. That is probably another reason why I don't want to look back at it. It is just so uncomfortable to think that it is someone we knew from the Boys Club.' He has admitted that it was hard to get used to the idea that someone he knew turned out to be a murderer, and that he too could have been one of his victims. 'From time to time, Andy would talk about it, but Jamie never, ever talked about it,' Judy has recalled. 'But it was very difficult to avoid it because it affected the whole town.'

For days and weeks, Dunblane was unusually quiet. And for years it was primarily known as the place where Hamilton, a former scout leader, had committed the most horrific of crimes. Some years later, Andy and Jamie moved away, not because they were trying to escape the memories, but because they were never going to have much of a future in tennis if they stayed in Dunblane. Andy, once he had returned from training in Spain, bought a penthouse apartment near the river in south London, and then a house in Surrey's footballers-and-commuters belt, while Jamie lived in a flat in south-west London. But the rest of the family stayed put. Their father Willie continued to live in the area, as did Judy and her parents. Andy and Jamie's uncle, Niall Erskine, has an optometrist business in the town. Andy's tennis, and Jamie's too, has gone a long way to changing how people look at the town, casting Dunblane in a more positive light. Even as a teenager, Murray was aware that Dunblane was 'known around the world for the wrong reasons', and spoke of his desire to change that.

The Murray brothers' accomplishments have also done much to change how Dunblane's residents see themselves. Locals take great pride in having the same roots as the Murrays. 'I know Andy and Jamie are both very aware that the success they've had, and the excitement they've brought to the town, has helped a lot with the moving-on process,' said Judy. As one resident put it, 'Of course nobody will ever forget what happened here, but it's lovely that people still think of something else when they hear of Dunblane.' The morning after Murray had won his first grand slam title, at the 2012 US Open, to become the first British man since Fred Perry in 1936 to win one of the four grand slams, residents gathered around the postbox which had been painted gold by the Royal Mail to commemorate his victory at the Olympics, and newspaper front pages were stuck on the inside of shop windows.

A few days later, some 20,000 people, more than the

population of Dunblane, were there to see Murray ride the open-top bus and to walk around greeting his public. At some points on Murray's route, the crowd was ten deep; fans had stood in the drizzle and the downpours for hours as they waited for Murray. A long wait and rain; this was a very British homecoming for a new grand slam champion. There were women in their seventies and eighties who called themselves 'Andy's groupies', there were old school friends, old neighbours, old fans and new fans, people who had travelled from across Scotland to be there when the Olympic and US Open champion returned home. To think that Murray had wondered whether there would be a crowd; that morning, he had had breakfast with his grandparents, and had become emotional when they had presented him with a miniature version of his golden postbox, which they had had engraved with the message: 'You're awesome. We're so proud of you.' Murray had said to his grandmother: 'Do you think there will be a lot of people?' to which she had replied: 'I think you might be surprised, Andy.'

Murray signed hundreds, perhaps even thousands, of autographs, he posed for pictures, he was introduced to someone's Jack Russell Terrier pup, he accepted hugs from strangers, he chatted and smiled, and he hit a few tennis balls in the rain with children at his first tennis club. About halfway through his walkabout, everything became a blur for Murray, but he carried on smiling, posing, signing and waving. If Murray didn't perform the politician's trick of kissing babies, he came close, having his photograph taken with one infant. He handed his Olympic singles gold medal and mixed doubles silver medal to children so they could take a closer look. Everyone wanted a piece of him; his walkabout lasted for the best part of five hours, almost as long as it had taken him to defeat Novak Djokovic in the New York final. Whatever happened at the All England Club in the summer of 2013, Murray had already done plenty for Dunblane.

Any list of the most influential figures in Andy Murray's tennis education must include Rafa Nadal, one of the greatest players of all time. It was when no one outside Majorca knew Nadal's name that he had a life-changing conversation with his Scottish friend. Life-changing for Murray, that is, as Nadal already seemed to be on his way.

Murray was 15 years old, and Britain and Nadal's Spain had been competing in the European under-16 team championships in Andorra. Spain beat Britain in the final, and Murray went off to play a friendly game of racketball with Nadal, and when that was over – no one can remember who won – they started chatting. Though Nadal's English was far from fluent and everything was delivered with a Majorcan accent, he had a large enough vocabulary to be able to communicate to Murray the benefits he was gaining from training in Majorca with Carlos Moya, also a native of the island, and a player of the class to have held the world number one ranking and the French Open title.

For a while, Murray had been thinking that he was in danger of falling behind his European peer-group. Most days, there was not time for more than two good hours of practice, once he had finished his schoolwork, had been driven to and from the centre in Stirling, and had arranged courts and sparring partners. And when he was on court, the available hitting-partners did not extend much beyond his brother, his mother and whichever county-level players were in the mood that day. Tim Henman and Greg Rusedski certainly never passed through Dunblane or Stirling looking for juniors to share a practice court with. The conversation with Nadal had confirmed in Murray's mind: he had to leave Scotland if he was to make the most of his talent. 'Rafa's out in the sun all day,' Murray said to his mother when he returned home. 'He hardly goes to school and he's playing four and a half hours a day. I'm playing four and a half hours a week. It's not enough.'

There was another reason for Murray to move abroad: to escape what he regarded as the catty, negative British tennis scene. Murray can remember playing tournaments when he felt as though some of the British players were willing him to lose. If they were not going to make it as tennis players, they did not want anyone else making a success of themselves either.

After what had happened to her other son, Judy was concerned how leaving home would affect Murray. When Jamie was 12, he had gone to the Lawn Tennis Association's boarding-school-style academy in Cambridge, but after just a few months he had returned home, disenchanted with tennis. Andy has recalled training with Jamie, soon after his return from East Anglia, and thinking that his brother looked fraught and unhappy. During the same practice session, Judy walked to the back of the court, and tearfully said to Andy: 'I can't believe what they've done to him.' Andy thought that the LTA had 'ruined' his brother, and he carried that anger around with him for years. While the Murrays considered sending Andy to the United States – possibly even to the Nick Bollettieri Academy in Florida, which Andre Agassi regarded as *Lord of the Flies* with forehands – as it was English-speaking, they believed that he would be too far away from home. So Europe it was, and they settled on the Sanchez-Casal Academy, just a short drive from Barcelona's airport.

A Spanish tennis education would not be cheap. The annual boarding fees were £25,000, with competition expenses on top of that. Though Sport England, Tennis Scotland and the LTA all contributed, and Judy found a couple of private sponsors, Murray's move would mean family sacrifices.

Before Murray left, his father gave him this advice: 'Don't take s*** from anyone.' As if that was ever going to happen. Willie's pep-talk was akin to John McEnroe's father imploring his son to express himself more forcefully when talking to umpires. The first time that Emilio Sanchez, one of the founders and a former doubles world number one, saw Murray, he thought he was wasting his time. Murray had recently gone through a growth spurt. 'Andy was tall and skinny, bandy-legged, he walked a bit slow, sloping with his shoulders. He didn't look like a tennis player. I thought he must have been talked up by his mother.' But then they stepped on court, and Sanchez realised that this skinny kid from Scotland had some talent. Murray beat Sanchez in straight sets, and the Spaniard was so impressed that he put the Briton in a squad of players aged between 19 and 26, with a spread of world rankings from 200 to 700.

A typical day for Murray at the academy – he would spend around 18 months there – involved three hours of tennis in the morning, an hour in the gym, lunch and the shortest of siestas, a couple of hours of school, an hour and a half of match play, and then another hour of school. There was the risk, when Murray went to the academy, that he would end up with no academic qualifications to fall back on; so if he failed to make a career in tennis, he would have nothing. Though he was supposed to be studying English, Maths, French and colloquial Spanish, he felt as though the schoolwork was holding him back with his tennis; the books came a very distant second behind the rackets.

Pato Alvarez, a Colombian in his late sixties who was known around those parts as 'El Guru del Tenis', had Murray working hard, putting the clay-court miles into the boy's legs. It was not unusual for elite tennis players to drop into the academy looking for some juniors to practise with. When they did, Murray more than held his own. Murray split sets with Moya, and beat Guillermo Coria, the 2004 French Open finalist, two days in a row; here was encouragement that he was not too far off their level. Never mind that Murray was not picking up much Spanish.

Murray once complained that he had been allocated the worst bungalow in the complex. It was a small wooden hut painted chemical yellow, with a bunk bed, a flower-print sofa and a Ukrainian stranger for a room-mate. But he had only himself to blame for the mess, with the floor covered in around a week's worth of empty food packets, dirty tennis kit, discarded rackets and used tennis balls. There was more debris on the sofa. When Judy came to visit, she brought news from home, and several bags of Milkybar Buttons and chocolate digestive biscuits (that was what Murray had meant when he had requested 'normal food'). She often struggled to fully open the door of the bungalow, such was the build-up of litter.

Murray liked the place. Here he could develop his game away from the British tennis mainstream. He felt that no one here was willing him to fail, or actively trying to bring him down. There was a good international crowd, all committed to reaching the top, but not wanting to step on anyone to get there. Murray was happy to keep his life low key. In that hut, it felt as though he could escape the gathering comparisons with Henman, and the rest of the attention he regarded as absurd. In Catalonia, no one could reach Murray. Or at least no one that Murray didn't want to speak to.

Some in Britain did not share the Murray family's view that Andy was doing the right thing by basing himself in Barcelona, and by playing Futures events, the lowest level of professional tennis, in Spain rather than in Britain. Tony Pickard, a former British Davis Cup captain, and Stefan Edberg's ex-coach, bumped into Judy Murray at a tournament and told her it looked as though her son was scared of his British contemporaries. 'What's Andy doing playing in Spain and not in British Futures events? He should be back here in Britain, competing at home. It shows fear that he's leaving his country. He will lose locker-room respect if he goes on avoiding British players.'

But it was not as if Britain's best male players at the time, Tim Henman and Greg Rusedski, had come through the LTA's system either. Henman was not a product of the LTA, and Rusedski, when he changed nationalities, arrived fully formed from Canada, with a fast serve, a Union Flag bandana and a professed love of Arsenal Football Club and James Bond.

On top of the tennis, Murray enjoyed being a budget flight away from home; for the first time in his life, he felt independent. Whenever he returned home, his parents were 'always telling me what to do', but in Barcelona he was his own man. He didn't abuse that freedom with late nights of beer, tapas and tequila along Las Ramblas ('going to bars isn't my scene'). Any free time he had was spent sleeping in the bunk, at the city's English-language cinema or watching DVDs with friends.

Murray appreciated the financial commitment that his family had made to allow him to train in Spain, and that he was not there to have fun. If this was about having fun, he should board the first plane back to Scotland. For several long months, he did have to stay in Scotland. That was when, in 2003, the cause of the pain he had been playing through was diagnosed as a bipartite patella, or split kneecap. As Murray was still growing, they could not operate, and so all he could do was rest his right knee, work on his upper-body strength, shoot some pool, take Spanish classes, and mope. 'That was the worst period of Andy's tennis career,' Judy has said, but when her son returned to the sport it was not long before he was alerting the wider tennis world to his potential.

When Murray returned to Spain after a trip to the 2004 US Open, he told his friends that he had won the boys' singles title – thinking that they might not have noticed – but he did not want to be treated like a superstar. Or for there to be any fuss. But, whether Murray liked it or not, the sporting world was starting to make a fuss over him. That December, he was put on the shortlist for the BBC Young Sports Personality of the Year award. Murray won, but the day was not without its dramas – he almost missed the ceremony after locking himself in his hotel loo.

So, the opening Monday of the greatest show in tennis, and Andy Murray was back on Centre Court, returning to where he had lost the previous summer's Wimbledon final and where, just a few weeks later, he had marmalised the same opponent, Roger Federer, to win gold at the Olympics. Plus, beating Benjamin Becker would mean that Murray would go to the top of the list of British men with the most match victories at the slams – reaching the second round would give him 107, one more than Fred Perry (him again). And yet, as it turned out, Murray opening his tournament wasn't even big news; this wasn't the grass-court premiere that everyone had supposed it was going to be.

Had you tuned in to the evening news bulletins, you could

easily have missed the short clip of Britain's world number two swinging away on the grass; this was a day dominated by the departure of Rafa Nadal – on the Richter scale of tennis shocks, this was a nine, with the former champion being skewered by Steve Darcis, a Belgian ranked 135 in the world. In the morning, one broadsheet would call this 'The Shock of the Century'. In truth, it wasn't even the most surprising result involving Nadal and a lowly ranked opponent in the past 12 months at the All England Club.

Yes, this was a round earlier than Nadal's defeat by Lukas Rosol at the 2012 tournament, and Darcis was lower down the rankings than the Czech, who had been number 100 at the time. But the Majorcan had been saying over the preview weekend that grass was now the toughest surface for him and his knee, as he was forced to get lower to the ground to strike the ball, and his body didn't like that. From the off, it appeared as though Nadal was in no great shape to fling himself around the lawns of London – his straight-sets defeat was great news for Darcis (though he wouldn't play his second-round match because of injury), and also for Murray and Roger Federer. Just think of all the time and energy that had been wasted discussing the seedings, grass-court formulas, and whether Nadal should have been promoted above David Ferrer.

In the early rounds of a slam, there is almost nothing to gain, and everything to lose, for the top seeds. Such had been the Fab Four's dominance, it had occasionally sounded a little disingenuous when Novak Djokovic, Murray, Federer or Nadal spoke of the dangers posed by a first-round opponent.

Darcis beating Nadal was a reminder that the unexpected can occasionally happen. No doubt, it was to Murray's advantage that he had recent experience of playing his opponent on grass, the pair having met just two weeks prior at Queen's Club. Murray could hardly have had a more uneventful match; this was a blissfully boring 6-4, 6-3, 6-2 victory. For surprises, you needed to be on Nadal's Number One Court. Or sitting on Murray's Centre Court with your eyes on the big screen between games – the Darcis-Nadal result was flashed up as Murray sat on his chair at a change of ends, and the spectators gasped as only a Wimbledon crowd can. You knew Murray's match was straightforward when the BBC put him on the red button, preferring to focus on events elsewhere.

So Murray was on the move, through to play Yen-Hsun Lu, and no one needed to remind him to guard against complacency (Judy is forever telling him how 'remarkable' he is, but he knew that a mother's admiration and love alone were not going to be enough). Nadal's departure had shown everyone what was possible. And Murray had prior knowledge of how horrible it felt to lose to his opponent from Chinese Taipei; their match in the early stages of the 2008 Beijing Olympics had been one of the roughest defeats of his career. Nadal was out, but Murray was not about to mentally fast-forward to the second Sunday, to start day-dreaming about kissing a golden cup.

2

The Coach that Everybody Cares About

Wild Wednesday. Weird Wednesday. Wacky Wednesday. Whatever your preference, this was a Wednesday that no one had foreseen; in his 'wildest dreams', John McEnroe had never imagined he would see a day like this at the All England Club. It would be all too easy to mock Pippa Middleton for her column published in the *Spectator* magazine later in the week, predicting great things for Jo-Wilfried Tsonga ('his game suits grass, and he's one of those players who's just unstoppable when he gets into what the pros call "the zone"') and Roger Federer ('I'm following my heart and backing Roger') – unfortunately for Mystic Middleton, by the time the piece appeared, her tips were already on the All England Club slagheap. But let's not hear anyone suggesting that Pippa had been talking out of her shapely posterior; sharper tennis minds than hers had not come close to calling day three. Lawn tennis can make fools out of everyone.

Big names kept going splat on the grass, literally and metaphorically. There were so many slips, tumbles, fumbles, injuries and retirements, and negative comments from the players, including an on-court microphone picking up Maria Sharapova saying 'this court is dangerous', that the club issued a statement claiming that the grass was in the same excellent condition it had been the summer before, and the summer before that. And, as former champion Lleyton Hewitt noted, the grass is always a bit slippery on the first few days, and dealing with that is just part of the challenge.

Even after such a day, no one of any standing in the locker-room was advocating the launch of the Rip Up The Wimbledon Grass Society, and arguing that, in the interests of the players' safety, they should concrete over the courts. For all the opinions expressed about the grass – it can't have been easy for the head groundsman in his first year in the job – here were some facts. Sharapova had lost. Caroline Wozniacki was beaten. Tsonga, who had been projected to play Andy Murray in the last eight, was out. Victoria Azarenka, who had slipped on the first day, decided against playing her next match.

Federer was supposed to have brought order to Wimbledon. And if you can't depend on the Swiss when he's playing the world number 116 in the second round, and on Centre Court, then who exactly can you rely on? Federer, whose victory over Murray in the 2012 final had put him level with Pete Sampras and William Renshaw on seven Wimbledon titles, had come to London attempting to become the first man to win this tournament eight times. Plus, Federer had reached the quarter-finals or better at his last 36 grand slams. So what happened? Sergiy Stakhovsky, a serve-and-volleying Ukrainian, is what happened; no one had ever bamboozled Federer like that on Centre Court before. Still, you had to wonder what difference it had made that Federer had been forced to change his footwear. Federer's Wimbledon outfits are planned months, perhaps even a full year, in advance, so it would have been a small drama when the Club told him he wouldn't be able to wear the orange-soled shoes he had used for his opening match, as they broke the predominantly white clothing rule.

With all this going on across the grounds, did anyone actually notice that Murray was out there on the grass, with his annual match away from Centre Court?

Murray, playing his first Wimbledon as a grand slam champion, would do everything in his power on Number One Court to avoid becoming part of this madness, and to swerve a defeat that would potentially torment him for the rest of his days. You didn't have to tell Murray's coach, Ivan Lendl, what it felt like to spend your middle age spooling back to the disappointments of your youth at the All England Club; though he won eight grand slam titles, a British audience will always remember him for his failure to win Wimbledon. As a player, Lendl had never made it to the Champions' Dinner, but perhaps, just perhaps – and this would be the next best thing – he would put on his tuxedo as the winning coach. But if that was going to happen, Murray would first have to survive Wild Wednesday, the closest that this smart bit of London had ever come to an insurrection.

Ivan Lendl tells some of the dirtiest jokes in tennis. People on the tour often remark on that; what they won't then do is repeat any of his jokes. Meet the man once described as 'an equal opportunities offender', whose locker-room gags were said by John McEnroe to have been 'dubious at best'. Lendl could make Jilly Cooper blush. Political correctness seems to be as foreign to Lendl as smiling when Andy Murray is on the match court.

To get his other kicks, Lendl launched tennis balls at Murray during training. Lendl the player had been known for drilling the ball at opponents in matches – he felt it was a legitimate tactic, and he also took some pleasure from causing mischief – and now, in his fifties, he was still doing it. A direct hit from Lendl stings like a paintball shot. Lendl would inflict pain, and then expect a laugh. But Murray was always looking to do the same back to his coach and just days before Wimbledon he had his chance. Has anyone ever seen Murray as happy on a tennis court as when, while playing a charity exhibition match at Queen's Club, he managed to smack Lendl with the meatiest of strikes, a shot hit with the force to bruise both body and ego? In the days that followed, Murray watched the clip a dozen times on YouTube, enjoying it more with every viewing.

The Coach that Everybody Cares About

Lendl has not always had the tennis world chuckling. And America was the most resistant to his gags. When he was winning US Open titles in the 1980s, he was seen as sour, robotic and humourless – he had all the charm of an Ostrava tower-block. He was about as much fun as communism. To mark Lendl's achievement of winning the 1986 US Open, *Sports Illustrated* put him on the cover with the headline 'The Champion That Nobody Cares About'. The copy inside was not much gentler either, with Lendl – who had moved to America just a few years earlier – accused of 'clearing the stadium like a bomb threat'. 'This was his second straight US Open title, and the fifth consecutive year he has reached the finals. In that time he has won 32 of 35 matches, and almost as many fans. In the early rounds of the Open a certain "Lendl Factor" emerged. As soon as his matches were announced, multitudes would abandon the stadium and the outer courts would jam up. Lendl may someday empty entire cities.' Another magazine writer who spent time with him reported: 'In a sport that had exploded in the 1970s on the gunpowder of personality, Lendl had none.'

Lendl thinks he was always funny, just that the public and media had been slow to realise. Were people aware that he used to roller-skate around the practice court in his back yard? Maybe the problem during the Cold War was that he was delivering his lines with a thick Czech accent. Or perhaps, back then, the jokes were just not very amusing. As Richard Hinds, of the *Melbourne Age*, has recalled of Lendl the touring professional: 'Occasionally you would see a picture of Lendl walking his German Shepherds or read about his wicked sense of humour. But when he tried to tell a joke at a press conference it would fall so flat you figured he should have let the dogs do the talking.' Sometimes the joke was on Lendl, such as when a friend arranged for an actor dressed as a traffic cop to knock on his door and arrest him for failing to pay a speeding ticket. Lendl's immediate response was to cry out: 'Get me my lawyer.' The friend told *Sports Illustrated*: 'Sweat was pouring off him; he was stuttering. We had to tell him it was a joke. We were afraid he was going to break down.'

When the news broke, on New Year's Eve 2011, that Lendl would be re-engaging with tennis, one satirical website ran a story about his appointment as Murray's new 'misery coach'. So, who had Murray hired, Mr Sour Face from behind the old Iron Curtain, the player who had once threatened to kill the sport off in America, or the funniest man in tennis? Both, perhaps. There have always been two Lendls: the man dedicated to his task like no other, whether that be playing or coaching, and the man who uses humour to relieve any social awkwardness, to score points (he will be the only one keeping score) and also as a way of showing affection. The harder he was hitting the ball at Murray, the more jokes he was telling him, the more he was in fact showing how fond he was of the Scot. Lendl was surprised at how Murray laughed hard, and kept on laughing. 'Andy's sense of humour is almost as sick as mine. That's helped our relationship. You don't have to tiptoe around if you want to tell a bad joke.'

Of course, professional tennis is not a Will Ferrell movie.

Murray did not imagine he was going to giggle all the way to grand slam titles.

Murray's decision to hire Lendl was not without risk. For all Lendl's achievements as a player – in addition to his eight slams, he had held the world number one ranking, and had had an enraged Jimmy Connors giving him the finger – he was a rookie as a coach. In a 15-year self-imposed exile from tennis, he had spent much of his time helping three of his five daughters with their golf, as well as working on his own swing. Did he now know more about golf than he did about tennis? Plus, having the unsmiling Lendl in his corner was bound to draw more international attention to his efforts to become Britain's first male champion since the 1930s. Lendl would become 'The Coach That Everybody Cares About'. It would, in Lendl's words, up the ante.

When Murray announced he was linking up with Lendl, his rivals were in established, long-term coaching relationships. Rafa Nadal has only ever had one coach – his uncle Toni. All of Novak Djokovic's grand slam titles had come while he was working with Marian Vajda. And when the 2012 tennis season began, Roger Federer was settled with Paul Annacone, Pete Sampras's former coach. Murray, still very much the fourth member of the quartet, was the one who had to try something new. A few saw this as a desperate move by a player who was running out of options. Since becoming a professional tennis player, Murray had had guidance from a number of different characters – Leon Smith, Pato Alvarez, Mark Petchey, Brad Gilbert, Alex Corretja,

Miles Maclagan and Darren Cahill. So what could Lendl possibly do any differently?

And if Murray was risking some of his personal credibility on this new venture, then Lendl was also going to have some skin in the game. Lendl was the joint most successful former player – the other being Connors, who worked with Andy Roddick for a while – to coach at the highest level. He didn't have to do this, to take the chance that the partnership could go badly wrong. Lendl said he had already turned down a number of other offers from players. But he was intrigued by Murray.

Time magazine once described Andy Murray's tennis as 'a concerto of arrhythmic disharmony'. His mother Judy put it more simply: 'He messes people about.' In an era of baseline bashing and slashing – when most are incapable of doing anything more imaginative than wellying their forehand – Murray is different.

From an early age, he knew all this: a tennis court's geometry and how to use angles and impart spin; how to infuriate opponents with 'junk' or deliberately low-grade shots; how to slow a rally down; how to then speed it up; a fondness for drop-shots. Andy Roddick once remarked when you played Murray it could feel as though you were playing points in reverse, because of his habit of taking the pace off the ball at the beginning of the point. So Murray had introduced himself to the tennis world as a counter-puncher – he would soak up whatever his opponent was throwing at him before waiting for his moment to strike. The elite didn't like it, and Murray was soon bamboozling those who just couldn't work out how to deal with his intelligent, creative game. The problem, though, was this: Murray had become so good at playing defensive tennis, at allowing his opponent to make the first move, that he was reluctant to be proactive in rallies. Winning a grand slam is hard enough already without trying to do it playing defensive tennis.

The ten months that Murray spent with Mark Petchey, from June 2005 until April 2006, was the time he went from an Andrew to an Andy – he used the back-page of the *Sun* one morning to say that his friends and family had always called him Andy, so could the press and public please do the same. Those ten months also saw Murray thrill and torment Wimbledon, become a top-100 player, compete in a first ATP final, and win a first senior title. But Murray and Petchey couldn't always agree on how Murray should be playing. Petchey would have liked to have seen Murray being more assertive and aggressive. Murray wasn't so sure.

Before Petchey came on the scene, Murray was making an impression on senior tennis. In March 2005, the 17-year-old had become the youngest-ever British player to compete in the Davis Cup when he appeared in a doubles rubber in a tie against Israel in Tel Aviv (as the team bus later overtook the media shuttle on the way back to the hotel, Murray turned and bounced on his seat, shaking his fist in triumph).

A month later, Murray made his first appearance on the ATP Tour, and to listen to the self-recriminations that followed 'a terrible, terrible match' was to begin to appreciate the ambitions he had for himself. With Murray living at the Sanchez-Casal Academy outside the city, the clay-court event at the Real Club de Tenis Barcelona was effectively his home tournament. The night before the wild card played Jan Hernych of the Czech Republic, his mother Judy had sent him this scouting report about the then world number 79: 'Your granny volleys better than he does.' This had been enormously frustrating and hugely encouraging: if Hernych could reach the top 100, there was no reason why he couldn't too.

Not long afterwards, it started to get 'nasty' between Murray and Pato Alvarez, his Colombian coach from the academy, who had once worked with the Romanian Ilie Nastase. Realistically, this alliance between a South American man in his sixties and a Scottish teenager was never going to last long, but it had become personal. 'Off the court we were arguing a lot,' Murray said at a press conference. 'We weren't having so much fun. There were a lot of problems. The last week we were together, it got a bit nasty. He was saying bad things about my tennis and bad things about me. I didn't really need someone that negative in my corner.'

One thing Petchey had in his favour was that he was half Alvarez's age, so would be willing and able to run and lift weights with Murray, as well as compete at pool and darts. Another was that, when Murray had been recuperating for several months in 2004 after being diagnosed with a split kneecap, he had spent much of his time watching tennis on Sky television, which meant he had been listening to the

The Coach that Everybody Cares About

Essex-born Petchey, himself a former top-100 player. To Murray's mind, Petchey, who was then also working for the Lawn Tennis Association, sounded as though he knew what he was talking about.

Their first tournament together was the pre-Wimbledon tournament at Queen's Club in the summer of 2005, though at that stage Petchey was just helping out, and was still employed by the LTA as their head of men's national training. The tennis that Murray played at Queen's would lead to Petchey resigning from his job at the governing body. At the time, other coaches had been telling Petchey that he was mad to want to work with Murray as, 'he'll never do anything, he's very soft'. Clothing manufacturers were reluctant to sponsor Murray because they felt that he did not have enough power in his racket-arm. Petchey, though, saw something in Murray.

People tend to have a better recall of Murray's third-round defeat at Queen's than of the two matches which preceded it, when he beat Spain's Santiago Ventura and America's Taylor Dent for his first victories on the ATP Tour. It was not just Murray's tennis which made his match against Sweden's Thomas Johansson, a former Australian Open champion, score so highly on the Pimm's-ometer; there were medical mini-dramas to add to the narrative. The first time Murray collapsed on to the grass, after falling awkwardly, he screamed so loudly that all of West Kensington put their drinks down. The crowd had barely had time to pick them up again when Murray toppled to the floor once again. For five minutes, he lay face down in the turf, and when he eventually pulled himself to his feet, he chose not to wipe the grass and mud from his face, giving him the appearance of a rugby forward who had just resurfaced from the bottom of a ruck.

London's grass courts have seen too many 'Brave Brits' over the years, but as the tennis-literate members returned to the bar they appreciated that this match – Murray had come within two points of victory – was not to be filed away under 'heroic cameo', an entertaining effort from a player who was never to be heard from again. So Tim Henman had been right before Queen's when he had told Murray, still sore from losing in the semi-finals of the boys' singles at the French Open the week before: 'Who cares about the juniors?'

The interest in Murray was such that he was invited on to breakfast television (he declined – too early) and had to change his mobile telephone number. But Murray's summer, the soundtrack to which was the Black Eyed Peas track 'Let's Get It Started', which he would listen to on his headphones as he walked on court, had much more to give.

Who could have imagined that Petchey would walk around the All England Club wearing a baseball cap promoting the *Sun* newspaper, that Murray would become friends with James Bond (tennis enthusiast Sir Sean Connery), or that the teenager would go deeper into the draw at the Wimbledon Championships than Henman or Greg Rusedski? Or that Murray would find himself politely declining John McEnroe's offer of part-time coaching, as he thought, rightly, that the New Yorker would struggle to fit him in around his other commitments, and because the Scot was sure in his mind that he needed full-time assistance? Or that Petchey would suggest that Murray could go on to be bigger than Wayne Rooney?

The All England Club certainly got value from the wild card they gave Murray, who at the time was ranked outside the world's top 300, who arrived for practice wearing a replica Barcelona football shirt, and who played with a nerveless ease which only teenagers, not yet knowing any better, are truly capable of. Murray was an All England Club innocent, still excited by the attendants offering him towels in the locker-room and the fact that, had he chosen to, he could have sat there all day drinking unlimited Sprite. Or the fact that, though he was staying a few minutes' walk from the club, in a rented flat up in Wimbledon Village, people kept asking him whether he wanted to be driven down the hill in one of the tournament's official cars.

Murray's senior grand slam career began on the old Court Two, which is known as 'The Graveyard of Champions', not because Fred Perry and others were buried under the baseline, but because, for whatever reason, seeded players had tended to fare worse there than on any other lawn at the club. The most famous of all the upsets had been when George Bastl, an unknown from Switzerland, had beaten Pete Sampras in the second round in 2002, and the American, who had won seven Wimbledons, never played in the tournament again.

Bastl had not done much in the three years that followed, but after qualifying for the 2005 Championships he found himself paired in the first round with Murray. That morning, Murray had got himself in the mood for Wimbledon, which styles itself as tennis at an English summer's garden party, by switching on the television and turning up MTV to full volume. There had been concerns about his ankle injury from Queen's, but he was moving freely among the tombstones of Wimbledons past. The reward for Murray's straight-sets victory was having to sign so many autographs that Venus Williams was kept waiting for Court Two, and for the first time having a crowd by his practice court ('Let's face it,' Murray said, 'the hype surrounding me has been over the top, as I haven't done anything – everybody's making out as if I'd pretty much won Wimbledon').

His other reward was to be promoted to a bigger stage, Court One, for a second-round match with Radek Stepanek, a Czech player who bore some facial resemblance to Homer Simpson, and who had something of a reputation for cartoon behaviour and gamesmanship. So Murray would have been prepared for Stepanek pulling funny faces at him, among other tricks. Stepanek, a top-20 player at the time, had not been helped by his coach Tony Pickard. Murray had been aggravated by what Pickard had said to his mother Judy about it looking as though he was training in Spain to run away from his British contemporaries. Plus, he had heard on the locker-room grapevine before this encounter that Pickard and Stepanek didn't rate him much. When Murray defeated Stepanek, Petchey walked over to shake Pickard's hand and to tell him, 'Tough luck.' According to Petchey, Pickard responded: 'That was a terrible match. Both of them played badly. It was embarrassing. I can't believe that was on Court

One.' When Murray heard about the post-match exchange, he was amused, but also regarded it as typical of the bitching in British tennis.

While Murray had been saying throughout that grass was not his favourite surface, there was no denying that playing his first match on Centre Court was a thrill. So far that summer, Murray had formally introduced himself to Britain's tennis public; his third-round match against David Nalbandian, a former Wimbledon runner-up, was the occasion that he launched himself at a wider audience. Sir Sean Connery, sitting in the Royal Box, was not the only person who got a little carried away as Murray took the first two sets. Murray was comfortable playing in the white heat of grand slam competition, before Bond and a television audience of millions. Unfortunately for Murray, who was playing only his seventh match on the main tour, fatigue and cramp began to take hold of his legs. Never before had Murray played a five-setter, and he was so exhausted after his defeat that he did not have the energy to stand up in the shower.

At least that happened behind the scenes; at the back end of summer, at the US Open, Murray's problems were all too public. New York also brought further signs that Murray was not going to mind his Ps and Qs with the tennis establishment. Both Murray and Petchey had expected that the teenager, the winner of the previous year's junior title, would be given a wild card into the main draw of the US Open. And the United States Tennis Association had indicated their willingness to do a trade with the All England Club, with one spot in the draw for the following summer's Wimbledon to be kept back for a young American. But the offer was rejected, and it was a moot point who was angrier, Murray or Petchey.

Murray, with a sore shoulder, and with a long American summer in his legs, would have to qualify. When he won his third and final match, he raised a finger to his lips, a gesture that was telling his critics, all those saying he was not fit enough, to be quiet. When Murray vomited on the court in his opening match in the main draw, against Romania's Andrei Pavel, he blamed it on his electrolyte drink: 'I felt like I was going to burp and then I threw up. It was pretty funny.' Some of the sick went over Pavel's bag. Murray was not so much embarrassed as surprised, and once the court had been wiped down, he scored his first five-set victory. Still, after the burn of lactic and stomach acid that Murray had experienced against Pavel, it was not altogether surprising that he was not at his freshest for his next match, against Frenchman Arnaud Clement, which he lost with a 6-0 fifth set.

That long summer in America, which Murray felt was almost like a road movie, had allowed him and his coach to form a fast friendship. There are few jobs that involve a man in his thirties sharing twin hotel rooms with his teenage employer, even spending Christmas together, but this was one of them. Still, their relationship was not without its strange moments; when Murray would not stop honking the horn of their rental car as they drove through a rough part of the States, Petchey felt as though he had no option but to whack the boy on the arm. He didn't want to meet his end outside a trailer park. On their return, Murray became a lodger at Petchey's family home in Wimbledon.

A recurring theme was Murray's desire – after feeling maligned and misunderstood – to prove people wrong. When Murray had openly declared at the start of 2005 that he wanted to break into the top 100 that season, there were a few who had told him he would have been wiser to have kept those ambitions to himself. It was at a tournament in Bangkok that autumn, when he defeated Sweden's Robin Soderling to reach the quarter-finals, that he collected the points to give him a double-digit ranking, and he sent his mother this text message: 'I did it, Mum.' Murray also collected a bonus of £400, as a group of friends had all pledged to pay £100 each to whoever was first to make the top 100.

When Murray won a couple more rounds, putting him in his first ATP final, where he would play Roger Federer, Judy could not help herself in Dunblane – she danced about her house in her dressing gown and slipper socks. For Murray, playing Federer was like 'being a character in my own video game', but he showed plenty of composure. The only time he lacked clarity of thought was during the prize-giving ceremony when he could not be sure whether to kiss the beauty queen who presented him with a bouquet of flowers. There was some blushing of Scottish cheeks. 'She wasn't that great up close, Mum,' Murray later told his mother, to which she immediately replied: 'I'm sure she said the same thing about you.'

As much as tennis is an international sport – look at where tournaments are played around the world, and you will see that the sport has colonised more countries than the Romans or the British ever did – it can feel parochial at times. The rest of the sport did not much care that Murray had been drawn to play Tim Henman in the first round of the Swiss Indoors in Federer's home town, Basel. By then, Henman and Murray were friends, their friendship born out of backgammon, and the 2004 US Open – while Murray had been winning the junior title, Henman had reached the semi-finals of the senior event for the first and only time.

Murray, who had first met Henman when he was 13, at a tennis clinic, had never understood why the British public were so hard on a man who had played in six grand slam semi-finals, including four at Wimbledon. Murray was grateful for the time that Henman had spent welcoming him to the tour. There are few occasions when someone will weep into a towel on making the second round of the indoor tournament in Basel, but this was one of them. Henman had a sore back and his post-match comments were cuter than the tennis that had come before it. 'Is it a torch? Is it a baton? Whatever it is, I've passed it on.'

Petchey would not have known it at the time, but his decision to miss the tournament in San Jose in California, which Murray played in February 2006, did not help him to stay in employment. In the opening month of the season, Murray had not had the Australian Open he would have wanted, playing some tame tennis to lose in the first round to Argentina's Juan Ignacio Chela, which had him calling out 'This isn't me' on the court and afterwards suggesting that the media were expecting too much from him (his future coach, Brad Gilbert, subsequently wrote a column for the *Melbourne Age* about how disappointed he was in Murray for his remarks). Petchey would have felt some extra responsibility for what had happened in Australia, as the decision to spend Christmas in South Africa – where Murray had only his coach to hit with – meant that he had been a little unprepared for the full weight of shot coming from his opponents as he began his first full year on the tour.

The tournament in San Jose fell during half-term, and Petchey chose to stay at home with his wife and children, and to talk Murray through his matches on the telephone. Murray's companion for the week would be Kim Sears, who had a week off from studying for her A-levels. One of her first tasks, on landing, was to do something about Murray's hair, which had not been cut for a year. Murray didn't want to go to the barber's, but did allow Sears to attack his mop with a pair of nail-scissors.

No one could suggest that Murray's first title on the main circuit came at a 'soft' tournament. In the last couple of rounds, Murray beat two players who had previously been the world number one, Andy Roddick and then Lleyton Hewitt. To celebrate, Murray climbed into the crowd and kissed Sears. If the tournament had strengthened how Murray felt about Sears, it had done nothing for his relationship with Petchey.

The week after San Jose, Murray played in Memphis (Petchey was now with him once again) where he gathered the points which made him the British number one. However, there were signs, on both sides of America, that all was not well with Murray and Petchey. Reports in California had them arguing on a practice court at the Indian Wells Tennis Garden, and eating separately – when once they would have had all their meals together. In Florida, at the tournament in Miami, Murray complained publicly about the heavy schedule set by his coach. There were differences of opinion over strategies. Just before the start of the European clay-court season, and with Murray entered to play in Monaco, they sat down at a cafe in the French Riviera and he sacked Petchey.

Murray, who had had the best months of his tennis life with Petchey, was keen that the situation did not drag on any longer. He did not feel good about doing it. After all the time he had spent with Petchey's family, including living in their London home, and pulling Christmas crackers, this felt very personal. Indeed, Petchey's wife and children were in Monaco when this happened, as they had flown out for a family holiday. From Petchey's side, this was not unexpected and it did not permanently sour relations between the two men. This could be seen from the interviews they did together during the 2012 US Open, for Sky television, that the split had not stopped them from going back to being friends again.

There is no more spectacular place to play tennis than the Monte Carlo Country Club, with the Mediterranean on one side and the limestone cliffs on the other. It is a setting to lift the spirits. Yet for his first match without Petchey, Murray wore all black. Even his towel was black.

*

Brad Gilbert calls himself 'a neurotic, redneck Jew'. The actor Robin Williams, a friend of Gilbert's, thinks of 'BG' as 'a tennis sensei'. Andre Agassi had credited Gilbert for turning his tennis life around. Nothing would have prepared the American for the barracking he received from Andy Murray – a verbal assault on his dignity – during the most expensive coaching experiment in tennis history.

Whatever Gilbert was being paid by the Lawn Tennis Association – he was said to have been invoicing them somewhere between half and three-quarters of a million pounds a year – this gig would not have been easy on his ego. Money, sunglasses and a baseball cap didn't offer much protection. In Gilbert's bestselling book *Winning Ugly*, subtitled 'Tennis Warfare – Lessons From A Master', he advises the reader on how to relieve tension on court: try breathing like you have asthma, have 'happy feet', or sing a song ('I'll get a Tom Petty song going to myself').

What the manual doesn't recommend is Murray's foam-flecked approach, which was to whirl around to Gilbert and to gob a mouthful of invective his way. On at least one occasion, Murray was heard raging at Gilbert, the man who had guided Agassi back to world number one, 'You're giving me nothing out here.' There is a YouTube clip that shows Murray at a low moment in a grand slam; as he gives Gilbert a sarcastic thumbs-up, he also says something rude in Anglo-Saxon.

Gilbert is the most talkative person you will ever encounter (or have a largely one-sided conversation with) in tennis; it has been said that he is probably capable of talking underwater.

Gilbert, an analyst for the American broadcasters ESPN, also has his own special way of 'calling' tennis, using colourful phrases as well as nicknames he has invented. It goes something like this: 'I smell a beatdown – Dr Ivo [Karlovic] is going to be taken to the woodshed.' Translating that from Bradspeak into plain English: it's bad news for Karlovic; Gilbert thinks he is going to lose heavily.

Francesca Schiavone, a former women's French Open champion, is 'Frankie Goes to Hollywood', while the Australian player Bernard Tomic is 'Weekend at Bernie's', and if you ever hear Gilbert talking or tweeting about 'Gael Force' he is referring to the French player Gael Monfils. In Gilbert's universe of beatdowns and woodsheds, Roger Federer is 'FedFan' and Murray 'Muzza' or 'Muzzard'. As John McEnroe once said to Gilbert, 'You do know that you are allowed to use the players' real names?' So Gilbert likes to talk almost as much as McEnroe does.

But, when Murray got angry and started to vent, and the television director zoomed in for a close-up of Gilbert, he would sit there in silence – neutered by a young man's anger. What was the alternative? Scream back? Walk out? Other tennis players register their frustrations by destroying rackets, threatening to stuff tennis balls down line-judges' throats, or snarling at the umpires. But surely few have ever abused their coach like Murray mistreated Gilbert. Not once did Murray remember to call Gilbert 'a tennis sensei'.

'Andy had the hunger. He also had the temper,' Gilbert once said. 'McEnroe got furious at everything. Andy mainly got angry at Andy for not doing it perfectly. Sometimes he took it out on me. That's okay. I knew it was mostly frustration with himself.'

But Murray had never screamed at Mark Petchey. The way that Murray was sometimes carrying on, Gilbert must have been almost nostalgic for those gentle days when McEnroe shouted at him over the net at New York City's Madison Square Gardens: 'You don't deserve to be on the same court as me.' That was a one-off, a match that sent a fried McEnroe into temporary retirement. With Murray, Gilbert was being verbally abused more regularly than that.

Maybe, in some ways, Gilbert had not been that different from Murray in his playing days; angry and with plenty to say. McEnroe once recalled: 'Eeyore had nothing on Brad; he had a black cloud over his head from the moment he went out there and never seemed satisfied until he got you pretty gloomy too. It almost seemed to be his game-plan. He'd look like he was going to commit hara-kari in the warm-up. Then he did a running commentary when he played, berating himself on every single point and justifying every mistake he had made.' The difference being, of course, that Gilbert's anger was not directed at a coach.

Initially, Murray had been attracted by Gilbert's past. Gilbert had coached Andy Roddick to the 2003 US Open title (the only grand slam title he would win) and to the world number one ranking, success which Gilbert partly attributed to talking Roddick into abandoning a sun-visor for a baseball cap. Murray was more interested in the work that Gilbert had done with his boyhood idol Agassi; in their eight years together, Agassi had harvested six of his eight grand slam titles.

The Las Vegan has often spoken of how much he owed to Gilbert. In 1997, Agassi had spiralled down the rankings to number 141 in the world, and he would later disclose in his memoirs how it reached such a low that he found himself snorting lines of crystal meth – a highly addictive stimulant more commonly associated with America's under-class than former Wimbledon champions – off the top of his coffee table. It was Gilbert who talked Agassi into dropping down to the Challenger circuit, the level below the main tour, so he could build up some confidence and momentum. Agassi took his advice, and rode the wave all the way to the top of the rankings.

Gilbert's Hollywood moment came during the 1999 French Open final, when Agassi, hoping to win the Musketeers' Cup for the first time to complete his set of grand slam titles, found himself two sets down against Ukraine's Andrei Medvedev. When the rain came, and stopped play, Gilbert gave the pep talk of his coaching life. Agassi has said that he would not have won that match if Gilbert had not found the right words. Murray knew all that. As a player, Gilbert had made the most of his limited talents – his highest ranking was fourth – but it was as a coach that he had made his mark on tennis.

Murray had found, after firing Mark Petchey, he missed having someone around to talk to, and felt down. As a temporary move for the 2006 French Open, he asked his boyhood coach Leon Smith to accompany him to Roland Garros. Smith's influence on Murray, when coaching the boy from 11 to 17, was such that Murray wanted peroxide hair too. 'Leon was a bit of a poser back then: tall, good-looking with bleached blond hair.' As with many of Murray's working relationships, he ended it because of the bickering. On this occasion, the root cause of the arguments was that Murray wanted more independence. But it was an amicable parting, and they remained friends, which was why Smith was pleased to help in Paris that spring. What Murray wanted, though, was a full-time coach.

One of the greybeards of men's tennis thinks that working with a new coach is very much like having a new girlfriend. Hope springs eternal. You think to yourself, 'This is the girl/coach for me.' Murray linked up with Gilbert after that summer's Wimbledon, where he had beaten Roddick to reach the fourth round, only to play a pancake-flat match against Greek Cypriot Marcos Baghdatis.

In the early days, such as when Murray achieved his first victory over Roger Federer, at a tournament in Cincinnati, Murray and Gilbert patted compliments back and forth at each other, the American talking fondly of 'The Kid'. Some wondered what the LTA was doing paying for a millionaire's coach. But Gilbert had a theory that the LTA's decision to fund the arrangement had improved the usual player-coach dynamic. The relationship between a player and a coach is an odd and often fraught one; though the coach is the employee, he is the one giving instruction. Gilbert's thinking was that, because Murray was not paying his wages, there would not be as much of the usual conflict and tension. That was the theory, anyway.

'With Andy and Brad's personalities,' Tim Henman said, 'it was never a bed of roses.' How Yen-Hsun Lu would have loved to have had someone of Gilbert's calibre to have screamed at, but that was how the other half lived. Gilbert was going to put some muscle on those Scottish arms. He was also going to give him the tactical guidance he needed.

Murray and Gilbert were spending an unhealthy amount of time together. They were together for breakfast, lunch and dinner, for practice sessions, matches, flights, car rides and while killing time in the player-lounges and locker-rooms of the world tour. When Murray yelled at Gilbert, it looked like a release after all those hours spent listening to Gilbert. Only in matches could Murray take the conversational lead.

Murray appeared to grow tired of listening to Gilbert. Gilbert was a morning person; Murray often didn't function properly until after lunch. Gilbert loved Cadillacs; Murray didn't even have a driving licence then. Gilbert was also somewhat neurotic, and had such a phobia for germs that he always carried a small bottle of anti-bacterial handwash with him. Making bets about British football – they had a £500 wager on the number of goals that the footballer Peter Crouch would score in a season – was not going to bridge this divide. 'Andy doesn't live an outlandish life and he has got to be the only Scottish guy ever who doesn't drink,' Gilbert recalled in an interview with the *Guardian*. 'His idea of a good time is studying his opponent's play on DVD. And then he plays video games seven hours a day. So if he is not playing video games or playing tennis, he is with his girlfriend. He lives a quiet relaxed life, focused on being a tennis player. But he is obsessed with video games. I don't play video games.'

From what Gilbert was saying to Murray, it was almost as if the coach thought it a problem that his player did not have any vices. So Gilbert suggested to Murray that he ought to consider blowing off some steam by sky-diving, bungee-jumping or stripping in public. How different this was to what Gilbert had been used to with Agassi. 'I knew Agassi years before I coached him. We were contemporaries. We were mates before we started. The day I started with Andy I didn't know him at all. It was the first time I had coached a non-American. Andy is very argumentative if he feels strongly about something. A lot of people in his team gave into him. I didn't so we would argue.' Even after they stopped travelling together, Gilbert and Agassi had stayed friends. But Murray would have been aware that Gilbert's relationship with Roddick had ended badly.

Even when Murray was playing well at the beginning of the 2007 season – he reached the fourth round of the Australian Open, where he took Rafa Nadal to five sets – he was not enjoying his tennis. Wasn't this supposed to be fun? He was tetchy and angry when he should have been happy that he was making decent progress in the profession he had chosen. It was almost as if he had forgotten the pleasure he could take from tennis, though it has to be said that any dissatisfaction in

Murray's head stopped a long way short of how Agassi had felt about the sport. Murray never hated tennis.

The greatest pain that Murray has ever experienced on a tennis court came when, playing on his 20th birthday on the clay of Hamburg, he hit what he had imagined was an ordinary forehand. The wrist injury, sustained in a match against Italy's Filippo Volandri, would wreck Murray's summer, and leave Gilbert wondering whether the Briton was depressed and psychologically damaged. Murray and Gilbert were in agreement that the French Open was a write-off; there was no chance of Murray being in Paris.

Wimbledon was a different matter. Murray thought he was not ready to play, but Gilbert believed that the Scot's wrist tendons were strong enough for him to have competed. Not for the first time, Murray thought Gilbert was not listening to him, and they were not communicating properly. Murray didn't like how, after he had lost at a tournament, Gilbert would occasionally get up early, put a note under Murray's hotel door, and fly home. So alarmed was Murray by Gilbert's suggestion he was depressed and might need help that he sought reassurance from his friends about his mental health, and even went to see a psychologist, who confirmed that he was not.

Murray wrote in an autobiography published when he was 21: 'Brad even wondered about the cause of my anger on court, whether it was just related to something in the past rather than just my frustrated perfectionism as a player. I know he meant all these things as a form of motivation and he has the best of intentions.' What Gilbert saw in Murray was 'one of the most negative people' he'd met, but that was not how Murray saw himself, and he found it difficult to relate to someone who saw him in that way.

In the circumstances, making the third round of the 2007 US Open, when he lost to Korea's Hyung-Taik Lee, was a decent little run. Eventually, Murray tired of all things Brad. When Murray fired Gilbert in the autumn of 2007, he did so through an intermediary at the LTA. Maybe Murray should have fired Gilbert himself, but they weren't really talking then, and Murray couldn't ask his agent to do it for him, since Gilbert wouldn't have taken the call as the two of them weren't on speaking terms.

If Gilbert was no longer Murray's coach, he was still on the LTA's payroll; for several months he found himself trying and failing to coax more from Alex Bogdanovic, a British player who has the unfortunate career record of having turned eight Wimbledon wild-card entries into eight opening-round defeats (for some 'Boggo' had come to symbolise everything that was wrong with British tennis's culture of welfare dependency, with his first-round defeats at Wimbledon becoming as much a part of the summer season as Henley and Royal Ascot).

'I could have done more with Andy, but that's the thing in coaching – it's one-on-one, and if they're not feeling it, you don't want to stand in their way,' Gilbert has said. Murray would later confess that his treatment of Gilbert had been immature and silly. So he had learnt from his mistakes. The image that lingers, though, is of Gilbert sitting in the stands, feeling what it's like to be on the wrong end of a monologue.

Call them Andy Murray's Cross-Dressing Years. They were also the Miles Maclagan Years. Maclagan had Scottish blood and a floppy sun-hat, but much more importantly than that, in a post-Gilbert world, was that he had an easy-going nature. Coaches don't come much lower maintenance than Maclagan, who until he was hired had been best known for having held, but not converted, three match points against Boris Becker at the German's last tournament, the 1999 Wimbledon Championships. Unlike Brad Gilbert, Maclagan wouldn't talk at all, at least not in public, with Murray preferring his new coach not to give interviews. Murray, though sensitive to the charge that he wanted to surround himself with yes-men, was plainly in much greater control than he had ever been with Gilbert.

After ditching Gilbert, Murray had resolved to put together a gang of good people around him. Maclagan was the coach and he worked alongside physiotherapist Andy Ireland, fitness trainers Jez Green and Matt Little and the occasional consultant, such as Alex Corretja, a former French Open finalist and world number two. They became known as Team Murray, a term which the player himself was not keen on. When Murray was playing a grand slam, and all his backroom staff were there, mischief could be had during a change of ends by counting the number of people in his guest box, and then suggesting that this Scottish tennis player had an entourage that would not shame a Saudi prince. This was often unfair; while it was reasonable to count agents and media advisers and anyone who worked for his management company, it was going too far to throw his girlfriend and brother into the mix just to reach double figures and get a cheap laugh.

This Team Murray made their own entertainment. To keep their training and off-court life interesting, there were forfeits riding on their games of football tennis, played with two people on either side of the net, and used as a warm-up. That was why you might have seen Murray, or one of his staff, going out to dinner at a restaurant wearing women's clothing or a chest wig, dressing in a pink velour tracksuit or choosing a Hannah Montana film as his in-flight movie. Other forfeits included kissing the winners' toes, taking an ice bath without shorts on, clearing the plates away at lunch and wearing a cricket helmet to practice. There was a strict rule: if anyone from outside Murray's circle enquired as to what you were doing, you weren't allowed to say it was for a forfeit; you had to tell whoever was asking that you simply liked going to restaurants with your clothes on inside out. It may or may not have been a coincidence that, around that time, Murray was watching a lot of *Entourage*, the American television series about a Hollywood actor and his posse.

Twice during Murray's time with Maclagan – they were together for two and a half years, from the end of the 2007 season until after the 2010 Wimbledon Championships, during which time his ranking peaked at number two – he came within three sets of winning a grand slam. At the 2008

US Open, Murray became the first British grand slam finalist since Greg Rusedski had been the runner-up to Australia's Pat Rafter in 1997, also in New York.

For Murray, wearing a grey shirt, and with what someone called a geography teacher's facial fuzz, the final went by in a blur, and he did not win a set against Roger Federer. That was not entirely unexpected. Murray was not used to the emotions and the choreography of a grand slam final, while the other guy was arguably the greatest player of all time. 'This was a good effort at my age,' said Murray, who was 21 at the time, but he wanted more: 'I don't want to be remembered for losing in the final of the US Open.' Even then, Murray was saying that the only goal he had left in tennis was becoming a grand slam champion.

The second occasion that Murray went close was at the 2010 Australian Open, and again he had the misfortune to play Federer. Had Murray won the third set – he had been 5-2 up in games and had five set points in the tiebreak – the match could have got very interesting. But he didn't. Once again, Murray lost in straight sets to Federer and it all got too much for him when he was making his thank-you speech. The previous year's final had had Federer, after a defeat by Rafa Nadal, weeping during the speeches: 'God, it's killing me.' And now it was Murray's turn to lose control of his bottom lip, though almost immediately afterwards he thought of a gen-uinely funny line and returned to the microphone: 'I can cry like Roger, it's just a shame I can't play like him.'

The way Maclagan tells it, the end came when he realised

there were three people in this tennis marriage. For a couple of months, Maclagan had been uncomfortable with the role played within Team Murray by Corretja. Though the Spaniard had initially been hired to help with Murray's clay-court game, as time went on his influence spread to other surfaces too. Murray had reached the semi-finals of that summer's Wimbledon Championships, losing to Nadal, and as Maclagan flew across the Atlantic to join his player at a training camp in Miami, he felt that it was the right time to speak openly about his concerns. He was aware that starting such a conversation could result in his unemployment.

'The issue was about Alex,' Maclagan recalled in an interview with the *Daily Telegraph*. 'Alex was a great player and he's a good coach and he had his ideas. And, with most of our ideas, there was some agreement between us. But there were a couple of things that we didn't agree on. The three of us sat down for a civilised chat and Andy and I decided to move on rather than coming to a compromise.' Maclagan was pleased that the trio did not try to throttle each other, and they parted amicably. 'I'm proud of the fact that we didn't have a big fight, that we didn't try to throw each other off the balcony. We ended things and shook hands. The next morning, I had breakfast with Andy and then flew home.'

For the second time, the first having been Brad Gilbert, one of Andre Agassi's former coaches played a role in Andy Murray's development. Darren Cahill was part of the Adidas team of coaches who were made available to anyone sponsored by the

German sportswear company. Murray often turned to the Australian for advice, and for a while it looked as though he wanted Cahill just for himself. The loose arrangement had its drawbacks. During grand slams, Cahill had his television commitments with ESPN and so was not always around when he was needed. Plus, there was the adidas versus adidas rule – if Murray found himself playing an opponent also dressed with three stripes on his kit, Cahill was not allowed to offer any tactical guidance. Where Cahill really helped, though, was encouraging Murray to consider appointing Ivan Lendl as a full-time coach.

The possibility that Murray and Lendl could work together was first raised in the spring of 2011 when the Scot, clearly still thrown by having lost to Novak Djokovic in the final of the Australian Open, was beaten by Alex Bogomolov Junior at the hard-court tournament in Miami. Lendl was the one who made the first move, not Murray, and there was initially some suspicion that Lendl was happy to have the idea floated in the media as a way of publicising his tennis academy. Without Cahill, though, Murray might never have entertained the possibility.

Cahill has recalled: 'I really encouraged Andy to consider. It's not easy, when players look at these former champions, to get their heads around the fact that they are going to fully commit to the coaching job because, to be quite frank, a lot of these guys can go off and in two or three days make the type of money that they can make from a full year of coaching. So it is unusual that a Lendl, a Connors or a McEnroe or any of

Giving his mother Judy a kiss after winning the title at Queen's Club in June 2009.

Murray found himself 'welling up big time' after winning a doubles title with his brother Jamie in Valencia in November 2010.

With his girlfriend Kim Sears during London Fashion Week.

Sacking Mark Petchey, a friend as well as his coach, was one of the hardest experiences of Murray's professional life.

Brad Gilbert wondered whether Murray was 'depressed'.

Murray reached two grand slam finals while being coached by Miles Maclagan.

The *New York Times* magazine called Murray and Ivan Lendl 'tennis's odd couple'.

Murray's fitness trainers, Jez Green and Matt Little, helped to transform the Scot into a gym- and track-hardened tennis player.

Murray flexes his bicep at the 2008 Wimbledon Championships.

Four key figures in Murray's life: his mother Judy, his manager Simon Fuller, his girlfriend Kim Sears and his physiotherapist Andy Ireland.

Playing doubles with Tim Henman, who has been one of the most influential figures in Murray's tennis life.

Punching his strings in anger leaves Murray's knuckles – and shorts – covered in blood.

For years, Murray didn't have the universal support of the British public, after a joke he made about the England football team.

these legends of the game would actually commit to somebody else's career. We felt that Ivan ticked a lot of boxes in what Andy was looking for. They had travelled down similar paths. Ivan recognised that what he went through was very similar to what Andy was going through. He wanted to make a difference to Andy's life and career. You can't buy that.'

Ever since Murray had stopped working with Miles Maclagan, he had been urged to appoint someone with standing and gravitas as his coach. For a while, Murray's good friend, Dani Vallverdu, was the closest to being the Scot's full-time coach. Murray and Vallverdu had first met when they were juniors training in Barcelona. 'The first day Andy got there, they made me practise with him. I thought: "Oh my god, who's this kid? He's very good." He always says that I gave him attitude that day and that I wasn't too nice to him,' Vallverdu has recalled. 'But I don't think that's true.' During Murray's years on the tour, the Venezuelan had been an occasional hitting-partner and even more occasional doubles partner, and he had started to travel to most tournaments.

But didn't Murray need a big-hitter? Wouldn't someone with more clout have possibly helped change the outcome of the 2011 Australian Open final, with Murray's straight-sets defeat to Djokovic giving rise to the unfortunate statistic that the Briton had not won any of the nine sets he had played in his first three slam finals? What Murray was looking for, when you boiled it down, was someone who had been there and done it. Vallverdu's ranking had peaked, in 2005, at 727; Lendl had won every major apart from Wimbledon. So

Murray was curious. But Lendl was not going to come to him. If Murray wanted to talk this over, he was the one who would have to travel. Some observers, including American former professional Justin Gimelstob, interpreted Lendl's demand as a way of showing that he was not beholden to Murray; that he did not need the job.

So Murray went to have lunch with Lendl, at a pizzeria in Florida, and there was no avoiding the symmetries. At that stage, Murray had played and lost in three grand slam finals, while Lendl's first four major finals had brought four defeats. Along the way, a clever sub-editor at the *New York Post* had him as 'Choke-Oslovakian'. Murray was, of course, encouraged by how Lendl had then gone on to win grand slam finals (though it should be noted that Lendl had some good fortune in his fifth major final when he found himself trailing John McEnroe by two sets to love at the 1984 French Open, only for the noise leaking from a cameraman's headset to drive the New Yorker wild). 'Ivan was able to look Murray in the eye and say, "I've been in your position." Very few people could say that,' McEnroe noted. Murray agreed: 'To talk to someone who had gone on to be a great player, but who had been in a lot of the same situations as me, that was so helpful.'

Would Murray have been so interested in Lendl, and vice versa, had Lendl won his first grand slam final? Probably not. But a rough run in slam finals was not all they had in common. All Murray wanted to do in tennis was to win a grand slam; everything he did on the match court, the practice court, in the gym or on the track was to further that aim. And

Lendl knew all about obsession. Such was Lendl's desire to win Wimbledon – to add to the three US Opens, the three French Opens and the two Australian Opens – he twice skipped Roland Garros to give himself more time to prepare for the grass. That didn't work either.

A couple of Stakhanovites, they also had self-discipline in common. Maybe there are tennis professionals on the tour today who are more committed to hard work and self-improvement than Murray, but they have kept themselves very well hidden; and Lendl had been the first tennis player to take diet, fitness and training seriously. Boris Becker regards Lendl as the first modern tennis professional. Lendl would make a schedule and stick to it. A friend once said of Lendl that 'if the Pope was in Ivan's living room at bedtime, he'd say, "it was nice meeting you," give you that blank smile of his and disappear into his bedroom'. Lendl's attention to detail was such that he would ask the man who laid the courts at the US Open to also lay the practice court at his home so that he would be practising on the exact same surface. For the first time in his life, Murray had met someone as obsessive about tennis as he was. That wasn't all they had in common – both had been coached by their mothers.

In other ways, they were very different men. When Lendl was playing, he had displayed what some saw as paranoid behaviour. If he heard clicking on his telephone, he imagined that the Czech secret services had him under surveillance again, and he would spend the next few weeks on the lookout for eavesdroppers in restaurants. But when you have grown up under a communist dictatorship, perhaps that is less surprising. When Lendl returned to his house, with its high stone walls, expensive alarm systems and German Shepherds for guard dogs, people thought him a recluse. For all Murray's unease with fame, he has never hidden himself away, or wondered whether the couple on the next table were spies. Murray is more popular with his peer group than Lendl ever was with his, though that needs qualifying: Murray is living in a more corporate and civilised age. The current generation don't spit insults like 'communist son of a bitch' at each other like the old boys did.

More than anything, what Lendl brought was authority. Miles Maclagan would later suggest that Lendl was probably telling Murray many of the same things that he had been, including to be more aggressive and assertive from the off, but that Lendl would have been doing so with a back-catalogue of achievement. Only Lendl, out of all Murray's coaches, was in the position to tell him what it was really like to win a grand slam. Murray was hoping that Lendl could assist with the mental side of playing slams, and how to deal with pressure and expectation. During that first meeting, Lendl had impressed Murray with his knowledge of the modern game, telling him how he would go about beating Roger Federer, Rafa Nadal and Djokovic. While Lendl had not been on the tour, he had clearly been watching enough matches on television, and talking to enough people, to have kept his tennis brain active.

*

The Coach that Everybody Cares About

Andy Murray could have beaten Yen-Hsun Lu 6-0, 6-0, 6-0, having performed cartwheels and backflips during every change of ends, and still he would not have elicited a smile from his coach. Ivan Lendl never smiled when he was watching Murray play. It was something he had copied from his parents; they had never shown any emotion as spectators. 'Smiling is over-rated,' he said. Maybe Lendl did not have the choice, perhaps he was no longer even physically capable of smiling while tennis was being played. This much was clear: Lendl's unmoving, unsmiling face had been having a calming effect on Murray. When Lendl was around, Murray was much better at controlling his emotions than when his coach had stayed at home to play golf. What would have happened, you wondered, if Murray had ever dared to scream at Lendl in the same way he used to tear into Brad Gilbert? 'I really wouldn't recommend that he ever does that,' Boris Becker said.

So no one expected Lendl to smile, or to clap, to move or to do very much at all when Murray competed for a place in the last 32. Dani Vallverdu was so excitable – up out of his seat the whole time – that Lendl wondered whether the South American might one day fall out of a guest box. Lendl, meanwhile, liked to hold the same position for as long as he could; with his chin resting on the upturned palm of his hand.

Still, there is plenty a coach can communicate to a player by doing nothing, as Chris Evert, once the ice queen of the women's game, and a winner of 18 grand slam singles titles, had noticed. 'When I first heard that Andy and Ivan were going to work together, I thought, "Oh yes, this looks interesting." Ivan is so poker-faced, so stoic and he never claps. Ivan's intense but in a low-key way. Andy used to get so down on himself, and that was having an impact on his tennis. Ivan has stopped that. Ivan keeps Andy mentally balanced,' Evert said. 'If Andy plays a good shot and looks over at Ivan at the side of the court, Ivan looks back in a way that says, "Okay, but keep going." If Andy is down, Ivan is saying to him, "You can get out of this." Ivan's message to Andy is, "Don't get so heated or emotional – just chill."'

It would be going too far to claim that Lendl never showed any emotion while Murray was playing. Take the occasion when Murray had looked to be in trouble against Marin Cilic in the quarter-finals of the 2012 US Open, and Lendl removed his baseball cap; that may sound like a small act, but for a coach who doesn't usually like to move, some read that as a sign of great concern. Or recall Murray's final against Novak Djokovic at the same tournament. That night in New York, Lendl thought he would help his player by doing something extraordinary: clapping. There had been moments during the match when Murray had glanced over at Lendl and thought he looked bored. That was just Lendl being Lendl; unmoved, with the same range of facial expressions as a net post. Lendl's decision to break with his own coaching protocol – this was an even bigger event than when he had taken his hat off a couple of rounds earlier – was to tell the Scot to keep on doing what he was doing. 'Andy started hitting better forehands and I tried to show him, "That's the way,"' Lendl would later disclose. 'It's a war and he needs every bit of encouragement.' When Murray won the match, Lendl wasn't exactly dancing on his chair, but the Scot did notice what appeared to be a small smile.

Murray's new calmness was the biggest change since Lendl's arrival. Lendl knew that to have made any great technical changes to Murray's game – to have broken his game down and then put it back together – would have been 'suicidal'. What Lendl could change was Murray's strategy, and his willingness to take risks, to play some shots, to be bold. 'When somebody tells you to go for your shots, it's one thing,' Martina Navratilova has said. 'When Ivan Lendl tells you to go for your shots, you listen.'

There were not many dissenting or sceptical voices towards the Lendl–Murray collaboration, but one of them was Jim Courier's. The American, a former world number one, had his theory about why Lendl had returned to tennis, and he shared it with a local television network during the 2012 Australian Open: 'There is a reason and it is a little bit mercenary. He hasn't been allowed to make any money from tennis for the past fifteen years because he had cashed in disability insurance. That's the reason Ivan is back.' Lendl responded that Courier was being ridiculous: 'Jim shouldn't be saying stuff like that. First of all, it's wrong, and he doesn't have the proper information. End of story.'

Behind the scenes, and on the practice courts, Lendl was tweaking, chatting and encouraging. Lendl had told Murray to take it easy with some of the service drills, asking him: 'Do you want your arm to fall off?' The idea was that the arm would stay fresher and he would serve better when it mattered, in matches.

One observer reported that Lendl and Murray often had 'deep' conversations at the practice courts. 'Andy asks a lot of questions,' Lendl disclosed. 'Sometimes he surprises me with his questions, because they come out of nowhere, so obviously he has been thinking about it. The more questions he asks, the happier I am. He shows he wants to learn. I don't like to push things on him unless I have to – as I do at times. He can pluck what he wants from this closet, that closet or that closet. I really don't know at times which is the best one for him – or whether any of them are right. Only he knows what he is struggling with inside.' During their first year together, Lendl had told the *New York Times* magazine, for a feature about 'tennis's new odd couple': 'I want Andy to tell me things that will help me work with him, and some of them are very private and go very, very deep.' Even after Murray has retired, Lendl will not share what was said between them, believing that a tennis coach should be following the same strict rules of confidentiality as a lawyer, a doctor or a priest.

Lendl has always been honest with Murray. 'Ivan has always told me exactly what he thought. And in tennis it's not always that easy to do in a player-coach relationship. The player is sometimes the one in charge. I think sometimes coaches are not always that comfortable doing that,' Murray said. 'He's made me learn more from the losses that I've had than maybe I did in the past. He's been extremely honest with me. If I work hard, he's happy. If I don't, he's disappointed, and he'll tell me.'

The Coach that Everybody Cares About

In the past, Murray had had his suspicions about sports psychologists, yet Lendl persuaded him to speak to Alexis Castorri, who had helped the Czech during his career. She did her best to bring back Murray's 'zest'. 'When I looked at early films of Andy playing, he played with such happiness and excitement. My initial thought when I worked with him was that he needed to bring back the zest. But I believe you start that off the court,' Castorri told the *Daily Telegraph*. 'Andy is a creative genius, a tactical and technical genius, so he needed to reconnect with his inner strengths. It's natural that when someone puts their heart and soul into what they're doing, they sometimes forget how much enjoyment they once took from it. Andy has lofty goals and is hard on himself. You need to remember that you love the battle, that's why you are out there.' As Castorri told The Tennis Space website: 'I am both a psychologist and a therapist as well as a sports psychologist. Therefore my interest is first and foremost the person. I prefer to "use" an innate strength a person already has within him to assist in attaining their life or sports goals. Your entire life should be a reflection of who you are, what's important to you, and what you bring to the table that we can tap into to attain success.'

Once a conversation or practice session was over, Lendl often left to play golf (he played every other day during Wimbledon). Lendl was not being unfriendly or a total golf tragic (though his interest in golf was such that he was believed to have had a clause in his contract allowing him to watch the US Masters live, irrespective of where Murray was playing or training). It was just he had noted how some of Murray's previous arrangements had been spoilt by spending too much time together and he wanted to avoid that happening this time round. Player and coach weren't hanging out in the evenings during the Wimbledon fortnight; Murray would go home to Surrey, while Lendl would have dinner with his wife Samantha.

At first glance it seemed that, under the Lendl regime, all fun and fripperies had been cancelled. Since Lendl had joined Murray's staff, no one had seen them playing games of tennis-football on the practice court, or carrying out any forfeits. The thinking went something like this: you weren't going to catch Lendl wearing a pink velour tracksuit or watching a Hannah Montana film, just because he had a lost a game of tennis-football, or whatever else, with his twenty-something employer. But let us not forget about the filthy jokes and the attempts to inflict pain by clocking each other with tennis balls. Or how Lendl, covered in sweat after a training session, would cast around for someone 'dry' to bear-hug.

You knew that Murray had formed some sort of bond with Lendl when you heard about the potential forfeit riding on some doubles. Murray and Lendl were planning a challenge match with the British doubles pairing of Ross Hutchins and Colin Fleming, and if they lost, Lendl was going to have to rollerblade into the All England Club while dressed in white Spandex. Lendl also tried to make New York laugh during the 2012 US Open. All who compete on the Arthur Ashe Stadium are invited to select three songs for the stadium's DJ to play during the changeovers. Serena Williams tended to ask for rockers Green Day, Laura Robson was open about her liking for boy-bands, but Murray did not want to choose in case listening out for the tracks would be a distraction. The offer was passed on to Lendl, who requested Wham! and Culture Club.

The fun should never interfere with the tennis, though. One of Lendl's recommendations to Murray during the 2012 US Open was that he should move to a quieter hotel. When Lendl was competing for US Open titles, he would spend as little time as possible in New York City. Rather than staying in a hotel, he would commute from his Connecticut estate, and he would try to practise at his house rather than at the tournament; about the only time he went to the venue was to play matches. As much as Murray has always enjoyed the noise and the chaos of Manhattan, he took his coach's advice over the hotel. What Murray had not counted on, as he sought peace and quiet in New York, was Prince Harry playing a game of strip pool in a Las Vegas suite. And maybe Murray's new status as an Olympic champion had brought extra attention, too. On stepping out of his hotel lobby one morning, Murray was intercepted by a group of cameramen. 'They asked me whether I had seen the pictures of Prince Harry. I said, "No comment." And then they asked me what I thought of the crown jewels. I didn't comment on that either. I ran away.'

S*** happens, Andy Murray was essentially saying about the first Wednesday of this Wimbledon, and the mayhem all around him. Yes, you can hurt yourself on the grass, but you can also hurt yourself falling down the stairs, or tripping over your shoelaces. Let's not blame the grass, Murray was arguing. People fall over, people lose tennis matches, that's tennis, that's sport.

This was Murray's sixth grand slam with Lendl (it would have been his seventh had he not missed Roland Garros), and before the second seed played Yen-Hsun Lu he would have gone through his usual routines with his coach and with Dani Vallverdu. Before matches, Murray tended to talk first, Vallverdu would go next, and if Lendl had 'noticed something about the opponent, or what's going on, I would add that, but very few times would I add anything – the boys have it covered pretty well'. The way Vallverdu tells it, preparing Murray for matches is very much a team effort, with no egos complicating matters.

Murray's first major under Lendl's guidance had been the 2012 Australian Open when he had led Novak Djokovic in the semi-finals – he wouldn't win the match, but at least he lost in the right way, playing aggressive tennis. After reaching the quarter-finals of that year's French Open, where he was beaten by David Ferrer, he was the runner-up to Roger Federer at the All England Club (he quickly recovered from that disappointment to beat the same opponent in the gold-medal match at the Olympics). Then came the glory of the US Open, with a five-set victory over Djokovic. Murray's victory was a validation of the decision to employ Lendl, a move which had not been without risk. Boris Becker went further than most when he argued that, without Lendl, Murray would not have won the Olympics or the US Open.

But winning that first slam was hopefully going to be just the start of it. 'I didn't come here to have a good time,' Lendl had said in New York. 'I came here to help Andy win and he did just that. So it's job done.' Except that, in Lendl's head, this was a very long way from being 'job done'. That night, Lendl was already thinking to the future, to what might happen next for the Scot. Lendl didn't need to be reminded of what had happened to him after he won his first grand slam title on his fifth appearance in the final of a major; he then lost his sixth and seventh, so in American sporting parlance that left him at 1-6 for finals. Lendl wanted Murray to avoid that fate.

It didn't matter whether you listened to someone from the tennis mainstream. Or to Irvine Welsh, the *Trainspotting* novelist whose tennis commentary on Twitter is so outrageous that he has been likened to 'Dan Maskell on acid' (the Scot expressed his thoughts and emotions on Murray's matches using the sort of imagery that E.L. James would consider too racy). Everyone was agreed. The summer of 2012 – that transatlantic romp through the London Olympics and then New York City – had transformed Murray. Was there any better illustration of this new Murray than the occasion he beat Federer in the semi-finals of the 2013 Australian Open, for what was his first victory over the Swiss at the slams? While Murray was poised and assured, the multilingual Federer, a sophisticate who can charm and love-bomb in several languages, was demonstrating that he also knows a little Anglo-Saxon. 'F****** stop,' he said to Murray. 'F****** stop.'

This was the closest that Federer – also venting at the umpire – ever got to being a Jimmy Connors tribute act. As a writer for the *New York Times* put it, hearing Federer using the F-word was a bit like a unicorn giving you the finger.

Murray felt good about himself at Melbourne Park at the beginning of the year. That was clear from the way he was carrying himself. You could also tell by reading the slogan on the front of one of his T-shirts: 'Prepare, Attack, Destroy.' That's not a top you would be advised to wear if you're still the guy who keeps falling short at slams. But as a grand slam champion, as someone comfortable with his place in the sport, why not? Murray did as the T-shirt promised against Federer. But he couldn't quite manage it against Djokovic and lost the final in four sets.

So, after withdrawing from the French Open, London was next on the grand slam calendar. For those members of the British public who think tennis is a fortnight and not a year-round sport, Murray winning Wimbledon would be the greatest moment of them all, above anything he could ever achieve in New York, Melbourne or Paris. And if Murray could succeed on what someone once called the strawberry fields of London, Lendl would accomplish as a coach what he had never come close to as a player; winning the affection of the British people.

Murray's message after his second-round match would have been different had he been one of those players who looked as if they were trying to compete in heels, or if his opponent had, to use the locker-room lingo, 'got hot'.

The Coach that Everybody Cares About

It would be an exaggeration to call Murray the forgotten man of the All England Club, but at this stage of the tournament he wasn't exactly drawing attention to himself, and that was just as he and Lendl would have wanted it. For the second time in the tournament, Murray's match was low down the news agenda. Just as he had dominated Benjamin Becker in the opening round, he was in almost total control against Lu; he was ripping all the drama out of his tennis with a 6-3, 6-3, 7-5 victory. The news from Murray's court was that there was no news. In the first round, Lu had beaten a British opponent, but there was a world of difference between playing James Ward, the son of a London taxi driver, and looking down the court at Murray (there was to be no repeat of the shocking result in the first round of the Beijing Olympics). So Murray played that day, but he was never a part of Wimbledon's Wild Wednesday.

With both Federer and Rafa Nadal now out, the tennis commentariat believed that a Djokovic–Murray final was now a near-certainty. Still, those same critics had imagined that Nadal would have little trouble against Steve Darcis and that Federer would be comfortable against Sergiy Stakhovsky. And, as coaches were warning, upsets are infectious. Next for Murray was Tommy Robredo, a veteran Spaniard whose father had named him after The Who's rock-opera, and who would have been very encouraged by what he had seen so far.

At this Wimbledon, the Big Four weren't untouchable.

3

A Body like a Machine

There are no prizes, not even a deep-fried Mars bar, for guessing which of these two characters – Andy Murray or Tommy Robredo – had had a large slice of chocolate cake and some vanilla ice cream just a couple of nights before their third-round match. If you're unsure, here's a clue: it wasn't the man who had once appeared in a video feature for a British newspaper, in which, naked to the waist, he had looked into the camera and said: 'My body feels like a machine.' Or the player who, a few months before this Wimbledon, had offered himself up as soft porn for middle-class women when he was photographed shirtless and smothered in stripper's oil for the cover of a broadsheet magazine; somebody wanted people to know he was in excellent shape.

Yes, there had been the occasional moments of indulgence,

such as devouring Feast ice creams when he was between tournaments (he was capable of eating three or four in a day). Or the time he was flying home from New York and, after one glass of champagne too many, the new US Open champion realised he was brushing his teeth with his girlfriend's face-cream (Kim Sears would affectionately call him a lightweight for letting the bubbles go to his head). But, for the most part, Murray could not have been stricter about how he fuelled his body for competition. There was a time and a place for eating cake and ice cream, and it wasn't as you prepared to play for a place in the second week of Wimbledon. Anyone who imagined that, after winning a first grand slam, Murray's work ethic had floated to the bottom of a glass of fizz, or was lost among the mint leaves of a mojito served on Miami's South Beach, or that his diet had been ruined by a thousand canapés, didn't understand the guy.

Murray's appetite for pain was greater than ever before when he did his pre-season training ahead of 2013. That wasn't because Murray is a masochist – he isn't – but because he knew all those sessions on the track, in the gym and in the Bikram yoga studio were worth it, and that his physical fitness had helped him over the line in New York. Hard work brings great reward. And the details mattered; when Murray had played an exhibition match at London's Hurlingham Club the week before Wimbledon, two bottles of water were placed on the table in front of him, one still and one sparkling; he was always going to choose a glass of still, as the carbonated stuff doesn't help with an athlete's digestion.

Andy Murray: Wimbledon Champion

You only have to pass by Wimbledon's Court Eighteen, where there is a plaque commemorating John Isner's 11-hour victory over Nicolas Mahut in the first round of the 2010 Championships, to be reminded of how brutal this sport can be, and how fit you have to be to play it. When Murray had appeared at his first Wimbledon, some eight years earlier in 2005, he had been the skinniest, gawkiest kid on the tennis block, but he had transformed himself into a gym-hardened modern professional. Going into the 2013 grass-court slam, there was just one concern about Murray's physical conditioning, which was the worry that the problem with his lower back, which had caused his withdrawal from the French Open, could suddenly flare up at any moment and render the Briton incapable of serving any faster than 60mph.

Inside the All England Club's version of the Eden Project – Murray and Robredo would play under the closed roof of Centre Court – there was intense scrutiny of the Scot's every move and facial expression; the crowd were looking out for the first signs of Murray's back threatening to hijack his Wimbledon.

Tennis has never been more violent, or more explosive. There has, of course, been an arms race in frames and strings; the polyester strings have forced the greatest change in recent years by allowing players to stay in control even when swinging with maximum power. Forehands can be hit without compromise. The manufacturers often aren't subtle; there is a range of strings on the market called 'Big Banger'. But the tennis that is being played today – real matches and tennis video games have become almost indistinguishable – would not be possible if Generation Murray did not take their physical conditioning so seriously. Maybe once it was possible to win a grand slam without knowing what cardiovascular meant, or how you would go about fixing yourself a protein shake, but not now. Buy a ticket to a grand slam and you will be watching some of the world's greatest athletes.

In the 1970s and 1980s, tennis players would have thought 'kinetic energy' was something that came served in a cocktail glass. It is a different sport now. Watch footage of matches from those years and you find yourself marvelling at how slow it was. Almost absurdly slow. So slow it can be frustrating to sit through. Back then, a first serve struck at 125mph was considered 'big'; now a delivery at that speed would not be worthy of comment. Television companies use the Hawk-Eye cameras and computer, based on missile-tracking technology, to measure the speed of forehand winners, many of which are travelling at 100mph-plus. Tennis's Studio 54 days, when a player could roll out of the nightclub and on to a practice court, have gone the same way as the haircuts. Every modern tennis player has to work as hard on his strength and fitness as he does on correcting any technical faults. If not harder. What would be the point of having grooved groundstrokes if, when a match goes into the fifth hour, your body fails you? If Murray was to have any chance of winning Wimbledon, he had to compete physically.

His rivals were dedicating themselves to improving their

bodies. Rafa Nadal is no longer the same player who, as a teenager, bounded on to the tour in three-quarter-length trousers and muscle-vests. In recent times, he has been having platelet-rich therapy to combat his knee pain, with the injections bringing tears to his eyes.

Nadal regards Roger Federer as a 'freak of nature' for never picking up the serious injuries that others do. There is no doubt that Federer's smooth style and movement have been a great advantage over the years, but a great deal of effort has gone into making it look easy ('When Federer is in full flight, he looks like he's gliding, almost like he's floating above the court,' said Jim Courier, a former world number one). Federer's longest-serving member of staff, who was with him before he started winning grand slams, is his fitness trainer Pierre Paganini.

Federer knows that without excellent fitness, genius can't flow from his racket. Excellent fitness means excellent footwork, and that means he can glide or float to wherever he wants to be on a tennis court. Over the course of every season, Federer will have a couple of training blocks, maybe more, when he will work on his footwork and speed around the court rather than on his strokes. The drills are designed to replicate movement during a match. Andre Agassi's hill-running around Las Vegas, as impressive as it undoubtedly was, now looks a little unscientific.

Tennis has witnessed some weird science and some bogus science. There was once a Swiss player on the women's tour, Patty Schnyder, whose coach (who believed he had found the cure for AIDS and cancer) convinced her that she ought to be drinking two litres of fresh orange juice every day. But there is no reason to snigger at anything that any of the leading men have done.

Anyone still using that mocking line 'anyone for tennis?' without irony, needs to sit down in front of a television showing replays of Novak Djokovic's last two matches at the 2012 Australian Open – all 11 hours of them. Djokovic was on court for almost five hours in beating Murray in the semi-finals, and then for close to six hours in defeating Nadal in the final. Djokovic's tennis was astonishing, with the Serbian reaching balls that he should not have even been getting close to, and then really cuffing his shots. Strange to think that Djokovic was once derided for being soft, for always whining about his physical ailments, for hating the heat, and for being too eager to retire from matches. A joke from Andy Roddick at the US Open one year – the American said Djokovic was dealing with 'cramp, bird flu, anthrax, SARS, and a common cold and cough' – would have stung. He knew he had to change.

It was a very different Djokovic who won three grand slam titles in 2011, putting together one of the greatest seasons in tennis history. Djokovic's parents used to run a pizzeria halfway up a Serbian mountain, so you could say he was brought up on margheritas, but a doctor persuaded him to cut the carbs and the gluten from his plate. The same physician told him not to eat in front of the television, but to sit at the table where he could be 'present with his food'. Djokovic has also occasionally sat in an egg-shaped, pressurised chamber that gave him some of the benefits of being at altitude. Djokovic's fitness trainer, Gebhard Phil-Gritsch, has been quoted as saying that the player's body ran with the power and precision of a Formula One car. He also said that he is forever looking for that one per cent change to Djokovic's conditioning that could 'make a big jump'. 'The better you get the more you have to go into details, to optimise every little angle of the game.'

Like Djokovic, Murray has transformed his body since joining the tour. Back when he was being called 'a scruffy Hugh Grant', it was not necessarily a compliment, but a comment on his need to bulk up.

In those early days, after reaching the third round of the 2005 Wimbledon Championships, where he lost a five-setter to Argentina's David Nalbandian because of cramp and fatigue, Murray was sensitive to the criticism that he was more familiar with the Starbucks drinks menu than the weights-room. Murray felt as though there should have been more attention paid to his achievement of going that far in the tournament, and less on any physical deficiencies he might have shown against a former finalist. Certainly, no one should have expected an 18-year-old, who just weeks earlier had still been playing junior tennis, to have been at the peak of his physical powers.

More recently, however, looking back at that summer, Murray has appreciated that some of the observations were fair comment (in 2012, he recognised that his upper body had been too small when he first played on the full circuit, but said he never had too much of a problem with his legs as he had inherited strong calves from his mother). He will surely also see that, at the time, he was not doing everything in his power to prepare his body for tennis. For all the hours he was doing on the court and in the gym at Barcelona's Sanchez-Casal Academy, he wasn't eating properly and on one occasion fainted in the loo. At the 2005 junior French Open, he had been running on baguettes and chocolate spread, and during his first senior Wimbledon he would send his mother Judy out for Starbucks frappuccinos. And while he hardened up over that long American summer in 2005, and did well to qualify for the US Open, he faded in the second round of the main draw to France's Arnaud Clement.

Here at the 2013 Wimbledon Championships Murray was a very different animal, thanks to years of dedication and a sophisticated training programme. You don't get to challenge for grand slams simply by upping your broccoli intake and doing more chin-ups.

One of Brad Gilbert's ambitions as Murray's coach had been to have his player wearing a Nadal-style muscle-vest at Wimbledon, with his biceps on show for the Royal Box. We will never know for sure whether Murray would have considered that even for a moment, as Gilbert and Murray's time together included only one Wimbledon and Murray did not play because of injury. What we do know is that, when Murray sustained that wrist injury, one of his concerns was whether there would be further debate about his physical fitness (or lack thereof); he felt considerable relief when he saw that it had been accepted as a freak accident, and that he would not come under further attack for supposedly being a slacker.

Indeed, Murray has not been at fault for other freak injuries over the course of his career, such as when he was involved in a minor car crash in New York that left him lying on the floor of a yellow taxi cab with a bump on his head and mild whiplash. Or the prang during the indoor tournament in Paris one autumn when he stepped out of the crumpled vehicle with a stiff back. Or the time at the French Open when he broke his tooth by biting into a baguette.

Early on in their relationship, or 'right off the bat' as Gilbert said, he told Murray that he wanted a couple of things for him: an extra four kilos in weight and eight more miles per hour on his service speed, and that 'the second won't happen without the first'. Gilbert introduced Murray to an old buddy and neighbour, who also happened to be a former Olympic sprint gold medallist: the American Michael Johnson. The day that Murray and Johnson spent on a track in California was, in Johnson's words, a great shock to Murray's body, as it was the first time that the Scot had done anything like it. They parted with Johnson giving Murray some exercise routines and warm words of encouragement. Murray spent more time with another of Gilbert's friends, Mark Grabow, a fitness coach for the Golden State Warriors, an American basketball team. You could not fault Gilbert's contacts. Despite all of this, Murray was still some way short of many of his rivals; there was always more that he could have done to improve his fitness.

A Body like a Machine

Soon after sacking Gilbert, and at a pre-season boot camp in Miami in the final weeks of 2007, Murray committed to whatever his new team – fitness trainers Jez Green and Matt Little, and physiotherapist Andy Ireland – demanded of him (Green and Little would still be with him in the summer of 2013, while Ireland wasn't at Wimbledon as he had taken a break because of personal reasons, and had been replaced by Johan de Beer, who had previously tended to Tim Henman and Federer). During those first few days together, Murray told them: 'Look, I've spent the last two years not pushing myself as hard as I should. If I don't do a session properly I want you to tell me straight out. Tell me: "Your attitude's wrong." Don't let me get away with anything.' Green has since spoken admiringly of Murray's 'total dedication': 'He came to me when he realised this was an area he needed to work on and from the very first day he was prepared to do anything I asked.' Even if that included Bikram yoga, which involved holding positions in a studio heated to an 'insanely hot' 42°C, while trying not to faint. Or the pain and nausea of the track. There was no torture, Murray kept on saying, that he wouldn't consider, which was brave, as Green used to be a kick-boxer. And because, just before the camp, Murray had been on a drip in hospital for two days because of an extreme case of food poisoning.

Other players require their fitness staff to sign confidentiality agreements, so fearful are they of any secrets leaking to the locker-room, and taking away any competitive advantage, but Murray and his team appear to have been very open about the work they have been doing. Mostly, because being secretive is not in Murray's nature. And also, you suspect, because he does not mind people knowing how hard he has been working. Murray once collaborated with *Men's Health*, a fitness magazine for office grunts obsessing about turning soft guts into hard abs, to take readers through his regime. Such as how he does chin-ups with weights wrapped about his waist, or tied around his neck. About the only legal thing Murray would refuse to do is to borrow one of Djokovic's books on New Age spiritualism, which Djokovic reads on his doctor's recommendation.

Murray was happy to share a video on his website from that training camp which showed him lying down on his back in the crucifixion pose after doing twenty 100-metre sprints around the track. When Murray got up, he had left an exact imprint of his body, in sweat, on the grass. Though Murray had previously spent a day with Johnson, this was the first time he had done a full programme of track work, and he became all too familiar with the pain of doing sprints with only short intervals in between. The 400-metre repeats tended to be the worst. There were longer runs, too, up and down the sands of Miami's South Beach.

'Andy has never thrown up – that's not the aim,' Green has said. 'But Andy will tell you that he's been in pretty dodgy shape at the end of sessions, he really pushes himself to the limit.' Only once or twice has Murray failed to finish a set of sprints. One of those occasions was when he could manage only seven of the ten 200-metre runs he was supposed to be doing. Green gave Murray a ten-minute break, and then made him go back to the track to do the rest. The other time was when Murray went out too fast when asked to do five 400-metre runs, and after three found himself lying on the ground and crying out for oxygen. And, at the end of every session, Murray had the horror of the ice-bath, when he would sit in water chilled to 10°C. Not for masochism's sake, but to flush the lactic acid from his muscles.

It was at the 2008 Wimbledon Championships that Murray first seemed proud of the shape he was in; after coming from two sets down to beat France's Richard Gasquet, a victory that had taken him to his first quarter-final at the All England Club, he rolled up his shirt sleeve and flexed his bicep as Popeye might when trying to impress girlfriend Olive Oyl. Murray hadn't suddenly become the Narcissus of men's tennis, and he also wasn't trying to tell tennis that he had the biggest biceps in the draw; that would have been extremely foolish when he was to play Rafa Nadal in the next round (a match Murray lost). The gesture, which was copied by teenage girls standing behind the wire fence at the practice courts the next day, was about Murray thanking his team, and also showing them all that time at the track had been worthwhile. The hard work has continued ever since. That celebration reappeared in New York at the 2008 US Open, and people took notice. Murray was playing a match on the Arthur Ashe Stadium when he looked up at the video screen and saw that the actor Will Ferrell was kissing his bicep.

*

Men's tennis has its secret smokers; there are others who like a glass of wine with their pasta. It's to Andy Murray's advantage that he has never smoked and he hasn't drunk alcohol in any quantity since his mid-teens. The night that put Murray off booze was when, at the age of 16 and living in Barcelona, he 'got completely hammered on vodka, wine and champagne', vomited outside a nightclub and 'tried to catch it in my hands – it went down my arms and legs and splashed on my shoes. Unbelievably, the nightclub let me in, but I can only imagine that I wasn't a popular clubber that night.' The headache in the morning was horrendous, and so was the self-loathing; he was embarrassed at how he had behaved.

Murray has been teetotal pretty much ever since. One occasion that alcohol passed Murray's lips was when he was having dinner with his girlfriend, to celebrate winning the title in Miami, and he had a sip of her strawberry daiquiri. One sip was enough (he prefers the taste of lemonade to alcohol), and he went back to his soda. The other occasion was on that transatlantic flight after the 2012 US Open, which was the closest Murray ever came to going on what the tabloids would call 'a bender'. The night of his victory, he hadn't drunk a drop.

By the time Murray arrived at Hakkasan, a Chinese restaurant in midtown Manhattan, his friends and family were already light-headed from a combination of the day's events and 'zesty martinis', other cocktails and bottles of Louis Roederer champagne. Murray would later say that everyone else was so drunk that there was no point even trying to catch up. To wash down the truffle-roasted duck, stir-fried Brazilian lobster tail and roasted silver cod, he drank nothing stronger than a six-dollar lemon soda. Generally, if Murray was thirsty on tour, he would have water – he would consume six litres daily – or a lemon-coloured, cloudy concoction, which was a special sports drink that had been created for his individual needs.

Someone once looked at the number of calories Murray was putting away when he was training in Miami – 6,000 a day – and thought it sounded as though he was on an 'Elvis Presley suicide diet'. At his boot camps, he has consumed almost 4,000 calories a day more than the average man. Breakfast alone was a slog, almost as much of a physical endurance test as running around a track. He started with protein shakes and bagels with peanut butter; the peanut butter would stick to the roof of his mouth. Yoghurt and fruit would follow.

Almost every professional tennis player seems to have a thing for sushi, but Murray is the king of the tuna and avocado rolls, capable of eating up to 50 of them at one sitting. There is a sushi bar on the players' lawn at the All England Club, and Murray had got into the habit in the summer of 2013 of ordering 30 rolls, costing a pound each, as a post-match snack. Murray has also tried cutting gluten and dairy from his diet – Novak Djokovic's 2011 season had started a gluten-free craze in tennis – and had even stuck to it when he had the torture of sitting in restaurants, waiting for his food to arrive and watching everyone else at the table eating bread smeared with butter. But Murray felt that he was losing weight and strength on a gluten-free diet so didn't persevere.

Murray doesn't have much love for the humble tennis banana, as he regards it as 'a pathetic fruit' (he even hates the fact they're not straight, that there's a black bit at the end, and that if you put them in your bag there's the potential for mess), but he still eats them during matches as he knows they're good for him.

During tournaments, Murray shows great self-discipline. One Wimbledon, an opportunistic British supermarket sent a crate of their own-brand jelly sweets to Murray's house, after reading how much he liked them, but they remained untouched for the fortnight, only to be opened when he had played his last match.

About the only time he eats processed food or sugar, which are usually on the banned list, is when he is resting between tournaments. 'When I'm home and away from tournaments I don't eat particularly well for a week or so. I'm not really into chips that much, and sweets hurt my teeth now – I had too many of them when I was younger. Ice cream is the only thing I'll eat a lot of when I'm back around the house, and I can have it from midday until I go to bed.'

Greg Rusedski's story has made many tennis players, Murray included, think twice about using supplements. Rusedski, who tested positive for nandrolone, was exonerated after a tribunal accepted that the banned substance had entered his system when he had taken a contaminated supplement. So Murray has always been wary of supplements, believing that it would be difficult to recover from a positive test, even if that 'positive' had come about because of a mistake made by a pharmaceutical company.

A Body like a Machine

Murray can't understand why anyone would choose to take an illegal chemical short-cut to success. 'I would never go down that route. In some sports it has been a cultural thing – that feeling that everyone has done it because they have been able to compete. I don't think tennis has that same culture,' Murray told British *GQ* magazine in 2013. 'It's possible there are some people who have done it, and have cheated. But I would never do something like that and I think that comes down to how you've been brought up – my parents would be livid at the very idea.'

As much as Murray understands the need for having a rigorous testing programme in tennis, he has often spoken of his annoyance at having his privacy invaded. Murray, like everyone else in the tennis elite, must tell drugs-testers exactly where he will be during a one-hour slot on every day of the year. For 365 days of the year, Murray's time is never quite his own. Players can choose any hour between 6am and 11pm, and most go for the earliest possible slot as that means they will be in bed and so won't forget where they are meant to be and miss a test. However, when the drug-testers do come visiting that means being woken up at what Murray would consider to be an ungodly hour.

After one early-morning visit to his home in Surrey, Murray, who had been in bed with his girlfriend, took to Twitter: 'Nice little 6am drug test to start the day off. Must be a weird job being a drug-tester – waking people up, staring at their privates and leaving. Surely there is a law against that.' The testers don't always come at that allotted hour, as Murray discovered one summer, three days before the start of the Wimbledon fortnight: 'They said it was an out-of-hours test. So you fill in the forms but they come when they want. It's pointless.'

There have been frustrations at tournaments, too. Within a couple of minutes of one defeat at Wimbledon, he noticed he had a new shadow: a tester, and Murray politely said to him, 'Can you give me some space? I'd like to be on my own for five minutes.' Murray did a urine test after his semi-final defeat to Novak Djokovic at the 2012 Australian Open; but then was told he could not leave Melbourne Park as he had to stay seated for half an hour before doing a blood test. If Murray is ever inconvenienced by a tester, you tend to know about it. Only Rafa Nadal has been more outspoken about the intrusion of the testers. 'I just want to enjoy a normal life,' Murray has said, 'without people bashing on my door [in the middle of the night].'

Andy Murray has never punched anyone in the face. But, for almost as long as he can remember, he has been fascinated by boxing. At his first Wimbledon, he watched videos of Ricky Hatton's fights between matches. And he probably knows as much about obscure boxers as he does about obscure tennis players, which is a hell of a lot. Nothing gives him an adrenalin rush like boxing; watching a world heavyweight title fight once, he became so alarmed at how much he was getting into it that he switched the television off.

There is a theory that tennis players are drawn to the sport because they like having the physical barrier of a net between them and their opponent, that they want competition but abhor contact. If that's true, then that fear of physical contact would make tennis players very different from boxers. But Murray has always thought there are plenty of similarities between tennis and boxing: 'agility, speed, aggression, co-ordination and tactics' play a key part in both sports. Murray has also taken inspiration from the way fighters prime their bodies and minds for competition.

On a visit to David Haye's gym in Miami, Murray was taken by how basic it was; whereas tennis can be very neat and nice, this was sport at its purest. Boxers, Murray has realised, train hard to fortify their minds. Murray has started to think the same; if he has worked hard, he knows that he can last five sets. 'Staying more controlled mentally stemmed from taking my fitness more seriously. When you're doing track work, sprints and so on, it's pretty painful, but that does make you feel better prepared and therefore mentally stronger when you're going into a match,' Murray said in an interview with *Men's Health*. 'You know, without a doubt, that you are strong enough to last.' In the life of a tennis player, some of the biggest mental and physical challenges don't come on court at the grand slams, and on live television, but away from the crowds and cameras, and in training. So when Murray walks on court, he knows that whatever happens, it's not going to be any worse than what he has already been through.

Murray's comparisons between boxing and tennis were shared by Brad Gilbert (so there was something they agreed on). 'Andy is a fighter. The great thing about tennis is that it's like boxing in the sense that you go into the ring and it's just you against the other person. One guy tries to pound the other guy out of the ring,' he wrote in the *Guardian*. 'It's beautiful because it's basic.' (One thing Murray has not copied from boxing is the pre-match trash-talking. Haye would never send Murray a 'good luck' text message before an important tennis match, as boxers don't believe in luck. Instead, he will urge Murray to 'smash in' his opponent.)

The 2008 Beijing Olympics taught Murray a lesson about what happens when you are 'unprofessional'. When Murray arrived in China, he was already dehydrated from the plane, and had skipped some meals during the journey. Going to the Opening Ceremony, sweating for hours in the Bird's Nest Stadium, didn't help either. The sights and sounds of his first Olympics – he was collecting pins from all the teams, he was running around speaking to other athletes, and asking to have his picture taken with them – meant that he wasn't as focused as he should have been on his preparation. By the time Murray played his first-round match, he had dropped four and a half kilos; after his defeat, he was concerned people would think that he had been cavalier about the Olympics, that it looked as though he didn't gave a damn about the five rings and a possible medal.

The disappointment in the singles tournament, plus losing in the second round of the doubles event when partnering his brother, left him with a new determination always to prepare properly for tournaments and always to travel on planes with his protein drinks. And always to stand on some scales on arriving at a tournament so he can then maintain that weight. 'When I lost, I thought, "Why was I doing all that stuff?" I was there to win matches, not to collect pins,' Murray has recalled.

Murray has never understood why other tennis players don't work hard. He can't stand the indolence of some other British players, or how he has turned up at the National Tennis Centre in Roehampton, south-west London, at the weekend looking for someone to practise with, but has found the place to be like 'a ghost-town'. There was the occasion when he called James Ward, who has been the British number two, to ask where everyone was. Ward was on the train home; he had already been at the centre but, also finding no one to 'hit' with, had left. Murray was grateful that Ward returned to Roehampton, as otherwise he would have gone without practice. Murray has undoubtedly benefited from the Lawn Tennis Association's wealth – as we have seen, Brad Gilbert came for free – but has wondered out loud whether the annual Wimbledon surplus has harmed players as much as it has helped them.

During Murray's time, some young British players had their funding cut after posting pictures of themselves on a social-networking site which showed them eating junk food and partying, including, in the case of one girl, with her leg draped around a condom machine in a nightclub toilet. Another player had his money stopped when he was spotted in a bar during the Wimbledon Championships. No one could ever accuse Murray of pissing the LTA's millions up against the wall.

It was a long time ago that someone called Andy Murray soft or a tennis weakling. Instead, in the spring and summer of 2012, a number of talking heads created another controversy about Murray's physical conditioning. Murray kept on hearing how he was making the most of any pain or strain, how he was trying to create the impression he was in a medical crisis, when he wasn't. While they did not allege that Murray had 'cheated', the implication was that he had been unsporting. Murray's irritation with Virginia Wade, with the former world number two Tommy Haas, and with John McEnroe, was revealing. Was Murray still as sensitive to criticism as he had been as a body-conscious teenager?

Wade won Wimbledon so long ago that the celebrations included the Centre Court crowd singing 'For she's a jolly good fellow' in her honour as she put her cardigan back on, and privately Murray probably considers that she has never experienced anything as physical as his matches. Wade, whose victory at the 1977 Wimbledon Championships is still the last time that a British woman won a grand slam title, was in the Eurosport studio during the 2012 French Open, discussing Murray's second-round match against Finland's Jarkko Nieminen, when she called him 'a drama queen'.

Murray felt as though his injury had been very real; his back had gone into spasm, he had been unable to put all his weight on one leg, and he was serving at 60mph, which is about the speed of delivery you expect from a veterans' competition at Dunblane Sports Club. Murray, after having treatment on the court, came from a set down to win in four sets, undoubtedly helped by his opponent's loss of concentration. When Murray was told what Wade had said, he was furious; one eye-witness reported him to have been 'red-lining just this side of apoplexy'. Suddenly, thanks to Wade, everyone was being invited to have their say, and just before Wimbledon Haas shared his views with a German television station (this debate had gone international): 'Sometimes he looks like he can barely move, then comes the trainer and then he moves like a cat.' McEnroe's opinion was that Murray's injury was possibly more mental or psychological than physical.

When that comment reached Murray, he responded by asking whether McEnroe and others (Boris Becker had also had his say) would care to have a look at his medical records? Or to consider why, if this had been an imaginary injury, he had gone to the bother – the extremely painful bother – of having eight-inch needles stuck in his back? Still, Murray's reaction did not stop his first-round opponent at that summer's Wimbledon, a Russian called Nikolay Davydenko who is one of the tour's eccentrics, from saying that other players occasionally 'laugh' at his behaviour. 'Sometimes he walks on court, he looks tired, like he doesn't want to run any more, and then he runs like an animal. He has done it all his career. Maybe it is a special Scottish thing.'

Murray's back and the clay-court swing just can't seem to get along. The problems he had encountered during 2012 returned in 2013. One theory is that, on clay more than on any other surface, Murray has to generate his own pace during rallies, and all that extra rotation doesn't do his back any good. For the second time in his life, a birthday spent on a Continental clay court was ruined by physical discomfort. On Murray's 20th birthday he had damaged his wrist while competing in Hamburg, an injury that meant that he didn't play at the 2007 French Open and Wimbledon Championships. On his 26th birthday, he had just won a tiebreak to level a second-round encounter with Spain's Marcel Granollers in Rome when he retired from the match. For a few days afterwards, he had difficulty getting up and down stairs, and realised that he was not going to be in any fit state to play at the most physically demanding of the grand slams.

Even at the peak of his powers, Murray would still trail Rafa Nadal and Novak Djokovic on anyone's list of the most likely winners of the Musketeers' Cup, so to have boarded the Eurostar for Paris not feeling close to full fitness would have meant that he had zero chance of success. Murray's results at Roland Garros had been far weaker than at the other three majors. The smart move was for Murray to save himself for the grass-court swing, to do everything in his power to prepare for Wimbledon, and that was the move he made, determined as never before to be in the best possible shape for a major. Missing a grand slam had made Murray realise just how much he loved playing them.

No doubt Ivan Lendl – who during his own career had twice skipped the French Open to prepare for Wimbledon –

had been in Murray's ear urging him to miss Roland Garros as that would be for the best. That was also the advice that Murray had received from Mark Bender, a back specialist who would be in the Briton's corner during Wimbledon.

Only once in every five matches does a modern tennis player walk on court free of all pain, with absolutely nothing to trouble the masseurs. Playing pro tennis is about degrees of pain. 'As athletes you spend a lot of your time carrying injuries of one sort or another. I'd say there are three categories: about twenty per cent of the time your body feels great and you feel nothing; quite a bit of the time you'll have something that might be a bit sore, but it doesn't affect your tennis at all; the rest of the time you can be carrying something that means you have to compensate and make adjustments to your game. Everyone has to deal with it,' Murray wrote in his column on the BBC website during Wimbledon. On the eve of the tournament, Martina Navratilova had advocated that men's matches at the slams be shortened from best-of-five sets to best-of-three, as the longer form was doing such damage to players' bodies. But, despite suffering for their sport, there wasn't a voice in the men's locker-room who agreed with her. Murray and the rest all wanted to stick with tradition.

Taking pain-killing pills or, if it comes to it, pain-killing injections, is one of the realities of playing professional tennis. Take Murray's bipartite patella, or split knee-cap, which has been causing him pain since his teens. Murray can only 'manage' the knee, which, every now and then, feels as though it's on fire. While no one talks about Murray's knee problems in the same apocalyptic way that they discuss Rafa Nadal's chronically cranky knees – the Spaniard has had to take lengthy breaks from competition to rest his body – he often finds himself in great discomfort. The pain is often worse when he is playing clay-court tournaments.

Many players, Nadal included, feel that soft clay is much more forgiving on their bodies than playing on hard courts, but that is the surface which makes Murray screw up his face. Sliding around the clay, Murray has to work much harder at keeping his balance, and that puts more stress through the knee. It is a problem that Murray has had throughout his time on the tour, and it is not one that is suddenly going to disappear like a puff of clay-court dust.

Murray has done what he can to avoid aggravating the knee, but that has led to the odd storm in a Pimm's cup in British tennis, such as when he skipped Britain's Davis Cup tie against Argentina in 2008. Murray didn't think that flying to Buenos Aires to play on clay, when he had just played the hard-court Australian Open and when he had indoor hard-court tournaments to come in Europe, was going to do his knee any good. He knew that his withdrawal would start another round of bitching, but he always remembered what Jean-Pierre Bruyere, a French chiropractor, had told him when they worked together: 'Don't let anyone mess with you. Take care of yourself. I don't want anyone to stop you by pushing you too hard when you're young. It's your body and your life. If you're hurt, regardless of what anyone says, don't play.'

As Nadal has observed, playing sport is good for most

people's bodies, but not for professional athletes, because of what they have to endure to compete. You only have to look at a tennis player's bare feet, gnarled and beaten up, to see it is not the effete sport that many people used to think it was.

Ever since that first Miami boot-camp in 2007, Murray has continued to put great emphasis on his physical fitness. He goes there every winter to work on his fitness. He has also got into the habit of having a mid-season training camp, after Wimbledon and before his first tournament of the North American hard-court swing, though that was not possible in 2012 because of the Olympics.

There are a few players on tour who are more flexible than Murray; he has often been astonished at some of the things that Gael Monfils is capable of on a tennis court, and how Novak Djokovic can almost do the splits on court. Murray isn't as quick around the court as Nadal, and he knows he doesn't move as 'effortlessly' as Roger Federer does. He is never going to be as good in the air as Jo-Wilfried Tsonga. And perhaps there are a few characters in the locker-room that Murray wouldn't challenge to an arm-wrestle. But Murray is a fine all-rounder. He has become increasingly flexible. Over a short distance – and most of the time in tennis you only need to travel a short distance to reach the ball – he is one of the quickest. 'In tennis you don't have to be incredibly fast or incredibly strong, you just have to be very good at many different aspects,' Murray has said. 'I'm an all-round athlete.'

Jez Green, writing in the *Daily Mail*, suggested that Murray had 'the stamina of a middle-distance runner, 800–1,500 metres, and the speed of a sprinter – his speed over twenty metres is exceptional. He is able to take incredibly quick steps.' In the gym, Green said, the 'prodigiously strong' Murray had 'the capability of a rugby player, even though he is a tennis player and cannot be that bulky. He is a ridiculously natural athlete and when you combine that with the work ethic he has, you come up with something very special. I suppose as an athlete you could call him the complete package.'

There is no doubt that men's tennis is getting taller. There are some, such as Ivo Karlovic (six foot ten inches), John Isner (six foot nine inches) and Juan Martin del Potro (six foot six inches) who have to duck under doors before walking out on court. And yet the leading four players from the past few years are not exceptionally tall. Murray, at six foot three inches, is the tallest of the quartet, with Djokovic an inch shorter, and Federer and Nadal each an inch shorter still. Murray is tall enough to get some extra pace and bounce on his serve, but not so tall that he struggles with his movement, or low pickups. Six foot three inches was a good height for someone aspiring to win Wimbledon. And it matters not one bit that Murray's body is not totally in balance; he has a weak left shoulder, because it never gets to work as hard as the right, and his left leg is a little stronger than his right. But that's just the way it is, with tennis being 'such a diagonal sport'.

As was the case during every other match Murray played at Wimbledon, when the Scot faced Tommy Robredo, his coach Lendl would get more 'air-time' than anyone else on his staff. But Murray would never have become the force he was if it had not been for his fitness trainers and physiotherapists. Surely they also deserved the occasional close-up?

Let's not pretend that Tommy Robredo was some tennis slob, a glutton or a greedy guts who had somehow fluked his way to this stage of the tournament. No one makes the last 32 at a grand slam if they have either a soft head or tummy, and he wasn't shy about showing his body off, having once posed nude for a women's magazine. So Robredo might not have taken care of himself as carefully as Andy Murray did, but then who did?

Robredo was nothing less than a model professional, and he certainly wasn't fuelled by Mississippi Mud Pie alone. Indeed, Murray had a great amount of respect for Robredo's fitness for competition, and especially for the way that the Spaniard had regained his conditioning and his form after a leg operation the year before had seen his ranking drop to 471. Once ranked as high as fifth, Robredo had prolonged his career by working hard, and he had demonstrated his mental and physical fortitude at the 2013 French Open by achieving an astonishing three consecutive comebacks from two sets down to make the quarter-finals. Between Murray's second- and third-round matches at Wimbledon, there had been plenty of chat about the possibility of Murray and Serena Williams playing an exhibition match in Las Vegas – the idea being that it would be a modern version of Billie Jean King and Bobby Riggs' Battle of the Sexes – but that wasn't going to distract the Briton from what he had to do here in England. Robredo was not someone to be taken lightly – in the previous round, he had beaten a decent grass-court player in Nicolas Mahut, he of the 70-68 fifth set with John Isner in 2010.

Jez Green has disclosed the attention to detail that goes into preparing Murray on the day of the match, including how the entire team is immediately informed when the Scot has rolled out of bed (perhaps, as the US Secret Service does for the President, Team Murray also have a code word for the tennis player for all radio communications). Murray isn't allowed to choose his match-day breakfast on a whim. 'The nutrition routine is set,' Green said. 'He has to get a certain amount of calories in, all monitored.' Next, the physiotherapist 'wakes up' Murray's body with stretches, before the player pedals on the exercise-bike in the gym to raise his pulse, and then does what Green called 'some dynamic flexibility work'. After a light hit on a practice court, he 'refuels'. Twenty minutes before he is due on court, he returns to the gym for an 'explosive work-out, sprinting and everything quick and fast, he gets a sweat on and he goes directly from the gym to the court'. Green, who was talking to the *New York Times* magazine, also disclosed that throughout match days Murray has an osmolarity check to ensure that he is properly hydrated, with the right percentages of water and minerals in his urine. Before Murray played Robredo, as before every match, nothing would have been left to chance.

If Robredo had been given the choice, he would have played Murray on red clay, on one of those Continental surfaces that almost seem to slow down time. Robredo wasn't daft; he knew that the grass of Centre Court suited his opponent. Playing inside was also to Murray's advantage; though the playing conditions were affected when the roof was shut and the air-conditioning was turned on, the greatest shift was in acoustics; the sound of the ball leaving the strings was different, and so was the sound of the crowd. Earlier in the week, Murray had observed – quite rightly – that an indoor grass-court looked and sounded weird, that his eyes and ears were still not sure what to make of it.

One thing was for sure; it was loud indoors. With the roof closed, there was nowhere for the sound of the crowd to escape to. Whether or not the crowd was actually making any more noise than usual was academic; what mattered was that the spectators sounded louder to Murray's ears, and that extra encouragement – whether real or imagined – almost seemed to give him a greater air of superiority. It was 15,001 (the 15,000 spectators plus Murray) against one lonely Spaniard. For the first time in the tournament – after previously being upstaged by Rafa Nadal and Roger Federer's departures – Murray's match was the biggest event of the day, and he did not disappoint as he played some fine tennis during his 6-2, 6-4, 7-5 victory. After Robredo's three Parisian comebacks, Murray concentrated hard all the way. Even more importantly than that, Murray's back behaved all match.

The first stages of post-match recovery – after a performance that meant he had reached the second week without dropping a set in his first three rounds – included an ice-bath, stretches, protein shakes and ordering some tuna and avocado rolls. Some players are so superstitious that they can go whole grand slam fortnights sitting at the same table in the same restaurant, ordering the same food – Goran Ivanisevic's victory at the 2001 Wimbledon Championships was fuelled by eating fish soup, lamb and chips and then ice cream with chocolate sauce every night. Murray, though, likes to vary his diet, and during grand slams he has been known to eat fish, chicken and steak in rotation. After long matches, he eats 'a lot', taking on around 150g of protein.

As Murray had defeated Robredo on Friday evening, and wouldn't play again until Monday afternoon, he had a couple of practice days between matches, but the nature of tennis tournaments is that you don't have long to sit back in your ice-baths and enjoy your victories. Thoughts quickly turned to Murray's next opponent, a Russian who had become infamous for self-harming with a tennis racket. If you want an example of how a tennis player shouldn't look after themselves, find the piece of film from a tournament in Miami a few years ago when Mikhail Youzhny, a hard-looking chap with a buzz-cut, was so annoyed with himself after missing a shot that he clubbed himself over the head until blood trickled down his forehead and nose. Thwack, thwack, thwack. The match had to be suspended while the tournament's medical staff attended to him. So something for the Centre Court crowd to look out for when Murray played Youzhny; if the Muscovite started bashing himself about the head, they could probably start to relax.

4

The Joke that Went Wrong

Andy Murray had often felt unloved at this garden party. There was the occasion at the All England Club one summer when he had walked past a woman and heard her hissing into her mobile phone, 'There goes that Scottish w*****.' Or the times he had read the letters sent to his locker telling him, 'I hope you lose every match for the rest of your life.' Those were extreme examples, yet for years a mutual unease had existed between many of the Wimbledon crowd and Britain's only contender for the golden trophy. When he was on court, he had regularly been reminded of the public's affection for a retired player, and how he compared (not so well). While Murray had always enjoyed competing on the other side of the Atlantic, as he appreciated what he regarded as the upbeat, positive nature of your Average Joe American tennis fan, his dealings with the London tennis set had never been so straightforward.

In any young athlete's media training classes, there must be a module about Murray's joke that went wrong, the one about supporting 'anyone but England' at the 2006 football World Cup. Watch out, Murray would advise, as 'the wrong choice of word at the wrong moment can cause you months, or even years, of hassle.' Somewhere out there, there is a parallel universe in which Murray chose not to say anything when asked which team he wanted to win the tournament (since Scotland wouldn't be there). But Murray couldn't resist. Throughout the joint interview, Tim Henman had been teasing Murray about Scotland's failure to qualify, and so he laughed at his friend's gag. It was not the funniest joke anyone has ever told, of the kind you could tell at the Edinburgh Festival and launch yourself into the stratosphere in stand-up comedy, but it was still a joke and anyone with an IQ above 17 should have been able to tell that Murray wasn't being serious. In Henman's words, that joke became 'a pain in the arse' for Murray. Among many other things, it would inspire the creation of the Facebook group 'Andy Murray hates the English, so we hate Andy Murray'.

'Not nice,' Murray has said of the abuse he suffered for daring to make a joke about English football, and that's putting it mildly. Not nice is walking through drizzle from Southfields Tube station to the All England Club; this was having his character ripped apart on the air, in print, in the blogosphere or in his ear. And Mark Petchey, his former coach, has always said that Murray is a much more sensitive soul than people realise when they are listening to him cuss his way through an appearance on Wimbledon's Centre Court.

It would take six years, and Murray's big fat grass-court summer of tears and Olympic medals in 2012, for the player and the British (or, more precisely, English) public to start showing some genuine affection for each other.

By the time Wimbledon 2013 rolled around, the relationship between Murray and the All England Club mob had become closer still. Murray had needed a lot of persuading to allow cameras into his life away from the courts, but there could be no doubt that the resulting BBC pre-tournament documentary, *The Man Behind The Racket*, had 'humanised' him in the minds of those who had previously found him tough to like (you might contend, perfectly reasonably, that the public shouldn't need to see someone breaking down as they speak about a massacre at their primary school before they decide whether that person is likeable or not).

It had also not been lost on the Wimbledon crowd that Murray had been hugely supportive of his close friend, Ross Hutchins, who was undergoing cancer treatment after being diagnosed with Hodgkin's lymphoma a few months earlier. Hutchins had let it be known – and he was simply being honest, not trying to improve his friend's image – how Murray had helped. 'People think of Andy as a driven and single-minded tennis player, which he is. But he also has a huge heart. He said: "You will come back stronger" and "We are going to beat this,"' Hutchins told *The Times*. 'Andy started researching the illness. From then on, any time I came to him with a problem he would say: "Don't worry, that's normal," or "I read about a guy who had exactly the same experience – it's nothing to worry about." Or sometimes: "That's a bit odd. Let me look into it." Then he would call back a few days later with another batch of research. At times he seemed like my doctor.' Whenever Hutchins sent Murray a text message asking how he was, the Scot would check himself before telling his friend that he had had a poor day – after all, if he had his health, what did it really matter if he had had a mediocre practice session?

Just eight days before Wimbledon started, Murray had happily appeared in his friend's 'Rally Against Cancer' charity exhibition at Queen's Club – alongside London Mayor Boris Johnson, businessman Sir Richard Branson, comedians Jimmy Carr, Michael McIntyre and Jonathan Ross, actor Eddie Redmayne, and Ivan Lendl, Henman and Tomas Berdych – to raise funds for the Royal Marsden Cancer Charity. Had Murray not committed to the event, you wonder whether it would have happened at all. In addition, Murray donated his prize-money for winning the Queen's title – just over £70,000 – to the charity.

Had the British tennis public finally got what they had craved: a hard man on Wimbledon's Centre Court lawn – who would play Mikhail Youzhny for a place in the quarter-finals – and a cuddly one off it?

Middle England had been a little confused as to what they wanted from their tennis players (apart from the obvious, a

The Joke that Went Wrong

Wimbledon title). Tim Henman was too straight, they said. The public applauded when John McEnroe urged Henman to show more emotion on Wimbledon's Centre Court, perhaps by effing and blinding beneath the Royal Box, or by putting more effort into those little fist-clenchers. They laughed when a comedian cruelly described Henman as 'the human form of beige', and they debated, often at dinner parties, whether a middle-class upbringing had held him back. And, as if that had not been enough, they gave him the worst possible nickname: Tiger Tim. Some thought him to be a loser, for having reached only fourth in the world rankings, and for having played in six grand slam semi-finals, including four at Wimbledon, but never in a final. When Andy Murray came on the scene, with that first Wimbledon in 2005, he was a tartan novelty and so he had a period of grace, 'with everyone saying to me, "You're a breath of fresh air." Whatever Tim Henman or Greg Rusedski were like, I was different.'

But it was not long – it began in 2006, during Murray's first full year on the tour – before Henman's supposed defects became virtues. Virtues to attack Murray with. Suddenly, Murray was having a tennis racket wrapped around his neck for not being Gentleman Tim (that was how the Judy Murray–Jane Henman comparisons got started). With Henman coming to the end of his career, maybe some realised they were going to miss him. Whatever the underlying reasons, Middle England said Murray should show some respect by shaving. He should get a hold of himself and his emotions. He should wash his potty mouth out.

McEnroe's advice – and, depending on your point of view, this was either a man speaking from experience, or the most hypocritical remark in tennis history – was for Murray to stop 'spewing negative energy'. Murray should ask his barber for a short back and sides. The Centre Court crowds were making it quite clear to Murray that they hadn't quite let go of Henman; in years past, Murray and his team had made bets on how long it would be before someone in the crowd cried out: 'C'mon Tim,' and whoever had wagered on the first minute would win. Aorangi Terrace was still Henman Hill. After Henman's retirement, it felt as though Murray was competing for oxygen with someone whose appearances on Centre Court now came while wearing a suit and sitting behind a BBC microphone.

Why all the fuss and fury? One reason: tennis was not immune to the modern cult of personality, and nothing reveals personality like playing a tennis match.

Perhaps it was just tennis's chattering classes wanting to make conversation. That was one theory anyway, that Middle England had grown so tired of discussing why no British man had won Wimbledon since the 1930s that they now entertained themselves by picking at the players' characters. Britain needed some 'proper conversational balls to hit back and forth over the net', Paul Hayward wrote in the *Guardian*. 'The tear-inducing British exit from the grand slam tennis event exhausted itself as a breakfast-table subject long ago, so the middle classes make merry with character assassinations . . .'

It had quickly become apparent that Murray was Britain's

greatest talent for 70-odd years, but that didn't give him a free pass. A good few newspaper columnists didn't want to get too technical or too tennis-y, because they didn't know enough about the sport, and also because they didn't think their readers would care about the mechanics of a backhand volley; far better to focus on Murray's behaviour or appearance. Henman was the warm-up act; no British tennis player has ever had his language and behaviour scrutinised as Murray has. 'McBrat' offered up plenty of material for armchair and laptop psycho-analysis, especially as the on-court microphones and television replays meant you never missed a 'f***', a 's***' or a mangled racket.

There had been the suspicion during John McEnroe's 'Superbrat' days that the British public had enjoyed being shocked by his language and behaviour, and maybe there was an element of that with Murray. When they said they were appalled, maybe they were actually thrilled by the naughtiness of it all. Was it the hypocrisy of a tennis crowd which likes to see a tennis player smash a racket, or fill the air with stars and asterisks, but then tuts when they do? Murray has his own theory, that tennis has a great fear of emotion, of letting it all out. 'It wouldn't make me feel good to bottle up my emotions. Saying nothing and standing there makes me feel emotional and flat. There is a fear of emotion in tennis,' he once told the *Daily Mail*. 'If someone boos, everyone looks at them as if to ask, "What the hell are you doing?" Yet in other sports it happens all the time.'

Some of the outrage was real, some of it artificial, after

Murray told an umpire at a Davis Cup tie that he was 'f******
useless'. There was the business of Murray cursing at Brad
Gilbert. But, mostly, the swearing was directed at himself, as
part of the longest running show in tennis, The Murray
Monologues. If a match wasn't going well, or even if it generally was but he had just played a couple of duff games, Murray
would mutter and chunter, using cuss-words as verbs, nouns
and punctuation. Effing this, and effing that. So consumed
was Murray by the moment, he would forget about the microphones, or that he should have been using the sound of the
crowd for cover. More often than they would have wanted, television commentators found themselves apologising for
Murray's language.

Murray, not accepting the charge that he was the anti-Christ
in tennis shorts, was taken aback by this obsession with his
swearing. There were plenty of other athletes, he said, who
cursed every week without launching a thousand phone-ins
and newspaper editorials. 'There are things I say on the court
that I probably shouldn't say, but off the court I'm not stum-
bling out of nightclubs or throwing up in front of the
paparazzi. I don't mean to upset people.'

When Murray was cross, words often weren't enough. He
went through a period of self-harm, when he would bloody his
knuckles by punching the strings of his racket. Sometimes he
slapped the palm of his hand against his face, or smashed rackets by swinging them hard against his shoe. Or he grabbed at
his clothes. Every sub-clause, comma and semi-colon of
Murray's body-language – the times when he moped, or when

his chin appeared to be staple-gunned to his chest – was debated. Murray could hardly walk on court without someone quoting P.G. Wodehouse's remark, 'It is never difficult to distinguish between a ray of sunshine and a Scotsman with a grievance.'

That was when he was venting; how about when he was happy? A few disliked Murray's celebrations – all those clenched fists and stentorian cries – about as much as they disliked his anger. The satirical magazine *Private Eye* did one of their lookalikes features on Murray, printing a photograph of him howling alongside one of a werewolf. The public and media scrutiny included detailed studies of his appearance. Was this really allowed, a British player walking out on to Centre Court with what one critic had called 'a bum-fluff tache'? It would have been a big event in the shires the first time Murray played at Wimbledon with a sensible haircut and a smooth chin, and without a baseball cap. In short, Middle England thought Murray was a moody, scruffy young man. Even before Murray made a joke about the English football team, there were grievances. 'Wimbledon,' said one Centre Court regular, in reference to the spectators rather than the committee men, 'used to be so snotty about Murray.'

Despite appearances – an American once looked at Centre Court and all he could see were Paul Smith stripes and Oxbridge educations – Wimbledon can be a tough crowd. Murray and Henman weren't the first British players to have felt the disapproval of the tennis public and establishment. And you can't simply put that down to Britain's post-imperial tennis angst, with the nation kept waiting since the last days of empire for another male singles champion.

Spool all the way back to Fred Perry, who called himself 'a rebel the wrong side of the tennis tramlines', and you will see that he was cold-shouldered too, perhaps more than anyone. In the 1930s, Perry, a son of a Labour MP, was no friend of the public school-educated members of the All England Club. After winning the first of his three Wimbledon titles, he was lying in a hot bath in the locker-room when he heard a member say to his opponent, Australia's Jack Crawford, 'This was one day when the best man didn't win.'

As the champion, Perry was due a club tie, but it was presented without a smile and a handshake; instead, he got out of the bath and found it lying on a bench. Perry's disenchantment with British tennis, even after winning three consecutive titles from 1934–36, would persuade him to turn professional and move to America, and that hardly improved his standing at home. Bunny Austin, the beaten finalist in 1938, was also not always made to feel welcome; for many years, he was blackballed by the All England Club for being a conscientious objector during the Second World War. Some haven't helped themselves, such as Buster Mottram with his politics; to quote the *Observer*, he once had 'a dalliance' with the National Front, and more recently he tried, when he considered himself to be working in the interests of the United Kingdom Independence Party, to broker an electoral pact with the far-right British National Party. Some had a decent ride – John Lloyd and Roger Taylor – but many others didn't.

The Joke that Went Wrong

Jeremy Bates never went deep enough into Wimbledon – the fourth round was his limit – for the public to have made any great emotional investment in him. The Canadian-born Greg Rusedski tried hard, probably too hard, turning up to his first Wimbledon in a Union flag bandana, but there was always a distance between him and the crowd. Though he played in a grand slam final, and Henman didn't, Rusedski's achievement of finishing as the runner-up to Pat Rafter at the 1997 US Open never received the attention it should have done, even if he won the BBC Sports Personality of the Year award. That wasn't his fault; the match had taken place on the same weekend as Princess Diana's funeral. Wimbledon has had its summer flings, its one-match stands, with the lowly ranked players who had beaten, or threatened to beat, a seed. But most were quickly forgotten.

Wimbledon is not unique as a grand slam for being hard on its own players. It was only at the 2012 US Open that Venus Williams, a 32-year-old, two-time former champion and world number one, 'felt American for the first time' at Flushing Meadows. Until then, she had never thought she had had the full backing of the crowd. Australian tennis fans have never all warmed to Lleyton Hewitt, despite his success, winning two grand slams and reaching the top of the rankings, as many considered him to be too difficult a character, lacking charm and refinement. The best young Australian, Bernard Tomic, is on probation with Melbourne Park. The Roland Garros crowds are notoriously hard on French players, which explained why talented, but perhaps emotionally fragile players such as Amelie Mauresmo and Richard Gasquet usually played better tennis on the other side of the Channel, at Wimbledon, than in Paris.

Admittedly, a Wimbledon crowd would never boo or slow-handclap Murray, as the Parisians have done with French players. They would always support the British player; it's just that they had been holding back, not quite putting everything into it. And the crowd inside the gates of the All England Club is one thing; those outside, who take a more casual interest in the sport, have been even trickier to please.

It's unclear whether Andy Murray should be allowed to make jokes or not. For years he was teased for being the grumpiest man in tennis. When Tim Henman called Murray 'a miserable git', it was said with affection, but critics, seizing on the quote, bashed him about the head with the remark; there goes Murray, The Most Miserable Man in Tennis. *Headcases*, the satirical puppet show, a modern version of *Spitting Image*, did a sketch about an Andy Murray Misery Chatline, with 'each call costing just a little bit of your hopes and dreams'. And another which introduced a Murray puppet with the observation, 'Andy Murray's joyless moaning is the sound of summer,' before having the doll sing in monotone, 'The sun has got his hat on.'

Turn on your television or radio halfway through an interview with Murray, and you can't immediately tell from his tone of voice whether he has won or lost. Why, critics said, couldn't Murray just sound happy? Pat Cash, a former

The Joke that Went Wrong

Wimbledon champion, thought he knew why: because Murray has the most boring, monotone voice in the history of the planet (Murray, when told about the Australian's comments, did agree that his voice wasn't that interesting, though he has wondered why people care so much about these things).

However, the caricature of Murray was just that, a caricature. It ignored the fact that Murray had a dry sense of humour and laughter in his life. Perhaps that's why it threw people when he made jokes. Take the time when he played an April Fool's joke in 2011 by announcing on Twitter that he had hired his good friend Ross Hutchins as his new coach because he felt as though he needed 'another yes-man'. The background to the hoax was the constant speculation about who Miles Maclagan's successor would be, as well as the accusations that Murray was surrounding himself with an entourage of pals who would never challenge him for fear of being bumped from the inner circle and the pay-roll. Hutchins, who was in on the joke, wrote on his Twitter page that 'having this opportunity to work with such a special player and such a close friend is one I have wished for all my life', and within minutes the story was breaking on the Press Association news-wire and in the Sky Sports television studio.

There was some embarrassment and irritation in those newsrooms when they had to retract their stories later that evening, and it was an episode that seemed to reinforce people's opinion of Murray. Those already sympathetic to Murray thought it cast him in a good light, showing that he did not take not take himself or his job too seriously. For others, it strengthened their dislike. They didn't stop to consider that they were trying to have it both ways: they were saying Murray was a misery, while also suggesting that he should take his responsibilities as a public figure more seriously.

Murray still remembers the time when a 'sexist' joke became a global news story. After Murray played a match at a tournament in New Zealand in 2006 that had featured a lot of service breaks, he told the crowd, during a jocular post-match interview, that he and his opponent had 'played like women'. Some of the ladies, and a few men, gently booed Murray, but they knew that he had not meant anything by it and that he had not just revealed himself as a male chauvinist pig. This was a long way from the opinions once offered by Richard Krajicek, a former Wimbledon champion, who had let it be known that he thought the majority of female tennis players were 'lazy, fat pigs'. Krajicek had meant what he said, though he did eventually apologise; Murray was joshing. Unfortunately for Murray, when the story was reported by a news agency, it was made to sound as though the crowd had taken great offence, as if he had been booed out of Auckland. Murray was woken up the next morning by a radio station wanting him to expand on his supposed sexism, and by columnists across the world harrumphing from several thousands miles away.

The different reactions to Murray's gags about English sporting teams was telling. When asked for his views on the Ashes cricket series, he replied: 'I'm Scottish. I wanted

The Joke that Went Wrong

Australia to win.' That played well in Australia. And the joke didn't annoy the Barmy Army, or have people torching his effigy outside Lord's.

But if England's cricket fans could take a joke, some of England's football fans plainly couldn't. Perhaps they were too dim to realise that Murray wasn't being serious, or maybe they were fully aware that he hadn't meant it, but had gone along with the outrage anyway. The story very quickly got out of control, with Murray's comments discussed on BBC Radio Four's *Today* programme. The fun went toxic. Even now, there are those who believe that Murray bought a Paraguay football shirt to wear for when they played England.

The worst of the abuse was online. The general rule for the comments underneath newspaper articles is that by the time you get to the twentieth message, someone will have mentioned Hitler; with articles on the tennis page, the rule is you can't get to the tenth post without 'anyone but Murray' graffiti. Offline, it wasn't pleasant either. 'I was still a kid and people were sending notes to my locker saying that they hoped that I lost every tennis match for the rest of my life. That's at Wimbledon. Even people within the grounds were saying stuff to me,' Murray has recalled. 'It wasn't nice and I felt as though I hadn't done anything wrong.'

For someone who is supposedly anti-English, he has been leading a curious life. He has an English girlfriend, many of his friends are English, several members of his entourage are English, and he has chosen to live in Surrey. If he hated the English, he would hate his English grandmother. The reality, of course, is that he doesn't loathe the English, or carry a membership card for the Scottish National Party in the back pocket of his shorts.

What Murray doesn't like – and he has been quite open about this – is when people think he's English. He is proud to be Scottish, and it annoys him when people get that wrong. Initially, as he made a life for himself on the circuit, and played international tournaments for the first time, he found some people thought 'British' and 'English' were one and the same. An American once asked Murray, then a teenager, to explain the difference between being Scottish and English. 'I was born in Scotland. If somebody says to me I'm English, I correct them because it's not true. And I don't mind when people call me British, but it really annoys me when I get called English. I'm not from there. It's like calling someone from France German.' At the 2011 French Open, he was not impressed when he was introduced to the crowd as 'L'Anglais'. But that's not the same as hating the English, not the same at all. As Murray has said, 'Being Scottish is just a fact, not a racist state of mind.'

Every time Murray has tried to explain himself, and reminded everyone about all the English people he has chosen to have in his life, it has not had the effect he would have wanted. The best example of this anti-Murray prejudice was a column in the *Daily Mirror* in 2008, written by Tony Parsons, an English author: 'If the English can survive the attentions of the Luftwaffe, the IRA and al-Qaeda, then I quite fancy our chances against Andy Murray. I don't really object to anyone despising the English – we can take it – but hypocritical back-tracking gets right up my Wembley Way and puts my Morris dancer out of joint. It's a bit rich for Murray to decide that he loves the English after all.'

The difficulty for Murray was that he was talking to two different audiences. The more he spoke of his fondness for the English, and how he was British as well as Scottish (there has never been any confusion in his mind over that), the greater the risk that he would upset a few Scottish opinion-formers. Take the column in the *Scottish Sun* in the summer of 2009, which was reacting to Murray's comment, another attempt at ending the cross-border sniping, that he had always got on well with the English. Under the headline 'He's one of us, not one of them', the columnist wrote: 'Andy Murray's new best mates? The English. Aye, but I bet he jumped for joy like the rest of us when Portugal knocked them out of the World Cup in 2006. I suppose Murray's climbdown from his anti-English comments before the World Cup three years ago is to appease relations with the notoriously snobby Home Counties set who hang out at SW19. Don't let them hijack you when you win by draping you in a Union flag.'

In the background during Wimbledon 2013 were the discussions about Scottish independence. If Edinburgh and London were to go through a messy divorce, and Scotland was to break away, where would that leave Murray, who would then be competing at all future Wimbledons as a Scottish rather than a British player? Would he see a dip in the support from the London crowd? Going into the tournament, Murray was yet to have expressed a strong view. 'I want to read more about the issue. I don't think you should judge the thing on emotion, but on what is best economically for Scotland,' he told *The Times* in the spring of 2013. 'You don't want to make a snap decision and then see the country go tits up. I am proud to be Scottish, but I am also proud to be British, and I don't think there's a contradiction in that.'

Murray's joke had been useful for something: revealing people's prejudices on either side of Hadrian's Wall. There was a clear attempt at hijacking by the English edition of the *Sun* in 2010, with the newspaper campaigning during that summer's Wimbledon to claim him for the Home Counties. They printed 'Come on Surrey' headlines, and a tenuous list of 25 reasons why Murray was 'more English than he lets on', including that he had played in front of the Queen at Wimbledon one year and he listened to music on an iPod, which had been designed by a Londoner. As the saying goes – and you hear this a lot from international tennis fans teasing the English – Murray is British when he wins and Scottish when he loses. When, during past Wimbledons, British papers had printed a daily swing-ometer for where Murray stood that morning – something like 'totally Tartan' at one end and 'Rule Britannia' at the other – it was hard to know whether they were being snide or just showing the whole thing up for how ridiculous it is. But then, as everyone knows, you can say what you like about Murray.

Andy Murray had never cast himself as the saviour of British tennis. He had politely declined, as one observer once put it, 'the role of darling to the middle classes and corporate lunch-munchers'. He had never chased popularity. When he resolved to tone down the on-court swearing and the gore (punching strings), it was not to endear himself to the Wimbledon queue, but because he thought that if he became more of an emotional flat-liner it would improve his tennis. Murray has made the odd concession to the mob, and for a while he took professional advice from Stuart Higgins, a former editor of the *Sun* turned public relations consultant who specialised in what his website called 'crisis management support' (his other clients had included supermodel Kate Moss after a newspaper had published photographs which they claimed showed her using cocaine).

Murray was willing to shave and to take his baseball cap off before playing at Wimbledon, but he wasn't going to manufacture a new personality (and Higgins didn't ask him to either). 'You need to try to be yourself as much as possible, but at the same time if people don't like you it's not really your problem. You need to stay true to yourself and the people around you and hopefully things will turn around,' Murray has said. So while Murray would naturally always choose popularity over unpopularity, and was annoyed that people had taken his jokes the wrong way, he had accepted he would never be universally loved or liked. Since he wasn't playing tennis for the love of strangers, he was okay with that.

It is to Murray's credit that he has never claimed to be the shining knight in Wimbledon whites, the player to rescue British tennis from the dark forces of failure and mediocrity. He hasn't spent his life obsessing about Fred Perry and British tennis. About winning Wimbledon, yes, but not directly about Fred. For the 2009 Wimbledon Championships, Murray's then clothing sponsor, the label which Perry had started, dressed the Scot up in retro kit which referenced what Perry used to wear. Had Perry still been alive, he would have been 100 years old that year, and Murray, thinking it was a bit of a fun, played along. Murray was relaxed about the stunt, and did not consider that it could possibly add to the expectation on him.

Murray has always been clear in his mind that tennis is an individual sport. Murray is British and Scottish but he plays primarily for himself; he wanted to win Wimbledon for his own personal satisfaction and sense of accomplishment; if that meant he would also end Britain's long wait for a male singles champion and would be the first since Fred, then that would be great, but that was not why he was enduring a lifetime of Bikram yoga and ice-baths. The 70-odd years that had passed without a British champion, that wasn't his responsibility. 'I want to win for the people I work with, and for my parents, who helped me when I was growing up,' Murray once said. 'Then, doing it for British tennis and British sport would be excellent as well.'

People have kept missing the point that singles players fly solo. Murray is the only British man with a respectable singles ranking, so you often hear how terrible it must be for Murray to be out there on his own. But, in an individual sport, it's hardly possible to be anything else but 'out there on your own'. About the only other time you will see other British men playing singles is during the first week of the Wimbledon fortnight, thanks to the All England Club's gifts of wild cards, as their rankings aren't high enough for them to have gained automatic entry into the main draw. Then, most years, they go back to the chorus line until the next summer's Wimbledon wild cards are announced. The lack of other British men is often presented as a problem for Murray, as if it has somehow been a barrier to his chances of maximising his talent. Wouldn't Murray benefit from sharing the spotlight, from watching it burn through someone else's whites for an afternoon or two each summer?

'Not really,' Murray will say, just as Tim Henman used to say when he was the only Briton thought to have had a shot at winning a grand slam. In tennis, you play for yourself, apart from during those rare weeks when you are playing in the Davis Cup and, rarer still, in the Olympics. Who could blame Murray for not prioritising the Davis Cup when, without a decent second singles player, Britain had zero chance of winning a competition which was last in British hands in 1936? (One person was former British captain John Lloyd, who said: 'Call me old-fashioned, but when is it an inconvenience and a not a privilege to play for your country?')

It's difficult to see how, in recent years, having a second British man around would have made any difference whatsoever to Murray's performances. At the 2006 Australian Open, where he lost in the first round, he said the media had been expecting too much from him, but he was young then, and he wasn't on his own either, as Tim Henman and Greg Rusedski still had not passed into the tennis after-life. Look back at how Murray has played at Wimbledon over the years, and you will struggle to find a match that he lost because he was fretting about the British public.

'I've never felt stress and pressure from playing in front of a home crowd. I've never made it an excuse, and it's not going to go away so deal with it,' Murray said in an interview with the *Daily Mail*. 'I think we as a nation expect to win and when we don't we look for these big reasons. Why did Tim Henman not win Wimbledon? Why has Andy Murray not won Wimbledon? Well, sometimes you're not quite good enough. I can't say exactly why it hasn't happened for me there, but I'll tell you what isn't the reason: the pressure of the people and the pressure of the media.'

In a way, Murray finds Wimbledon to be one of the most relaxing tournaments of the year as he gets to sleep in his own bed. He has learnt to insulate himself. He tries not to read the sports section of a newspaper. If he is watching television, and a story about himself appears on his screen, he zones out or turns over. He didn't become carried away by what the public were saying, thinking or Tweeting. Every year, when Murray is the last British player left in the tournament, it is said that he has been left 'carrying the flag'; it's an embarrassing phrase, and one which, in an individual sport, is almost devoid of any meaning. As Murray sat on his chair during his fourth-round match against Mikhail Youzhny, he wasn't worrying about the state of British tennis, or feeling any great sense of responsibility for improving the sport (that is the Lawn Tennis Association's concern, as well as the concern of an all-party group of MPs and peers after Parliament got involved). And that was just as it should have been.

Had Tim Henman's dealings with the media been different, then Andy Murray's would have been, too. In addition to Stuart Higgins, Murray has taken professional advice from three different management companies during his career: Octagon, Ace Group and then XIX Entertainment, founded by Simon Fuller, who had managed the Spice Girls. And yet the figure who has arguably had more influence than anyone else on Murray's media relations has been an interested amateur, an Englishman who once went on the record to say that the British press is 'probably the worst in the world'.

'Unfortunately, that's part of the culture,' Tim Henman said in an interview with a Swiss newspaper. 'When you speak to tennis journalists, you notice how little they understand. I have asked them technical and tactical questions, and it was embarrassing. I was embarrassed for them. They knew nothing about the game. I've never been influenced by their opinions anyway, but now we are talking tennis and they didn't know anything.' Every Christmas during Henman's career, his parents would have a little treat for him; they would open up the box of newspaper cuttings they had collected from that year's coverage, and the family, looking back at what they regarded as that year's worst excesses from the broadsheets and tabloids, laughed all the way into Boxing Day. One of the cuttings they treasured was the front page of the *Daily Mirror* during one

Wimbledon that declared: 'No Pressure, Timbo, But If You Choke Now, We Will Never Forgive You.'

The first time that Henman felt as though he had got burned by Fleet Street was after being defaulted from the 1995 Wimbledon Championships when, in a moment of anger, he had smacked a ball away and inadvertently struck a ball-girl. The next day, he bought her flowers and kissed her on both cheeks during an awkward photo-call, but that didn't stop what Henman saw as an over-reaction. His views were also shaped by the hysteria which followed his comments about equal prize-money and why there was a case for keeping a pay gap; the next day at the All England Club, he could not move for camera crews. The next time the subject came up, he decided to be 'boring' rather than 'sexist'. Henman had resolved to save himself the bother of being open; he never really lied, just deflected. Henman had enough to think about without inviting more drama and distraction into his life. 'If someone asked me a question, there might have been a truthful question and a correct answer. I would give the correct answer, then I wouldn't have to deal with all the extra attention. I felt I had to protect myself all the time.'

That, in turn, became Murray's coping mechanism. At first, dealing with the media was an exciting game. The day after Murray lost to David Nalbandian in the third round of Wimbledon in 2005, he left with friends in a car for a day's go-karting, and immediately several paparazzi vans with darkened windows pulled out and followed them down the street. During that grace period, Murray knew he was saying things in interviews that he probably shouldn't have, such as the time he returned the kindness of a wild card into a tournament in Newport in America by being critical about the quality of their grass courts. He got away with that because of his age. But that did not last long, and soon enough, after the fuss over his jokes, he believed that the best approach was to be careful and guarded in interviews. Press conferences had once been 'fun'; now he was on alert for the 'traps'.

He could be confrontational. For a while, Murray imposed a period of radio silence with the BBC, refusing to speak to Auntie because he felt they had taken his remarks about suspected match-fixing in tennis out of context. Murray's quote that 'everyone knows that it's going on' was presented as if he was suggesting it was common knowledge in the locker-room that players were being offered bribes to throw matches. What he had meant by that was that it had been in the public domain that a few players had been approached.

Murray could not immediately forgive what he thought were underhand tactics by the BBC, especially as the radio broadcast led to a minor tiff with Rafa Nadal (they soon made up) and being called in to speak to executives at the men's tour about any new information he had (absolutely none). According to his account, the BBC had not told him they were researching a programme about alleged corruption in tennis, and had given him the impression they had wanted only a general interview. Plus Murray had other quarrels with the corporation, such as the article which had appeared on their website after he had been nominated for the shortlist for the

2007 BBC Sports Personality of the Year award. There was a 'did you know?' trivia-box for each of the nominees and Murray's was: 'Did you know that Murray was called "Lazy English" when he trained in Spain?' That was the first time Murray had heard that insult.

There was also a public falling-out with a couple of Sky's commentators, former world number four Greg Rusedski and Barry Cowan, best known for having once taken Pete Sampras to five sets at Wimbledon. Around the time of the 2009 year-end championships in London, Rusedski and Cowan were urging Murray to play with more adventure. Murray's response was that he didn't care for their opinion, or value it: 'Yeah, who are these experts? Barry Cowan? Greg Rusedski? I think I know more about tennis than Barry and Greg.'

Murray has laughed off some of the newspaper attacks on his character and his appearance, including the one that commented on the shape of his skull. But he couldn't laugh off all of them. Mark Petchey, on seeing how upset Murray had been by some of the criticism, once said to him: 'I don't envy you as a person. You're going to go through so much in your life that will be difficult. You're going to be incredibly successful and yet often you're going to read stuff that makes you sound like a failure.'

There had been two Henmans, Public Tim and Private Tim, and so there would be two Murrays, one of them more interesting, candid, funny and personable than the other. One consequence of Henman's pursuit of an easier life was that the public thought he was boring. They never really got to see the

Murray at an academy in Barcelona, where he could escape the bitchy world of British tennis.

Murray's victory in the boys' singles tournament at the 2004 US Open meant he would always love playing in New York City.

Murray's first title on the main tour came in San Jose, California, in February 2006.

Murray's first grand slam final came at the 2008 US Open, against Roger Federer.

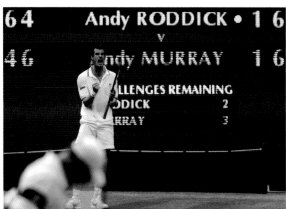

Murray played his first Wimbledon semi-final at the 2009 Championships, when he lost to Andy Roddick.

(LEFT) In tears after losing to Roger Federer in the 2010 Australian Open final, Murray said: 'I can cry like Roger, it's just a pity I can't play like him.'

(RIGHT) Murray and Novak Djokovic meet at the net after the Serbian's victory in the final of the 2011 Australian Open.

Murray serves to Jo-Wilfried Tsonga during the semi-final of the 2012 Wimbledon Championships.

Murray's tears, after ultimately losing to Roger Federer in the final, helped him to 'reconnect' with the British public.

Murray speaks to Roger Federer at the net after beating the Swiss in the gold medal match at the London Olympics.

Murray poses with a post-box in Dunblane, painted gold by the Royal Mail.

Murray serves to Novak Djokovic during the final of the 2012 US Open final.

Murray is in shock after becoming the first British man to win a grand slam singles title for 76 years.

devil in Henman, or to appreciate his humour. Murray, however, thought Henman had done a fine job in covering up his 'real personality'.

So Murray stopped making jokes, because of the trouble they could cause him, and became reluctant to give much away. This became tennis's biggest secret: that Murray had a gentler side, that he could mind his Ps and Qs, that he was perfectly capable of polite conversation. If Murray was really as grumpy as his popular image had suggested he was, he would have been living alone in Surrey, and he would never have had friends popping by.

Most people who have met Murray away from the tennis court have been struck by his manners. One lady who bumped into Murray on Wimbledon Common, where they were both walking their dogs, described how when she said hello, Murray immediately pulled down the hood of his tracksuit top – he wasn't a snarky young 'hoodie' – before making entertaining small talk. While Murray is not a reader of books (something else he has in common with Henman), he has always been interested in the world around him and the people he has met, and made an informed decision about who he would vote for in the 2010 General Election (but he never let on which party secured his vote; his politics have stayed between him and the polling booth). To borrow a phrase from Richard Williams, father of Venus and Serena, Murray could see there was a whole world out there beyond the baseline.

For a sign of Murray's good nature, you have only to look at how he gets along with his rivals. Which is just fine, as friendly as it is possible to be when you're competing against one another. That is despite some people's best efforts to will a feud between Murray and Roger Federer into existence. Those who had been brought up on the bad-ass tennis of the 1980s, when John McEnroe, Ivan Lendl, Boris Becker and Jimmy Connors went rat-a-tat-tat with the insults, were still hooked on the idea of animosity in the locker-room. They wanted players to hate each other.

The British author Martin Amis wrote an essay in the *New Yorker* in which he elegantly riffed about the cult of tennis personalities: 'I have a problem with – I am uncomfortable with – the word personality and its plural, as in "modern tennis lacks personalities" and "tennis needs a new star who is a genuine personality". But, if from now on, I can use "personality" between quotation marks and use it as an exact synonym of a seven-letter duosyllable starting with "a" and ending with "e" (and also featuring, in order of appearance, an "ss", an "h", an "o" and an "l"), why, then personality and I are going to get along just fine.'

Using the Amis definition, the top of modern tennis has been free of 'personalities' for some time. Anyone who wants aggro in tennis will have been left feeling disappointed by the Federer era; the Swiss would much rather start a bromance than a feud.

Clearly, Murray was unhappy when Federer observed, after Murray had just beaten him at a tournament in Dubai in 2008, that the Scot needed to change his defensive playing style, and stop 'grinding' several feet behind the baseline, if he was ever going to win a grand slam. Murray didn't think that it was Federer's place to criticise his tennis when he had just lost. But that was as vicious as it ever got. Federer, who thought he was just being honest, apologised for his critique. For years, people kept looking for tension between the two. Innocent comments that Federer made about Murray were dressed up as being little digs at the Scot. While Murray and Federer have never been the best of friends, it would be going too far to imagine they loathed each other. Even to say they disliked each other would be a stretch.

Murray and Nadal have always got on well, apart from those few days when Nadal was unhappy at hearing what Murray was supposed to have said about corruption in tennis. Murray and Nadal have known each other since they were on the junior tennis circuit, and they remain friendly. Murray has disclosed that he loves watching Nadal play. And, before they played a Wimbledon semi-final, Nadal said Murray was 'one of the good guys' of tennis, 'not one of the bad people or arrogant people – Andy is a normal guy who hasn't changed after all his victories and that's important.'

But the clearest sign of the collegiate atmosphere in the men's game came at a tournament in Miami in the spring of 2011, when Murray chose to play doubles with Novak Djokovic. This was the same man who, just weeks earlier, had beaten him in straight sets in the final of the Australian Open, and put him in a funk. There were no hard feelings on Murray's side, and his doubles partner said: 'I like the guy.'

*

Andy Murray: Wimbledon Champion

Andy Murray is the only one of the big four in men's tennis who has a home grand slam. There isn't a major in Spain, Switzerland or Serbia. Everything has been on a smaller scale for Rafa Nadal at Madrid's Caja Magica, for Roger Federer at Basel's St Jakobshalle, or for Novak Djokovic when his family used to own a tournament in Belgrade, than it has ever been for Murray at Wimbledon. The first time Ivan Lendl experienced Wimbledon as Murray's coach, in 2012, he was shocked: 'There was incredible pressure on Andy, from the media, from the spectators, from himself. It was just incredible. There were days after the matches when my head was just spinning.'

When Murray first came on tour, he would openly declare that the US Open was his favourite grand slam ('Everyone says Wimbledon's the best tournament – it's not'). And all this was before his joke about English football went toxic. This wasn't Murray being a teenage contrarian, and hoping to upset his elders, as he meant what he said.

Clearly, his views of the US Open had been coloured by his victory in the junior competition. He made comparisons between how the US Open and Wimbledon treated their juniors. At the US Open, the boys and girls stayed in hotels in Manhattan and were free to be in the same changing-rooms and lounges as the seniors. At Wimbledon, the boys and girls were housed in student digs and changed in the pavilion at the practice courts, not in the main locker-rooms. Murray was upset with the All England Club in 2005 when they declined a wild-card trade with the United States Tennis Association, which meant he would have to play in the qualifying tournament for that summer's US Open.

Murray has always adored playing in New York. The first time Murray saw a night-session match at the tournament, which was in 2004 when he was in the city for the junior tournament, he sat near the back row of the upper section; up there, spectators have a better view of the Manhattan skyline than they do of the tennis, so far are they from the court. But Murray was not as interested in following the ball as he was in the energy and the noise, in the music being played over the sound system between games, and how the spectators grew ever more vocal, fuelled by the beer and the atmosphere. The first time Murray played a night match, as a senior, only reinforced how he felt about the city and the grand slam.

There were other reasons, too, why he had once liked the hard-court championships in New York more than the grass-court tournament in London, one of which was that he thought his game was better suited to concrete than to lawns. Another was that he didn't like the all-white clothing rule at Wimbledon; he wanted to be free to wear whatever colour he pleased (there were echoes, here, of Andre Agassi's complaints at not being able to dress in ripped denim on Centre Court). A third was that he liked what he regarded as the friendly and enthusiastic nature of the average American fan; those weren't characteristics that he would necessarily have attributed to an average British spectator.

With time, though, Murray came to appreciate Wimbledon for what it was, down to the silence around Centre Court as he prepared to serve (there's never complete quiet at the US Open). His views softened; he no longer expressed a preference for one tournament over the other. He has not lost any of his adoration for New York, just gained plenty for Wimbledon.

What of the other two slams? When Murray has played at the Australian Open, he has been 'Muzza', and Melbourne Park has always been friendly. But it has sometimes seemed as though Australians can't shake off a fascination with how the 'English media' have been beastly to the Scot. Americans wanted to watch Murray play tennis; the Australians wanted to see whether the mother country was crushing him with their expectations. And while Murray has been booed at Roland Garros, that doesn't make him special.

If Murray had to select one match when he first realised the power of having the Wimbledon crowd on his side, he would probably choose when he came from two sets down to beat Frenchman Richard Gasquet in a fourth-round encounter in 2008. That was also the same occasion when Murray, standing by the side of the court, with his eyes popping out of his head, and with engorged veins on his neck, looked for half a second as though he was about to do a stage dive.

During the high that followed, Murray and others thought he had formed an emotional bond with the Centre Court crowd. Murray lost heavily in the next round, a quarter-final with Rafa Nadal, but he went further at the next three Wimbledons, making the semi-finals each time. After three semi-final defeats, to Andy Roddick in 2009, and then to Nadal in 2010 and 2011, there were concerns that he was becoming what Tim Henman had been, a serial beaten semi-finalist. The defeat in 2011, when Murray appeared to be in control against Nadal, only to miss one forehand and then lose his way, was the hardest for the crowd to take. Still, away from London, he had been in three grand slam finals by then – one at the US Open in 2008, and two at the Australian Open in 2010 and 2011 – and the public seemed to accept and appreciate Murray for what he was: an exceptional talent who looked to have the rare ability to win a major, and who had his faults, just like everyone else.

Andy Murray's tears after the 2012 Wimbledon final shouldn't be thought of as the moment that British tennis lost its stiff upper lip. It certainly wasn't the moment that Andy Murray lost his stiff upper lip – who had ever considered that he was emotionally buttoned-up, that he had been keeping his feelings hidden?

What was different this time, though, was that the British public were seeing a softer side to Murray. They had become accustomed to watching him growl and gurn, to seeing him bounce around the court and pump his fist, but now they were watching him weep. For many, that was suddenly the moment, as Murray wiped his face with his hands and shirt-sleeves, when they came to like the guy. How disappointing, a friend would later say, that it took Murray sobbing into a microphone for the public to realise 'he has a heart'. But, in an age when you cannot turn on the television or flick through a magazine without seeing the puffy eyes or smeared mascara of another 'celebrity breakdown', it was almost as if the public had forgotten that it was possible to engage with someone without first seeing them blub. The next morning, Roger Federer's achievement of winning a 17th grand slam title almost became a footnote in some of the British newspapers, with pages and pages dedicated to Murray's failure to stop the tears. And to the images of his girlfriend Kim Sears, who at first had bitten her lip and put a hand over her mouth, but had then needed a hug from Murray's physiotherapist, Andy Ireland. 'It was horrible seeing someone you care about going through that,' she would later say. 'The immediate aftermath of that match wasn't pretty.' Indeed, Murray carried on crying when they were back home in Surrey.

Everything at Wimbledon is new; you learn that every summer. Something hasn't happened in tennis until it has happened at the All England Club. It was not the first time that Murray had sobbed on a tennis court. He had cried as a teenager after winning his first meeting with Tim Henman in 2005, and there had been tears after he lost the final of the 2010 Australian Open to Roger Federer (so the 2012 Wimbledon Championships was the second grand slam at which the Swiss had made the Brit cry). And when Murray had the rare opportunity in 2011 to play in front of a Scottish crowd, at Britain's Davis Cup tie in Glasgow against the Grand Duchy of Luxembourg, he was just in the middle of a post-match interview on the court, 'I don't get the chance to come back here very often so . . .' when his voice trailed off.

And those were just the tears in public. As Murray has

observed, 'Lots of great players go back to the locker-room and cry – it's just that the crowd don't see it too often.' Murray had cried as a teenager when he had a pain in his knee and thought there was a chance he might never play again (he would also have a quiet cry when he was alone in a hotel room in Toronto, just days after the London Olympics, as he reflected on winning a gold medal). So, in tennis circles, Murray's softer side was well known. But, until 2012, he had never sobbed on court at Wimbledon. There was a British television audience of 17 million in the weepy aftermath of Murray's first Wimbledon final. For most of those armchairs viewers, this was Murray crying for the first time, and they realised that these weren't the tears of a spoilt child wanting pity and attention.

Even before the tears that fortnight, there had been indications that attitudes towards Murray were shifting; a writer for the *Guardian* spotted what he regarded as 'perhaps the ultimate sign that Middle England has clasped Murray to its bosom', which was the sight of a couple holding up embroidered cushions with the Scot's name on. By beating France's Jo-Wilfried Tsonga, Murray became the first British man to appear in a Wimbledon final since Bunny Austin in 1938; no longer could you say, entirely truthfully, that the last player to have lost to a Briton in a semi-final at the tournament had died in the Battle of Stalingrad. So Murray's Wimbledon career had been moving in the right direction, ever closer to the prize of that golden cup. And, while Murray had not lost all of his rage, he had become a much calmer soul since working with Ivan Lendl; some of the rough edges had been smoothed away. The Wimbledon crowd, who had learned to love Jimmy Connors, John McEnroe, Andre Agassi and other assorted tennis vulgarians, were coming around. Perhaps it was always going to take time for the crowd to get on with Murray. It had taken Tim Henman a few years of tea-time thrillers before Wimbledon truly formed an attachment.

But the great, almost total, transformation in public opinion would not have happened if Murray had not cried. If the tears did not change everything, they changed a hell of a lot, with John Lloyd arguing they showed that Murray was 'not a grumpy geezer'. Murray's father Willie believed his son's speech had 'been good for Andy – I think it was good for other people to see, it was a defining moment for him.' The Hollywood actor Kevin Spacey thought Murray had shown great 'class and grace', and that the tears had 'humanised Andy for the public'. A column in the *Daily Mirror* by Tony Parsons, who had previously been so scathing about Murray, illustrated this change in mood: 'For those of us who had never warmed to Murray, it felt like, for the very first time, we were seeing the full man. It was a moving and humbling experience. The end of Wimbledon resembled the final reel of *Avatar* – where everyone says "I see you" and then breaks down ... Like the young McEnroe, Murray just made the leap from being widely disliked to being unanimously loved.'

In the Royal Box, British Prime Minister David Cameron shook hands with Scotland's First Minister Alex Salmond without anyone starting off another debate about where

The Joke that Went Wrong

Murray stood on the British–Scottish spectrum. This was as it should have been from the beginning; Murray playing at Wimbledon and enjoying the crowd's affection, without any background nonsense.

Just a few days after showing the British public he could cry, he demonstrated another important truth: that he could take a joke. There can't be many other beaten grand slam finalists who would dry their eyes and head to the filming of a comedy panel show where there was every chance they would be 'picked on'. All those who had changed their minds about Murray probably liked him even more after he accepted an invitation to sit in the audience for the BBC's *Mock the Week*. 'Keep it light when discussing the Wimbledon final,' the host of the panel show had said after informing the comedians on either side of him that Murray was sitting in the audience. And perhaps the teasing was more gentle than it would otherwise have been for Murray, who was given a standing ovation. 'The three most emotional things I've ever seen on television,' said one of the panel, 'are *Terms of Endearment*, *Philadelphia* and Andy Murray trying so hard in his speech not to call Roger Federer a bastard.' Between rounds, one of the regulars behind the desk put a towel over his head and peeled a banana. And there were a number of references to how Ivan Lendl had no emotional range during matches. 'This is Ivan Lendl happy,' said one comic, and keeping the same non-expression, 'and this is Ivan Lendl sad.' Throughout the programme, the director was able to cut to images of Murray and his girlfriend laughing.

Murray's rehabilitation continued at the Olympics. There were some extraordinary sights at the All England Club during the London Games. Serena Williams celebrating her gold medal in the women's singles by shaking her booty on Centre Court grass with a 'crip-walk' dance taken from the Los Angeles ganglands. There was the bright pinky-purple Olympic signage around the grounds, making it seem as though Wimbledon had been hijacked by the Teletubbies. And there was Murray – clear-eyed, no tears – looking as happy and as self-assured as anyone has ever seen him on a tennis court. For the first time, Murray was completely at ease, relaxed and assured, when playing against the world's best in front of a home crowd.

So Murray played some accomplished tennis to beat Novak Djokovic in the semi-finals and then gave Federer a horse-whipping in the gold-medal match (there was an hour-long period in which Federer, the greatest grass-court player of all time, did not win a game). It was undoubtedly true that the Olympic crowd was not quite the same as a regular Wimbledon crowd; during the Games, Centre Court was more international, perhaps a little younger, certainly quite a bit louder. But that should not be over-stated; this was still a tennis crowd, and not just people who had bought tickets to anything at the Olympics and who didn't much care whether it was archery, Greco-Roman wrestling or tennis. For the first time in his life, he felt loved by a Centre Court crowd.

Murray had felt as though his tears, and the reaction, had allowed him to 'reconnect' with the British tennis public. It mattered that Murray's first significant victory had come while he was wearing the red, white and blue of the British Olympic kit designed by Stella McCartney, and not just a regular outfit. Over the years, Murray's withdrawals from British Davis Cup ties had led some to imagine he was selfish and unpatriotic. But his reaction to the victory – climbing up to the guest box to embrace his lover, entourage and family, as well as accepting a hug from a little boy in the crowd – demonstrated that he cared deeply about being part of a British team. Indeed, he had been inspired by the events in the Olympic Stadium the night before, when Jessica Ennis, Mo Farah and Greg Rutherford had all won gold medals. Soon after winning his first medal, Murray earned another – silver in the mixed doubles with Laura Robson.

Murray's victory at the US Open made some sections of the public consider their feelings for him all over again (but that tournament didn't have anything like the impact on public opinion of his defeat in the Wimbledon final and his Olympic triumph). Was affection turning into adoration? In *The Times*, Matthew Syed argued: 'It is time to stop fretting about his voice, his hair, his tantrums and his relationship with his mother and to embrace him without inhibition.'

Did Andy Murray need a crowd's affection if he was going to have a chance of winning Wimbledon? Perhaps, but you could not be certain. Maybe Murray was capable of winning Wimbledon without Centre Court's universal, unconditional love. But there could be no doubt it would make it easier if he could spend the changeovers listening to chants of 'Andy, Andy, Andy' bounce around the place; if the All England Club could generate the sort of noise you would expect from a Glastonbury mosh-pit. During that emotional speech to the crowd in 2012 he had told the crowd how their noise had propelled him. Throughout the 2013 Wimbledon Championships, Murray implored the crowd to make as much noise as they could, for Centre Court to feel like it was the Olympics all over again. Such a request to the Wimbledon spectators would once have been ridiculous ('Who's he to ask that of us?' Centre Court man would once have thought). It wasn't ridiculous now; not now Murray was as popular as he had ever been, and the crowd would surely oblige with his request to turn up the dial.

Murray's popularity was obvious from the reception he was given on the middle Saturday when he appeared on Centre Court in a dark suit instead of in his Wimbledon whites; as Murray wasn't playing that day, he had accepted an invitation to sit in the Royal Box along with a number of other Olympians (there had been a little panic beforehand when he had cut himself shaving in the locker-room, but he managed to stem the bleeding with loo paper before it was time to take his applause). This is totally unscientific, but it also looked as though were more bottoms wedged on to Henman Hill – outside Centre Court, this was the most sought-after real estate in south-west London – than there had been in previous years.

For irrefutable evidence of how the public now felt towards Murray, just consider the 2012 BBC Sports Personality of the

Year Award show, when he came third in the phone vote, behind only the cyclist Bradley Wiggins, the first Briton to win the Tour de France, and athlete Jessica Ennis, the face and the abs of the London Olympics. Almost a quarter of a million people had punched keypads for him. Some had worried that Murray's decision not to attend the show in person, and to only take part via video link, would be a PR disaster, but it seemed as though the public mostly accepted it was important he didn't cut into his Miami training camp. In most other years, Murray would surely have won the prize. Soon afterwards, there was an acknowledgement from the establishment in the New Year's Honours List when he was awarded an OBE.

Perhaps a line or two is needed here on the strange evening in Greenwich in November 2012, when Murray was booed by sections of the London crowd as he played Roger Federer in the semi-finals of the season-ending championships. This was Murray's welcome home party, his first tournament in Britain since he'd won a grand slam, so what were the crowd doing treating him like the villain of the piece, even if it was just light booing (there was no real venom behind it)? Why was there more positive noise for Federer than there was for Murray? They could have played this in Basel and the crowd would hardly been cheering much harder for Federer.

But let's not allow some rowdy Swiss fans to twist or skew this narrative. The reality was the crowd was not representative of the opinion of the British tennis public; don't put Murray's reception down to unappreciative British fans. Large numbers of Swiss fans – this comes from the tournament's executives – had bought up blocks of seats weeks or even months in advance. The Roger Federer Fan Club had got organised; they had mobilised and taken over whole areas of the stadium. The crowd wasn't so much anti-Murray as pro-Federer.

The most extraordinary thing about Murray's match with Mikhail Youzhny, and with all his other appearances during the fortnight, was that he didn't have to listen to cries of 'C'mon Tim' from all around him. That, surely, was the biggest sign that everyone had moved on from Tim Henman, and come to accept and admire Murray. For the first time, Murray could be certain he was competing at Wimbledon and not – apologies in advance – Timbledon.

More than anyone else during the fortnight, Youzhny had done his homework before playing Murray. Indeed, he had gone so far as to have received a doctorate from Moscow University for writing a thesis on professional tennis players, and the psychology and tactics – 'it's like chess' – that determine matches ('I looked at how Murray and others would change their games when facing certain opponents, and it was very interesting').

For the first time in the fortnight, Murray experienced some hairy moments on court, such as when he winced and held his back, and when, trailing 2-5 in the second set, it looked as though he was about to drop his first set of the Championships. Still, Murray didn't turn a drama into a crisis. Everyone in tennis had been a bit uptight and on edge during that manic first week of the Championships, Murray thought, but he had felt calm before he played Youzhny, thanks in part to the two days on the practice court between matches.

The Centre Court crowd were unsettled as he walked on, the spectators still taking in what had happened – in the biggest shock of the women's tournament, Sabine Lisicki had beaten defending champion Serena Williams – but Murray wasn't going to allow that to throw him. The back turned out to be fine (though he didn't hold his press conference until two hours after his match, after having an extra 20 minutes of ice-baths, massage and generally 'taking care of my body', he said there was no reason for anyone to fret) and Murray managed to win that second set in a tiebreak, including recovering from a 5-3 deficit in the shoot-out by taking the last four points. No one can expect to play brilliant tennis all tournament, and in some ways Murray's 6-4, 7-6, 6-1 victory was more impressive for the fact that he had shown he was capable of getting through when playing average tennis; he wasn't above scuffling and scrabbling his way to a Wimbledon title.

While the crowd were perhaps not as animated or as vocal as they had been for his third-round match against Tommy Robredo, they were certainly engaged, especially during all the 'to-ing and fro-ing' of the second set. Judy Murray had been invited to sit in the Royal Box. Ladies aren't supposed to wear hats in the Royal Box, as to do so would block the view of those seated behind, and cries of 'C'mon' aren't exactly the done thing either. As for pumping your fist, Debrett's doesn't even begin to cover such behaviour. Judy didn't last a whole match, preferring to sit with the Centre Court 'commoners' where, if she felt like it – as she surely did – she could make herself heard.

Once again – this was the sixth consecutive summer he had reached this far or beyond – Murray was into the quarter-finals of Wimbledon. And few on Centre Court or on Henman Hill would have been that surprised if you had told them, after the draw was made, that Murray would end up playing a left-handed Spaniard in the last eight. The surprise was the identity of that Iberian lefty, as instead of Rafa Nadal – who by now was messing around on a boat off the coast of Majorca – Murray would play Fernando Verdasco, who was then the Spanish number nine (the British number nine probably lost in the first round of the pre-qualifying tournament, which is where you start if you're not ranked high enough to gain direct acceptance into qualifying proper).

Strangely, for we were already halfway through the tennis year, Verdasco would be the first lefty Murray had encountered all season, and to prepare the Scot his staff cast around for southpaw hitting partners until they found Johan Brunstrom, a Swedish doubles player who was more than happy to help. If you discounted his meetings with Nadal, Murray had a very respectable career record against left-handers, a result of all the hours he had spent playing with his lefty brother Jamie, 'so the way the ball comes off a lefty's racket almost feels more natural to me than a righty'.

Show the crowd you're vulnerable, Mats Wilander had urged Murray before he played Verdasco. Wilander, a former world number one, was of the view that Murray should 'be prepared to show people that he's not perfect, that he's bothered and that he's vulnerable, and then people will get behind him'. 'If Andy is showing that he really wants to win, the crowd will get involved,' he said. 'And if they get behind him, we saw what happened at the Olympics. He's still going to have to hit his shots, but the crowd can definitely help him and hurt the other guy. If the crowd get involved, it's going to be very difficult to beat him. He needs to let them know, "I need you and I want you to be with me, so please help me out."' Little did Wilander realise quite how 'vulnerable' Murray would be during his quarter-final.

5

Lover, Painter, Driver, Hairdresser

In the style of Anna Kournikova – who once predicted that female tennis players would eventually have to give the public what they wanted and compete topless – some kept on confusing Wimbledon with a beauty parade. Live on the radio, the BBC's John Inverdale would cause much consternation over the final weekend by remarking that Marion Bartoli, the winner of the ladies' title, was not 'a looker'. But was that as invidious as those who now focused their attentions almost exclusively on the women sitting off court, and who kept on comparing Andy Murray's girlfriend, Kim Sears, to his opponents' other halves? This was how one tabloid previewed Murray's meeting with Fernando Verdasco: 'Think the quarter-final showdown between Murray and Verdasco is the big match today? Well, stand by for the Battle of the Babes.'

Lover, Painter, Driver, Hairdresser

Why would you want to read about the ferocity of Verdasco's forehand (capable of putting dents in the Centre Court backstop), or how a new racket meant there was now even more zing in his shots, when you could discover more about his girlfriend, Jarah Mariano, 'a Victoria's Secret model who had stripped off for a series of sizzling shoots', who had appeared in the latest Bond movie *Skyfall*, and who, rather daringly, liked swimming with sharks? She was compared and contrasted with Sears, who, in her own words, specialised in 'quirky yet emotive' portraits of pets, who had called her business 'Brushes and Paws', and who was terrified of modern art (someone had made the observation that she was a well-groomed young lady painting well-groomed cats and dogs – Sears knew herself that she was on the other end of the spectrum to Damien Hirst's pickled sharks and cows, and that she was no *enfant terrible* of the art world, the Tracey Emin of pet portraiture).

As Hadley Freeman, a *Guardian* columnist, rightly observed in a piece examining how Wimbledon had exposed the sexism women face as players and girlfriends, 'Perhaps some day the media will be able to deal with the idea of high-profile men having girlfriends and not treat them as accessories or sad desperate harridans waiting anxiously for their wayward menfolk to marry them – but that day has not yet come. Throughout Wimbledon, the girlfriends of the male players were gawked at and purred over, their attributes detailed as clinically as discussions of the players' diets. Whenever Murray would play, newspapers would compare all of his qualities with those of his competitors and among those qualities would be his girlfriend – whose advantages and disadvantages were listed alongside the girlfriend of her boyfriend's opponent.' As Freeman noted, television directors also kept cutting to Sears between points.

No one should make the mistake of regarding Sears as mere accessory. In the opinion of Jean-Pierre Bruyere, a chiropractor who had worked closely with Murray for many years, Sears was 'the greatest asset in Andy's team'. 'Kim is special, as Andy is. She is always polite and she has beautiful clear-blue eyes which illuminate her nice face. Kim is a modern lady who can be independent but also very supportive. She is the best supporter of Andy, but she is never angry towards his opponent or the people around them. Kim is a well-balanced young lady. Her personality brings some leadership to the team. The team may not always appreciate her, but she is there and, as a person, her silent presence can be felt. Kim is a star in her own right.'

Andrew Castle, a former tennis player turned television commentator, who was covering the tournament for the BBC, and who had also known Sears since she was a baby, had come to think of her as 'Andy's anchor'. 'I think her importance to Andy is that she's been present throughout his journey, from the early days all the way through to now. That has given Andy a stability. Every man needs somebody to civilise him, and I think Kim has done that for Andy. She's been around tennis all her life so she understands the madness of an individual sport, the celebrations, the triumphs and the disasters – she's been there every day as a constant.'

*

Lover, Painter, Driver, Hairdresser

Fred Perry, a Hollywood swordsman as well as a grand slam champion, had four wives and lots of flings with actresses, including romancing Marlene Dietrich, whom he taught how to play tennis 'with great patience and lots of little passionate hugs, punctuated with rapid kissing between flying balls', so her daughter said. Ilie Nastase has claimed to have slept with 2,500 women. Boris Becker, who at one time felt he was being 'hunted' by female admirers, fathered an illegitimate child on the stairs of a Japanese restaurant in London (just not in a broom cupboard, as first thought; he has corrected that version of the Nobu conception). The first time that Bjorn Borg played at Wimbledon, so many teenage girls ran on to the court after his matches that the All England Club felt compelled to write to the headmistresses of the local schools to ask them to control their pupils; their heels were ruining the grass. In years to come, Borg's coach would take the hotel room next to the Swede so that he could hear any midnight knocks on the player's door. And, somehow, people kept a straight face when talking of how Bjorn had sexed-up tennis with his 'Borgasm'.

Like so many other facets of tennis from yesteryear, the womaniser and playboy had largely disappeared from view – in the modern game, there weren't many 'modelisers' left, though one of those was Fernando Verdasco, who had appeared on billboards for Calvin Klein underwear, and had posed naked for *Cosmopolitan* magazine. There cannot be many better adverts for monogamy than the fab four of the modern game; at the time of the 2013 Wimbledon Championships, Roger

Federer, Novak Djokovic, Rafa Nadal and Andy Murray were all in long-term relationships, and each had credited their girl-friend or wife for giving them the calm and emotional support they needed to play their best tennis. 'You absolutely cannot become a grand slam champion if your personal life is all over the place, and Murray's had been settled for years now,' Greg Rusedski has said. 'Continuity is key to winning major tour-naments and that goes for your relationship with your girlfriend as much as with your coaches.'

None of the four took Andy Roddick's route to love, which was to use his agent as a romantic go-between; after seeing the swimsuit model Brooklyn Decker while flicking through *Sports Illustrated* magazine, he instructed his agent to call her agent to set up a date. Or Ivan Lendl's approach during his early days on tour, which, according to that same publication, was to ask friends to talk to women for him: 'If a woman inter-ested him, he sent someone he knew to risk the opening line. He didn't trust his English, his face or his crooked teeth.'

All four had found companions without calling Jerry Maguire or using their friends to make the first introductions. Federer's first kiss with his future wife Mirka Vavrinec hap-pened in the athletes' village at the 2000 Sydney Olympics. Federer and Mirka, a former top-100 player, now travel the world with their twin daughters and nannies. Mirka is said to have stopped Federer from being such a tennis obsessive; he had been in the habit of spending his time off either playing tennis computer games, often selecting his own avatar, or re-living real matches to consider what he should have done differently. For a while, Mirka helped to organise Federer's interviews and media relations, and occasionally stepped in as a practice-partner.

Djokovic, who has been in a relationship with Jelena Ristic from around the time he broke into the top 100, has said that she has helped him to win grand slams: 'Our love and emotional stability has much to do with my success.' Before Wimbledon 2012, he took Ristic to Scotland for a couple of days to celebrate her birthday ('I sent Andy Murray a picture, and he replied, "What are you doing there?"'). Djokovic and Ristic, who has studied finance to masters level, live together in an apartment block in Monte Carlo; she doesn't go to every tournament he plays, though when she does you can see the angst on her expressive face.

Nadal's circle of friends in Majorca struggles to remember the time before he was in a relationship with Maria Perello, also from the same town of Manacor. Perello has rarely been seen on the tour; she has a full-time job and no desire to follow him everywhere. As Perello said in Nadal's autobiography, 'He needs his space when he is competing, and just the idea of me hanging around waiting on his needs all day wears me out. It would asphyxiate me. And then he would have to be worrying about me. No, if I followed him everywhere, I think there's a risk we might stop getting along.' She added that she didn't want to get caught up in the celebrity environment, a factor that she believed strengthened her relationship with Nadal. It was not until the 2010 Wimbledon Championships that she sat by the court to watch him play a grand slam final; before that, she had been happy to follow his matches on television.

Murray met Kim Sears in 2005 and they got to know each other by spending some time together in South Africa that Christmas; he was there to train with his then coach, Mark Petchey, and she was on a family holiday. They have been together ever since, apart from a short break of a few months that left both of them utterly miserable. Like Federer, Nadal and Djokovic, Murray has found that he is happiest in a long-term relationship.

Perhaps because he is essentially teetotal, and has no interest in hanging around bars, he has never had any desire to spend his evenings chatting up girls (his fitness trainers wouldn't allow it either). And no one has ever accused Murray of being a sex symbol. But that doesn't mean that he has been without female admirers; at his first Wimbledon Championships 'there were girls shouting out that they wanted to go out with me, and that was fun'. Another year, there was the opportunistic female fan who slipped a piece of paper with her number on it into his racket bag. 'I put my racket bag down to sign some autographs and when I went to get some grips out of it later on, someone called Natalie had left a note with her phone number on it,' Murray wrote on his website. 'So, Natalie, I'd appreciate a photo before I consider making a phone call because you could be a complete stinker.'

Before he broke on to the main tour, Murray was briefly in a relationship with a German girl he had met when they were both tennis students in Barcelona. He recalled: 'I liked this one girl. Then a different girl came and I started spending time with her. Then the first one got jealous and decided to go out with me. It just sort of happened.' But, with their training and playing commitments, they hardly saw each other, so Murray does not regard that as having been a proper relationship. However, he was relieved when the interview she did for a Sunday newspaper, for a fee, was revelation-free; it was perhaps not the kiss-and-tell that the publication had been looking for when they handed over the money.

While it may be true that a Miss Scotland came to watch Murray play at Wimbledon one summer, the relationship was purely platonic – Katharine Brown was an old school friend from Dunblane. Sears is the only serious girlfriend Murray has had. He has said he is aware that some professional athletes want to go out 'with a thousand girls rather than one', but that doesn't interest him.

'It isn't that I have anything against people who want to go drinking and find as many girls as they can – I know that's what most guys of my age do ... I don't know whether that's because I've got an older head on my shoulders or because I'm lucky enough to have Kim, but the last thing I'd want to do is go out looking for women,' Murray wrote when he was 21, in his 2008 autobiography.

Cups of tea, chocolate biscuits, Classic FM and Jilly Cooper are what excites Kim Sears, not the prospect of a photo-shoot in *Hello!* magazine. She would much rather spend her days painting cats and dogs, or reading, or listening to the radio, than pose in a photographer's studio or be strafed by flashbulbs outside a restaurant. Drawing attention to herself is not her style, so when she was sent some gold wellington boots – presumably to be accessorised with her boyfriend's gold medal – she decided they were too flash to be worn out of the house, writing in her blog: 'I'm sure they would look great on Lady Gaga at Glastonbury, but they will not be featuring on Wimbledon Common anytime soon.' Sears doesn't care for fame, or for following her boyfriend around the world to every tournament, and that's the way Andy Murray likes it. In this regard, Murray is no different to Rafa Nadal; it is unlikely he would have stayed with a girl who sees every match sat in a guest box as a promotional opportunity.

The highlight of the year, Sears has said, isn't one of the four grand slam tournaments, but Bonfire Night in Lewes – near her parents' house in Sussex – which she describes as 'a totally ridiculous, offensive, amazing tradition that links our whole community and I wouldn't miss it for the world'. Unlike her teetotal boyfriend, Sears drinks alcohol, and is said to make an excellent sloe gin from the berries picked by her mother, but she is not known for her partying.

Only very occasionally, such as when they are invited to sit on the front row for Burberry's collection at London Fashion Week, do they take up the perks of Murray's fame, and the next day it's back to the brushes. Of course, every time she watches him play a tennis match, her clothes, hair and make-up are closely scrutinised by the fashion pack; until one critic mentioned it, Sears was presumably unaware that she was part of the 'glossy posse – a group of girls whose long shiny hair, bright eyes, luminous complexions and dazzling smiles make men sigh and women gnash their unbleached teeth in envy'.

During Wimbledon 2012, one fashionista noted, with approval, that Sears had the Duchess of Cambridge's knack for successfully mixing High Street clothes and designer pieces. Hair salons reported during that same tournament that more women were asking for 'The Kim' than for 'The Kate'. And during the summer of 2013, she won a magazine poll for 'The Best Hair at Wimbledon', and one paper asked on its news pages, 'So how does Kim's hair stay that glossy?' Someone had even gone to the trouble of setting up a spoof Twitter account for her hair. But none of that is her doing; it's an unwanted consequence of taking her seat on Centre Court.

The first time that most people would have heard Sears speak would have been when she appeared in the BBC film about Murray which was broadcast on the eve of Wimbledon. She generally declines interviews, saying 'it's about Andy, not me', and about the only reference to Murray on her 'Brushes and Paws' website is a photograph of the bouquet he was given at the Olympics ('It was so beautiful I couldn't bring myself to throw it away, so I dried it in the airing cupboard and now have it hanging in the office'), but even then it's an indirect reference as she doesn't mention him by name. And only once could you say that Sears has upstaged her boyfriend at a tournament, and that was one autumn at the Paris Masters, an indoor event in the east of the city. Even then, she hardly engineered it. During the warm-up, her face suddenly appeared on the giant video screen, several thousand Frenchmen wolf-whistled, and she immediately started to blush. When a member of Murray's entourage jokingly fluffed up her hair with his hand, there were more whistles, and more blushing.

There have been no scandals or controversies, not unless you count how much she enjoys Jilly Cooper's bonkbusters – she bought a second copy of *Polo*, as she has read the first so many times that the pages were falling out. Another favourite is *The Man Who Made Husbands Jealous*, and when Sears was studying English literature at the University of Sussex, she would have liked to have done her dissertation on Cooper (the author said she was thrilled when she heard that).

She may like Cooper, but Sears is not a fan of *Fifty Shades of Grey*, the sado-masochistic bestseller by E.L. James. 'One book you can't judge by its cover – as it is impossible to prepare yourself for what lies inside – is *Fifty Shades of Grey*. Proof of that is that my brother "stumbled" across it when download-ing books for his Kindle, according to Mum. Worse still is now knowing that my mother has read it too. Luckily Dad doesn't own a Kindle, or possess the adequate know-how to download anything,' she wrote on her website. 'I'm not here to mas-querade as a literary critic, but I do want to say that I was left cold by the book.'

'Kim's good for Andy because she's not looking for fame,' Murray's father, Willie, has said. 'And she has a good sense of humour, which she has needed. I have a lot of time for her.' When Murray first introduced Sears to his father, he just said, 'This is Kim.' It was only a few months later that Willie realised that she was his son's girlfriend. 'Kim's a gorgeous, lovely girl and they get on so well. At the time, I thought she might be his agent or something like that. She's a very beautiful girl. To be honest, I wasn't sure if Andy entering into a relationship was a good thing for her because of the amount of time he is away. But Kim is the best thing that has ever happened to him,' Willie said in an interview with the *Mail on Sunday*. 'She has her own life, and she's not a hanger-on.' Murray's grandmother Shirley has told how Sears 'keeps herself quiet in the background, but is tremendously supportive – she's a lovely girl, she really is.'

Sears and Murray's mother Judy have become friends, and have sat next to each other during his matches (Sears knows that Judy doesn't like a running commentary from those around her, so recognises not to discuss every shot and shift in momentum).

Like Rafa Nadal's girlfriend, Sears wants more from life than being a tennis player's consort, and has no desire to be defined only by her relationship with her boyfriend (on one of the occasions Sears was on the tour with Murray, they happened to be in the same restaurant as Nadal, who played a joke on his friend and rival by sending messages to Murray's phone saying 'I love you' and 'I want to see you', obviously hoping that Sears would ask to take a look). Murray has said that having so much time apart has meant that they appreciate each other even more when they are together, and that there is always something to say to each other. It has kept the relationship fresh.

For a while Sears aspired to be an actress, and Murray – despite being as bewildered when reading Shakespeare's *Measure For Measure* as when Roger Federer speaks Swiss German – would help her with her lines. She has also expressed ambitions to write a novel. But, as recently as the 2011 summer grass-court season, she was still casting around for a job, and she was helped in her search by Andrew Castle, who asked on the air during one of Murray's matches at Queen's Club whether anyone watching would like to employ her.

'I've just been speaking to Kim's dad, and he said Kim is struggling right now to find a job,' Castle told BBC viewers. 'So if anyone out there is listening, there's a lovely young lady who wants a job. This could be the first time that someone gets a job via a TV commentary.' Castle never did report back on whether anyone contacted the BBC offering her employment.

Not long afterwards, Sears chose to make a career from her art. Sears, who as a teenager had created a Warhol-inspired print of three dairy cows on a five-foot piece of cardboard, had always found that her pencils and drawing had given her a release. Sears has been happy to paint cats and dogs, even though she has a slight aversion to cats, thanks to watching the Disney cartoon *Lady and the Tramp* as a child and being frightened by the Siamese cats: 'Even now, that song still gives me the heebie-jeebies.'

Only very rarely does she paint humans, but she made an exception when she produced a picture inspired by a photograph of her and her brother Scott dancing at a wedding. 'My comfort zone is definitely hairy animals and not humans, but Scott's questionable facial hair meant a hairy human would do. Mum and Dad had asked me to try to paint it as they loved the photograph and all the memories associated with it. It was quite liberating to play around with my brushstrokes and colour palette, as when I'm painting animals I'm quite restrained. But when I critique it now I'm pretty sure what I thought was a cool lighting effect actually makes me look like I've been swimming in chlorine without washing my hair.'

Sears, who at times was so busy that she had to stop taking on new commissions, clearly enjoys her work, though in her quieter moments she does sometimes find herself wondering whether, in another life, she could have been a country singer as she loves their values and their hats.

As Sears has been there from the beginning, it's clear in Murray's head that she's not with him for the money or the profile. When they met, introduced by Murray's then coach, Mark Petchey, Murray was ranked outside the top 100 and had had to qualify for the US Open rather than going straight into the main draw. And Sears was still at school. The week that Murray and Sears 'went public' was the same week that Murray won his first title on the main tour, in San Jose in February 2006.

With Petchey staying at home with his wife and children, Sears used her half-term holiday to spend time with her new boyfriend. Murray hadn't had his hair cut for a year, and the

Sun had started to compare him to Coco the Clown, so one of the first things she did on arrival in California was to give him a trim with a pair of nail-scissors.

To celebrate beating Lleyton Hewitt in the final, Murray walked into the crowd to kiss Sears on the lips, and the television commentator said, 'I'm not sure if he's going to come back on the court.' While she is believed to have later used a photograph of the kiss as the basis of a painting for her A-level art coursework, she was bewildered by the fuss over the embrace, saying it was 'nothing, and wasn't planned'. 'It was a great week, we had so much fun. I went with Andy thinking he was never going to win the tournament, and that I would be back in time for school on Monday, and then he did win the tournament,' Sears told the BBC. 'I remember saying to Mum, "you've got to call in and tell them that I've got the winter vomiting virus and that I'm not going to be in". But it ended up on the front page of the papers, so it was, "oh no, busted, sorry". The few days that followed were a bit weird. We had a few people following us around and people came to my school.' Wanting to carry on with the celebrations the day after winning that first title, Murray bought Sears a bag and a pair of sunglasses. Murray tries to be romantic. So if they are shopping and 'something catches her eye', he will try to pop back later to buy it for her; however, he has said that he has tended to ruin the moment by saying something stupid.

In a rare disclosure about the intimate aspects of their relationship, Murray once told the Spanish newspaper *El Mundo* that he is 'not one of those sportsmen who practises a strict policy of sexual abstinence before playing. Tennis is not like boxing. I remember a former world heavyweight whose trainer banned him from having sex for the six weeks before a fight. In tennis we play every week, so with a boxer's mentality we'd always be saying "no".'

Some six and a half years after that kiss in San Jose, there was another public display of affection, this time at the London Olympics. When Murray won the gold medal, he did what most do in the moment of triumph on Wimbledon's Centre Court, which was to climb up into the stands and find his guest box, where he kissed Sears (and hugged everyone else). 'At Wimbledon, everybody does it, especially the first time, as you want to share that moment with the people who have been with you all the time. Those are the guys who see what you are like after losing a Wimbledon final, and see how tough it is. It's nice to celebrate those special moments together.'

More than any other girlfriend or wife on the men's tour, Sears understands the sacrifices that go into being a tennis player, as she grew up around the sport. Or as Murray has said, 'She just gets it.' Her father, Nigel, has coached some of the world's leading female players, including the former world number one Ana Ivanovic, and former top-five players Daniela Hantuchova and Amanda Coetzer. 'It's good because her dad is a tennis coach and he still travels on the tour. She understands the sport well and from a young age was used to being away from her dad. She understands that sort of long-distance relationship,' Murray has said. In a sign of how small a world tennis is, when Judy Murray became the captain of Britain's Fed Cup (the women's team competition) she was taking on a position that had been vacated by Nigel Sears. Another was that Ivanovic had once been in a relationship with Fernando Verdasco.

Kim Sears understands that Murray will be away for around two-thirds of the year, and when he is at home, he must concentrate on his training. A couple of days after Murray's tears at the 2012 Wimbledon Championships, Beverley Turner, the wife of Olympic rowing gold medallist James Cracknell, said she knew what life would be like for Sears. 'Living with an elite athlete can be a lonely, emotional and challenging business; the Murrays of this world tend to be intense individuals who bring their day-to-day vicissitudes home, where the partners have to soak up the disappointments and offer platitudes over a teetotal dinner of steamed vegetables and pasta,' Turner wrote in the *Daily Telegraph*. 'When they win, you can share the joy – even though it can feel strangely hollow as it is ultimately their own achievement – but if they lose, you'd better be tough . . . She must arrive at numerous birthday parties and weddings on her own and probably no longer questions the need to check Andy's diary with at least three other people.'

On a practical level, Sears has done much for Murray. Before he had a driving licence, she drove him everywhere (he bought her a Mercedes as a thank-you present). She has done his laundry (even when finding bags of dirty kit that have been sitting there for weeks), and she has been his hairdresser. And when Murray moved house the week before one Wimbledon –

there couldn't have been a worse time – Sears and Murray's mother organised everything so he wouldn't have to interrupt his preparations for the tournament.

On top of that, Sears has helped to soften and improve Murray's image, though that was not part of some master-plan to repackage her beau for public consumption; it just happened naturally over the course of their relationship. If Sears was so pleasant, people thought, can Murray really be the difficult customer he has been made out to be? Sears has also helped Murray from being consumed by tennis, of thinking and talking about nothing other than winning grand slams. In the evening, Murray actually likes being able to talk to someone about a subject other than tennis. Sears is a much calmer soul than Andy Murray, his father Willie regarding her as a 'stabilising influence' on his son. Sears, as the daughter of an experienced coach, and now a portrait painter, manages to stand both inside and outside tennis. However, they don't play each other at tennis, because, as he has said, 'She's not very good.'

Sometimes – and this has generally happened only around Wimbledon – the paparazzi have trailed Murray and Sears, but the images have never been more rock 'n' roll than the pair buying sushi in Kensington, strolling around Surrey with their dogs and takeaway coffees, or shopping for groceries at a local supermarket. 'The last few Wimbledons, photographers have waited outside the house to see what we're doing on the off days. I think after about the fifth or sixth dog walk, they realised they were wasting their time, and they didn't come back,' Murray has said. They live a quiet life. 'We definitely don't court the spotlight,' Sears has said. 'For the most part, people do leave us alone. They probably think we're boring.'

Occasionally, Murray does wonder – or at least he says he does – what Sears is doing with him. While Murray is bright, he has recognised that she is considerably more intelligent than him. She is much better read than he is, but that is not too difficult, considering that he is known to have scanned only boxing magazines, a few passages from Harry Potter books, and part of a wrestler's autobiography. That must have been why Murray was so pleased with himself after beating her at Scrabble once that he announced the victory on Twitter (his winning move, 'hernias', was definitely a sportsman's word).

Central to Andy Murray's domestic life with Kim Sears are their dogs, a couple of Border Terriers called Maggie May and Rusty. 'Andy hasn't always been good at waking up in the morning – he has got better – but I can always send in the dogs to jump on his face,' Sears has disclosed. Once, when asked by his brother Jamie what he would save first if his house was on fire, Murray jokingly replied: 'I would save my dogs, probably. Is that wrong that I said that over my girlfriend? I'd take my dogs, I'd take them for sure.'

One of the happiest days of Murray's life was when his girlfriend's parents gave her Maggie May as a present for her 21st birthday. Murray's affection for the dogs – Rusty came along later – has been such that he has forgiven them for chewing everything in the house, for working up huge vet's fees by swallowing pebbles, and for peeing on his shoes. Between tournaments, Murray can often be found walking the dogs and encouraging them to jump up to lick his face, and he further demonstrated his love for all things canine in the week after his defeat in the 2012 Wimbledon final when he and Sears went on a private visit to the Battersea Dogs Home. Occasionally the dogs have gone on tour, such as to Paris for the French Open, but most of the time they have stayed in England, running around the Epsom Downs, or the Devil's Punchbowl in Surrey, with Sears.

In a sign of the madness of modern life, Maggie May has more followers on Twitter than some of the players that Murray encounters on the tour. Maggie May has used the Twitter account – written by Sears – to flirt with Pierre Djokovic, Novak's pet poodle (naturally, he is also on Twitter), and also been open about her jealousy of other dogs: 'Kate Middleton's dog is stealing column inches. This has not gone unnoticed, and I'll step out without underwear tomorrow to compensate.'

Named after the Rod Stewart song, Maggie May has tweeted pictures of herself and Rusty wearing Murray's Olympic medals, one getting a gold and the other a silver, and has written a column for The Tennis Space website: 'Let's get this straight, I'm not your ordinary tennis player's dog. I don't even like tennis balls for a start. I'll chew them, sure, and rip them to pieces – but don't even think about asking me to fetch. Ivan Lendl came round for dinner the other night, which I was pretty excited about. I'm a soft touch when it comes to men, you see. I flirted my Border Terrier socks off and even allowed him on my sofa, but he didn't let me kiss his face, which I thought pretty harsh. Maybe it's a Czech thing ... We get to jump on Dad's face in the morning and there are plenty of socks and ankle braces to play with.'

A happy home life has always been hugely important to Murray; having, in his words, 'gone through' his parents' divorce, he had resolved to 'work hard at having a successful relationship'. When Murray moved out of London, from his penthouse flat with a roof garden in Wandsworth, it was to a Surrey village and a house that he would share with Sears. Leaving London would mean more space and more privacy, and it would also mean better sleep; in the flat he was often woken up early in the morning by the noise from the nearby skips.

As the estate agents around Oxshott like to say, it has gone from being a hamlet for pig farmers to one of the most expensive villages in Britain, if not the most expensive. They also say that Oxshott, sandwiched between the A3 and the M25, is part of the 'wealth corridor', with the village populated by footballers in their twenties and fund managers in their thirties. The other line, although not one used by the estate agents, is that the village is 'divorce central'.

The house that Murray bought, which had been on the market for around £5 million, is a mock-Regency property with an indoor swimming pool, sauna, jacuzzi, gym, library, cinema, games room, six bedrooms and a triple garage. It was also Murray's castle, which he thought needed defending one night when the alarm went off at 2.30am; while wearing just his boxer-shorts, and having picked up a tennis racket to use as a weapon, he ran downstairs to confront the intruder. He felt some relief on realising there wasn't a burglar, only that the alarm system was faulty.

Just a few months after they moved in, in the summer of 2009, Sears returned to live with her parents. When Murray and Sears broke up, his mood would not have been improved by the suggestions – entirely false – that the relationship had ended because she was fed up with him spending so much time with his PlayStation. Murray's 'camp' strongly denied accusations that he would spend up to seven hours a day playing computer games.

It had been an amicable break-up and, as the publicists were saying, no one else was involved, but both were miserable apart. 'I work better in a relationship,' Murray has said. And he and Sears were not apart for long. By the 2010 Wimbledon Championships, the relationship was back on. Soon the press's attention would turn to whether Murray and Sears would marry. Murray had seen how happy his brother was as a married man. Murray had been the best man when Jamie married his Colombian girlfriend, Alejandra, in Dunblane in 2010; even though he doesn't usually drink, he had fulfilled his duties of organising a boozy stag night. Murray would joke – remember how dangerous jokes could be for him – how Sears was 'pushing for marriage'.

Apart from when Prince William was still at the boyfriend-girlfriend stage of his relationship with the then Kate

Middleton, has there ever been as much speculation about whether a young man is about to propose? When Murray returned to Britain after winning the US Open, he and Sears were welcomed home with front-page – and inside-page – speculation suggesting that he was to keep the party going by proposing. 'Wedding Smasher,' said the *Daily Mirror*, which reported: 'Andy Murray may have sealed his place in history, but he is already planning for his next big match – his wedding.' It wouldn't be the last time that speculation about their relationship would be served up as light entertainment.

'What the f*** are you doing? What are you f****** doing?' Andy Murray asked himself as he sat down on his chair to a two-set deficit against Fernando Verdasco. And there would have been a few sitting on Centre Court, or watching through their fingers from their sofas at home, who would have been asking Murray pretty much the same question, and with similar language. Murray was so angry with himself he was almost laughing. In the BBC's commentary box on Centre Court, Andrew Castle said sorry on the Scot's behalf: 'I do apologise for the language of course, but you can understand the frustration Andy feels at this point. He really is torturing himself.'

Murray wasn't the only one; this wasn't fun for those watching him from his guests' box; you could understand why Kim Sears had said she no longer looked forward to Wimbledon as much as she had done in the early years. Murray would have known that he was probably looking at a fine for what the rulebook calls 'audible obscenities', but any financial punishment wasn't his concern during that changeover; all he cared about what was finding a way to stay in the tournament.

John McEnroe's view – one he had formed after Roger Federer had followed Rafa Nadal out of the All England Club during the first week – was that it would be 'an absolute catastrophe' if Murray didn't go on to make the final. Of course, that wasn't a view shared by Ivan Lendl ('I wouldn't call Andy's draw open'), or by Murray, who was aware of how talented Verdasco was. After all, Verdasco had once been ranked in the top ten, he had toppled Murray at the slams once before – in the fourth round of the 2009 Australian Open – and had the sort of game that could hurt the world number two. Plus, no one ever reaches the quarter-finals of Wimbledon if they don't know what they're doing on grass, so Murray certainly wasn't going to underestimate the guy. We weren't looking at someone from the tennis underclass here, a grass-court nobody who could just be rolled over.

For all that, the quality of Verdasco's tennis – the ambition and the execution – was surprising; he wasn't supposed to play as fabulously as this. Two things never wavered on Centre Court during the first couple of sets – Verdasco's gelled hair and the Spaniard's resolve to keep on going for his shots. There was only one player embracing risk, only one player who was playing aggressive tennis, and only one who was trying to dominate the lawn. Yes, Murray had been too passive in the first two sets, which was perhaps a result of the circumstances. Would he have played with greater freedom had he, as the draw had projected, been facing Jo-Wilfried Tsonga for the prize of a semi-final against Nadal or Federer?

But, for all that, Verdasco more than played his part; he kept on hitting big serves close to the line. Even when Verdasco was break-point down on second serves, he wasn't, as Murray observed from the other side of the net, either taking some pace off or going for the middle of the box. Being so ballsy with his serve gave Verdasco plenty of opportunities to tee off with his forehand – and there aren't many players who clump the ball much harder. Verdasco just kept on ripping winners. Was the weirdest Wimbledon about to get even weirder?

When Murray dropped the second set, he noticed that the crowd 'definitely got behind me' and tried to spur him on. One of the noisiest spectators was Sir Alex Ferguson, the former Manchester United manager, and a guest in the Royal Box (sitting in the smart seats was hardly going to stop him from roaring his encouragement). Pat Cash thought that Murray had 'been trying too hard. It's really tough when there are fifteen thousand people and the whole nation cheering him. His brain is going a million miles an hour and he can't focus.'

Another former Wimbledon champion, Boris Becker, urged Murray to 'find a way – it doesn't have to be pretty'. If Murray was going to survive, he would have to come from two sets down for the seventh time in his career (however, one of those previous comebacks had been on Wimbledon's Centre Court when he had beaten France's Richard Gasquet in the fourth round of the 2008 Championships). Murray swore, but he didn't panic. 'You're concerned you may lose,' Murray recalled, 'but when you've been in that position a lot of times you know how to think and not get too far ahead of yourself.' In Murray's mind, it was a good sign that he wasn't trying to rush; in fact, he was doing the opposite and slowing down between points, taking his time and making sure he was ready. Murray was determined to hang in there.

And if anyone was getting ahead of themselves, it was Verdasco. The psychology of the match had changed when Verdasco had taken a two-set lead. Previously, he had been under no pressure whatsoever, but now he was a set away from producing the latest shock result of these Championships, and in the early stages of the third set the sense was that he wasn't serving or smacking his forehand with the same abandon as he had done before.

When the umpire appealed to the crowd to be quiet between points, he was just wasting his breath; Centre Court wasn't going to be silent on a day like this, as Murray took the third set for the loss of just one game. If Murray's first four matches had lacked drama, this more than made up for it. Murray took the fourth set, then the fifth set and the match, his 4-6, 3-6, 6-1, 6-4, 7-5 victory putting him into the semi-finals for the fifth summer in a row.

For those watching from the edge of their sofas, there was more tension to come during Murray's post-match interview with the BBC's Garry Richardson. Murray didn't look too impressed when Richardson asked him whether Lendl would 'say some things to gee you up', just as Ferguson used to 'go into the dressing-room after matches to give his players a bit of hair-dryer treatment'. Within minutes Richardson was trending on Twitter, and, in a sign of the new bond between the public and Murray, there could be no doubt that their sympathies lay with the player and not the media. To Murray's credit, he later used his Twitter account to ask his fanbase not to be 'too hard' on Richardson as 'he had a bad day and apologised afterwards'.

So Murray was through to play Jerzy Janowicz, the winner of the all-Polish quarter-final with Lukasz Kubot, and a young man who would terrify Middle England with his 6ft 8in frame, his Bond villain looks, his fierce serve and his terrifically light touch on the drop shot: think Jaws with a racket, just with the ability to serve, rather than eat, through the roof of a cable-car. So there was much to discuss ahead of the match, with McEnroe speaking of Janowicz as 'the real deal' and a possible grand slam champion of the future. Some of the British newspapers, though, spent much of their space and energy worrying about Sears 'facing a titanic battle in the glamour stakes', or sounding concerned that Janowicz's girl-friend, Marta Domachowska, a former player who had recently posed topless for *Playboy* magazine, 'may yet prove a rival to Miss Sears's title as Queen of the Wimbledon Wags' (did Sears even know this was her trophy to lose?). And so on we went.

6

Fame and Fortune

There's no room for the brigadiers in the Royal Box these days. While the All England Club aren't as celebrity-obsessed as the United States Tennis Association – it sometimes feels as though the core objective of the US Open is to show images of Eva Longoria on the big screens – the men in purple-and-green-striped ties certainly aren't above stuffing the Royal Box with luvvies. That space above one of the backstops often ends up looking like the cover of *Vanity Fair* magazine. The All England Club's thinking appears to be along these lines: if you're going to hold a garden party, you may as well have some interesting guests, who will then sprinkle their stardust all over our lawns. We'll give them VIP seats and sandwiches. They'll give us a front-page photograph or two, and their faces will fill some air-time during the changeovers.

Andy Murray: Wimbledon Champion

Wimbledon's fondness for celebrity certainly wasn't doing Andy Murray any harm (though his help came from someone who should never be described as a luvvie, especially not to his face). Indeed, Murray's preparations for his semi-final with Jerzy Janowicz included a pep talk from Sir Alex Ferguson, the recently retired manager of Manchester United Football Club. Ferguson, who had been a guest in the Royal Box during Murray's five-setter against Fernando Verdasco, had happily spent 20 minutes in conversation with his fellow Scot after the quarter-final, passing on tips that the tennis player regarded as 'gold dust'. 'He was giving me advice on how to handle certain pressures and expectations. Sir Alex said to me that one of the things he built his sides on was consistency and concentration. If you can concentrate throughout an entire match, you'll gain that consistency,' Murray disclosed. 'That is something I will always try to do, but it emphasises the point a bit more when someone like Sir Alex says it to you. He did it his whole career.'

It wasn't the first time that Ferguson had offered his personal encouragement to Murray during a grand slam; at the 2012 US Open, Ferguson had provided Murray with one of the most surreal moments of his career. Murray had been sitting in the main press conference room at Flushing Meadows, having just reached the final, when suddenly a couple of knights, breathing Merlot and mayhem, gatecrashed. Whoever had drawn up Murray's carefully choreographed schedule of post-match print, radio and television interviews hadn't made room in the schedule for Ferguson and Sir Sean

Connery dropping in to pass on their congratulations. Sir Sean and Sir Alex could have waited until after the interview was finished, but then where would the fun have been in that? While Murray had previously been in email contact with James Bond and Ferguson, it was the first time they had met. At the time, this almost felt like a tartan takeover of the city; as the *New York Post* would later observe, here were the three most famous Scotsmen – 'with apologies to Ewan McGregor' – in one room. 'We just went in,' Ferguson recalled. 'It was so funny.'

Watching all this, the American writer S.L.Price 'half expected Jackie Stewart, Fat Bastard and a blue-and-white faced Mel Gibson to come barrelling in next, flinging handfuls of haggis'. 'Excuse me for interrupting,' Connery said, and no one was going to stand in the way of James Bond's interlude. When Murray's mother, on the encouragement of Ferguson and doing her best Miss Moneypenny, moved forward to hug her youngest son, Murray told her, clearly enjoying this, 'Mum, you smell of wine.' Looking over at Ferguson, Judy said: 'He made me have wine. He's just been telling me that Scotland invented the world.' Ferguson responded: 'I explained how Scotland invented the world, and today we invented the wind.' And that was Connery's cue to say: 'Today we conquered the world.'

So at the US Open, Ferguson's intervention had been extremely public. When Ferguson was finished, he turned to Murray and said: 'Continue your interview.' And if anyone couldn't quite believe that had really happened, a full transcript was soon available from the stenographers who record every word of every interview at the US Open. Or, alternatively, you could have gone almost immediately to YouTube to watch one of the strangest episodes ever seen at a grand slam tournament.

Ferguson returned for the final, as a guest of Murray. Here on the other side of the Atlantic, Ferguson's contribution to Murray's slam may have been in private, but it had greater impact than in America. Murray wasn't about to forget what Ferguson had said to him. The Glaswegian, who had once said that he became more emotionally involved following Murray than he had ever been while watching Manchester United, observed that, for a sportsman, ability was never enough: 'It also requires that inner belief, a passion and a desire to get over the line.'

Ferguson wasn't the only public figure taking a close interest in Murray's wellbeing during the 2013 Wimbledon Championships. One of his guests for the semi-final was James Corden, an actor and comedian who had met Murray when they had made a sketch together for Sport Relief, the charity telethon, and who had bonded with the tennis player while double-dating in Nobu: 'We got on like a house on fire.' There wasn't a more animated spectator on Centre Court than Corden, who has been very open about his adoration for 'the most unassuming elite sportsman I have ever met'. 'For me, to be in the top five of anything in the world is such a difficult thing and he has achieved so much, and yet to meet him you would never know he was one of the world's best sportsmen.

He just has no ego. I've never known anyone who is such an unassuming and polite guy, and who is misrepresented in the eyes of the public,' Corden told *GQ* magazine. 'Ultimately, what you see with Andy is what you get. I think he might be the purest sportsman we have ever had. He is just so comfortable in his own skin.'

And, for much of the tournament, Murray had been playing text-message tennis with David Beckham, pinging missives back and forth. This was quite a collection of famous friends for someone who considered himself almost an anti-celebrity, and who once said he wouldn't wish fame on anyone. Before winning his first major at the US Open, Murray had spoken to Ivan Lendl about his fears of what becoming a grand slam champion could do to his life; would he become burnt up by celebrity, followed wherever he went by professionals with long lenses and amateurs with smart-phones and Facebook accounts? Lendl had told him not to worry, saying that the only significant change would be that he would be offered free rounds of golf and the best tables in restaurants. Still, winning a slam outside Britain was one thing; becoming Britain's first men's singles champion at Wimbledon for 77 years would be quite another.

How was it possible for Andy Murray to maintain that he did not care for fame when he was represented by Simon Fuller, the creator of the *Pop Idol* television franchise, and the former manager of the Spice Girls? When Murray had the same management team as David and Victoria Beckham, Jennifer Lopez,

Annie Lennox, Steven Tyler, Will Young and Lisa-Marie Presley? When his manager was the very same man who had spawned Simon Cowell? And hadn't Murray idolised Andre Agassi, who had willingly appeared in a campaign for a camera with the slogan, 'Image is everything'?

Murray's decision to sign a contract with Fuller's XIX Entertainment, which was announced in 2009, was certainly intriguing – it was a move that invited speculation that he hoped to turn himself into a serious player in showbusiness as well as sport, that this was Tennis Spice making a move on Hollywood. Up until that point, Murray had been represented by management companies who specialised in sport; first Octagon and then Ace Group, a more boutique company, and he had never intimated that he had any great desire to establish a Brand Murray along the lines of Brand Federer or Brand Beckham. The major players in the sports industry, such as IMG or Lagardere Unlimited, would have been disappointed by Murray's news. Perhaps a little surprised, too.

Why had Fuller, who had built his business empire on pop music and reality television formats, and who was said by the *Sunday Times* Rich List to have a personal fortune of £375 million, been interested in a 'mere' tennis player? Here was someone who had once been named by *Time* magazine as one of the 100 most influential people in the world. That was mostly off the back of his *Idol* creation, which was first seen in Britain as *Pop Idol*, became a huge ratings success in the United States as *American Idol*, and which was then sold in more than 100 other countries.

Fuller launched Cowell on the British and American public by employing his friend as a judge on both sides of the Atlantic. But there was a great, high-stakes falling out when Cowell launched a rival show, *The X-Factor*; Fuller sued for a reported £100 million, dropping the lawsuit only after a substantial out-of-court settlement. When you hear it called 'The Clash of the Simons' it sounds quite unremarkable, but theirs is an intense rivalry. A story has done the rounds in Los Angeles of how Fuller told Cowell he was on the waiting list for a sports car worth hundreds of thousands of pounds. So Cowell found one in Germany, had it shipped to Los Angeles and drove it to the set of a television network where he knew Fuller would be.

There is not another tennis player on the tour whose manager is frenemies with Cowell, or who has a star on the Hollywood Walk of Fame. Or who had discovered Amy Winehouse. The music promoter Harvey Goldsmith had picked Fuller as Britain's greatest entrepreneur. You could question Fuller's taste – he was also the Dr Frankenstein behind S Club 7 – but you could not knock his power or his influence. In short, Fuller was a big player, who the *Evening Standard* has described as 'The Man Who Wants To Rule The World' and 'the Mephistopheles of modern pop music'.

David Beckham wrote a piece for *Time* about how Fuller had helped to shape his career. 'We're both committed to being the very best at what we do – he's very hard-working and knows you rarely get an easy win in life,' Beckham wrote. 'He enjoys dealing with unexpected challenges. It's no surprise that he's as successful as he is because, despite being a nice guy and a modest character, he's also a real fighter for what he believes in. I admire him for that.' Beckham added that he had much to be grateful to Fuller for, not least that the entrepreneur had provided him with an introduction to Victoria Adams, who would become his wife. Fuller was also instrumental in driving through Beckham's move to the Los Angeles Galaxy football team, in a deal which was reputed to be worth a quarter of a billion dollars.

While Fuller didn't want any personal publicity – Goldsmith said that you won't see the Englishman 'hanging out with stars at parties, as his modus operandi is seeing opportunities, quietly grabbing them, staying under the radar, and delivering' – he has been brilliant at turning his clients into brands. When the Spice Girls were at the height of their popularity, he was seen as the 'Svengali Spice' or 'the man behind girl power'; he was the one who drove all the marketing and merchandise deals, including the dolls and the deodorants, and the movie.

When Murray made the decision to sign with Fuller, the only other sportsman under XIX Entertainment's management was Beckham and it was a while since he had been 'just' a footballer (the racing driver Lewis Hamilton would follow Murray). Fuller had never worked with a tennis player before, so he did not have anything like the same knowledge of the tour as he did of the music industry. But Fuller was intrigued by Murray, believing that if this young Scottish player could ever win a grand slam title he could become – and he used the

L-word here – 'a legend'. It had always been Fuller's intention to work with the 'hottest' designer, the 'hottest' singer and the 'hottest' footballer, and he believed that Murray had the potential to become the 'hottest' tennis player. To become iconic. 'I had seen a young man who was potentially a champion, someone who could make history. He had been so close, he was so young and I was projecting that if he were to win a grand slam tournament, I wanted to be part of it and I thought I could help. I was imagining a Brit winning a major and how massive that would be, and that's what appealed to me. My job is to complement sporting excellence with an understanding of what goes into being a superstar,' Fuller told *The Times*.

There could be little doubt that Fuller was giving Murray advice and strategic thinking that no other tennis player was getting. As part of the deal, Murray's brother and mother would also be represented by XIX Entertainment, but the company would say that they had no plans to expand in tennis, that they were content to concentrate on this potential 'legend' of the future.

It was certainly never Fuller's intention that he would travel the world with Murray, accompanying him to every tournament; he was the celebrity overlord – or the Svengali of tabloid imagination – giving occasional, long-term guidance. Matt Gentry of XIX Entertainment handled most of Murray's week-to-week media relations, while other company employees helped to organise the rest of his life.

Sport had become a key part of the entertainment business,

that's if it hadn't always been one; what exactly would be the point of tennis if it wasn't entertaining people? Tennis had certainly always had links with Hollywood. Take the man that Murray was hoping to emulate. Fred Perry had a very different take on fame from Murray; Perry embraced everything. Well, almost everything, as he turned down a film studio's two-picture deal for £70,000 because the Lawn Tennis Association talked him out of it. 'When Perry goes to Hollywood,' one American columnist noted, 'male film stars go to sulk in Nevada.'

Perry had actresses on his arm, he partied with Errol Flynn and David Niven, and, such was the strength of his own brand, he set up his own clothing label (as a pipe-smoker, he almost chose a pipe as his logo, before settling for a laurel wreath). Perry had never felt welcome in British tennis; he was much more at home in the world of showbusiness and entertainment, where they actually appreciated his looks, his success and his swagger.

Anyone who imagined that linking up with Fuller signified Murray's intention to take the Fred Perry approach or to air-kiss on the red carpets of film premieres had it all wrong. Certainly Murray would have been attracted to the idea of doing things a little differently from how the established sports management companies would have advised, but he was not interested in having parts of his life whipped up into celebrity froth.

Murray, for all his emoting and cussing on a tennis court, is naturally shy. And there was little chance – make that no chance – of Murray's girlfriend Kim Sears ever pushing for the couple to be sold as tennis's version of Posh and Becks. The only real equivalent to the Beckhams in tennis was Andy Roddick and Brooklyn Decker, who had had Elton John sing at their wedding (she was arguably now the more famous of the pair, after a couple of films).

Murray had liked what he had heard from Fuller about how XIX Entertainment would help to position him, and how they would look after his image and business interests in the long term, rather than concentrating on the short-term and medium-term buck. During the getting-to-know-each-other stage of the business relationship, Fuller had visited Murray's home, and Murray had made it plain that he did not care for empty celebrity, that he didn't crave a bigger profile just for the sake of it. The last thing Murray wanted was for anyone to think he had become a 'fake', as buffed and polished, as rebranded and repackaged, as a Posh Spice doll. As Murray told Fuller during that meeting: 'For me, it's not about becoming a celebrity, it's about becoming the best tennis player I can be.' What would concern Murray would be if those around him ever told him he had 'changed, and become an arse'. As James Corden had said: 'The worst thing that could ever happen to Andy Murray would be for him to have his teeth veneered, and to start acting like a superstar.' But, as Corden knew full well when he made that remark, that was never going to happen.

One aspect of stardom that Murray has always been happy with is the personal interaction with the fans when they approach him at the practice courts, in a restaurant, in the street or at an airport departure lounge. He has signed every body-part he has been asked to, including foreheads. He has posed for pictures. He has never knowingly been rude.

Murray never had the option of becoming a celebrity refusenik. Publicity stunts are a regular part of an elite tennis player's life, with Murray and others called upon to promote tournaments beyond the tennis hardcore. In the course of his work, Murray has met the Miami Dolphins cheerleaders, he has stood on top of London's O2 Arena, he has tried Thai kick-boxing, he has played tennis with Venus Williams on Miami's South Beach, and he has stood on the helipad of the Burj-al-Arab hotel in Dubai, hundreds of feet above the Persian Gulf.

Murray hardly had much choice in any of the above, as the players are contractually obliged to do promotional activity for the sport. But maybe he felt more comfortable about doing it because he felt as though he wasn't just selling himself, but the tour and the sport, too. Murray clearly cares about tennis, its image and its place in the world, and how the sport can possibly go about looking less elitist in Britain. When Murray has appeared on television talk shows, it has sometimes taken him a while to get warmed-up – he looked very nervous, for instance, when he sat down on Jonathan Ross's sofa – but then he has gone on to do a decent job of showing that he has a personality, a dry wit and a racket-bag of anecdotes to dip into.

And in the months leading up to the 2013 Wimbledon Championships, it appeared as though Murray had even started to enjoy some of his promotional activity, realising that this is part of his life – and in likelihood was going to be for a while – so it was probably for the best if he didn't find the whole business a drag or a nuisance. He certainly had fun during a photo-shoot for *GQ* magazine, in which rackets, balls and god knows what else were set on fire, and on another occasion, when he was in the studio for *The Times*, he giggled and smiled as an assistant sprayed him with oil.

If ever there was a television appearance which showed what Murray can be like in private, it was the interview he did with his former coach Mark Petchey in a corridor at the US Open one year. It was one of those rainy, dull days when no one has any idea when they are going to get on court, and Murray and a couple of his friends, the British doubles pair Colin Fleming and Ross Hutchins, had been killing time in the players' restaurant by laughing at each other's faults. Their off-camera conversation continued on the air, when Petchey asked the three of them to do a live chat for Sky Television. Murray disclosed that he had been under attack from Hutchins for 'losing my hair quite early', but countered by mocking Hutchins' shoes. Telling Hutchins that his 'banter on Twitter' was poor, Murray then looked into the camera and advised viewers against 'following' the Englishman. Fire up YouTube for a five-minute clip which is, at once, entertaining, silly to the point of being puerile, and probably the best insight you will ever get into what Murray is 'really like' (that's not to say, in that trite phrase, that it's the real Murray, as the tennis player in business mode during his normal post-match media commitments is just as much the real Murray, too).

Murray's appearance on the BBC comedy series *Outnumbered*, for the Sport Relief charity fundraiser, showed that he could be a good sport. A little girl asked Murray what he did, and he replied: 'I play tennis.' So she said: 'But what do you do for a job?' A teenage boy, having already taken one photograph of himself standing next to Murray, then asked the tennis player to pose for another, 'because my friends are not going to believe it's you. Can we do another one when you're not smiling, where it's a bit more you?'

The first time that many of the fashion crowd would have been made aware of Murray was when he featured in American *Vogue* (anyone wondering what he was doing in the magazine should consider that the editor-in-chief, Anna Wintour, loves her tennis). The piece, which was published before the 2010 US Open, showed how Murray would look if he employed a stylist. The photographer Mario Testino, best known for his portraits of Kate Moss and the late Princess Diana, shot Murray in his Surrey home, in the garage, which also doubles as a weights room, as he wanted to capture him where he worked. It would have been the first time, though, that Murray has worked out while wearing a tuxedo and a bow tie, which Testino had to help him with. When Testino looked at the images of Murray, he thought 'raw'. The writer of the piece noted Murray's 'green eyes, hot and fierce', and Christopher Bailey, the Burberry designer who had supplied the tuxedo, reported the Scot was 'sharp, strong and sexy, and had scrubbed up well', and would go on to become a 'global brand' and an iconic British sportsman. So this was Murray being love-bombed by fashion, with Bailey saying: 'He's so focused and driven in his craft. He's laser sharp: a wonderful person for the nation to celebrate.' Murray's appearance in American *Vogue* was certainly more successful than Laura Robson's in British *Vogue*, when the teenager had been quoted as calling some female players 'sluts, who go with every guy and make such a bad name for themselves' (she would later apologise).

There is a line that Murray won't cross, or pirouette over. Greg Rusedski's appearance on *Dancing on Ice*, a reality show on British television, only confirmed in Murray's mind that he would never do anything similar; it also confirmed the same in Tim Henman's head, and whenever Rusedski was on, Henman and Murray sent each other text messages. 'Andy and I are pretty united in our certainty that we would never, ever appear in a programme like that,' said Henman.

Murray looked at Andy Roddick's cameo on *Sabrina the Teenage Witch*, and when the American hosted the comedy show *Saturday Night Live*, and thought: no way. Murray knows what he is capable of and what he isn't. Murray would not have been comfortable – and he almost certainly wouldn't have been asked either – to have played the love interest role that Rafa Nadal did in a music video for Shakira, a Colombian pop star. Murray's adventures in music have been restricted to an unfortunate rap on the album produced by doubles players and identical twins Bob and Mike Bryan ('During Wimbledon it really gets crazy. My hand cramps up and my mind gets hazy. I sign and I sign but the line doesn't end. Wake me up tomorrow and let's do it again. Autograph.') When Murray appeared on a TV show that embarrassed him by playing a recording of his rapping, he leant forward and buried his head in his hands.

Other players were happy for their images to be updated, but not Murray. Nadal's collaboration with Shakira and subsequent cross-over into MTV – the video saw him pouting like crazy, while a wind-machine blew his hair, and later misplacing his shirt – was part of The Sexing-Up Of Rafa. It was a process that he had presumably consented to. Nadal had once dressed as if he had just stepped off the beach in Majorca, with those cut-off piratas trousers, the vests and the bandanas, and he had the cartoonish enthusiasm and endeavour of Mowgli from *The Jungle Book*.

Nadal's image had arguably been too young and too cartoony for him to have appealed to middle-aged, middle-management tennis fans, the ones that potential sponsors want to reach. Now Nadal wears conventional shorts, he has sleeves on his shirts and he does things that would make Mowgli turn bright red with embarrassment. An advert for Armani had Nadal stripping in a car-park, while his campaign for an aftershave depicted him as a *demi-mondaine*. The sexualisation of Nadal appeared complete when *Sports Illustrated*'s 2012 swimsuit edition carried images of Nadal nuzzling with the Israeli supermodel Bar Rafaeli. Undoubtedly Nadal would have grown up anyway without the intervention of his advisers, but they pushed him along and they cannot be displeased with the result, an image which Bloomberg called a rare mixture of 'humility and virility', while others considered the Spaniard to be a 'safe rebel'.

Over time, Roger Federer had gradually become a citizen of the world. In the beginning, he didn't have Anna Wintour on speed-dial, and he didn't have perfect hair and the cool demeanour. As a teenager, he had been happy to slob around in jeans, he had experimented with hair-buns and peroxide, and he had had a reputation in Swiss junior tennis for being a hot-head throwing tantrums and rackets. No one is born a sophisticate, and Wintour and Federer's wife Mirka have had their parts to play. But that is not say that Federer has become a 'fake' or something he isn't; he has clearly changed, but he has never looked anything less than well suited to the adulation, the private jets and the 'RF' monogram. Superstardom fits Federer as well as a white jacket with gold trim.

Since Djokovic started to make the most of his talent, and fully appreciated the connection between an appealing image and the size of his endorsement contracts, he has toned his personality down. The Djoker side of him hasn't quite disappeared, but certainly doesn't come out to play as often as it used to. There was a time when he couldn't resist any invitation to perform one of his impressions of tennis players – his Maria Sharapova is particularly good – but now there is a more serious, measured air to him (word would also have got back to him that Federer was displeased with the impersonations, saying that the Serbian was 'walking a tightrope').

Like the other three, Murray's appearance and image have clearly developed over the years, but any change had always seemed a bit more organic, and a bit less calculated. Anyone could see that he had been held back by that joke about the England football team, and as he lost trust in the media he became less inclined to be interesting. All that controversy happened before Fuller's time, so one can only speculate how he might have handled that situation differently. Fuller's challenge, after signing a contract with Murray, was to help turn the tennis player into a brand without his client freaking out that he had lost some of his integrity. One of the key moves that Fuller's XIX Entertainment made before the 2013 Wimbledon Championships was persuading Murray to sign up to do the behind-the-scenes BBC documentary, knowing full well that the programme would do much to soften the Scot's image. Murray's management company also had to prepare him for what might happen if he ever won Wimbledon.

In Murray's mind – and it is impossible to refute this – there is nothing hypocritical about being shy and wanting to meet those he had seen on his television screen. Murray has always been interested in talking to actors, comedians and sportsmen, and the more successful he became, the more others asked to be introduced.

As a child, Murray had listened to cassettes of Billy Connolly's stand-up routines during long car journeys, so when he heard during the Australian Open one January that the comedian was in Melbourne for some live shows he gave him a guest-pass. Connolly, who enjoys his tennis, accepted the invitation and appeared to enjoy the experience, apart from when the host television broadcaster put a microphone under his nose and asked him for his thoughts. 'Leave me alone,' Connolly bellowed, though he even managed to make that funny, and there was laughter all around the Rod Laver Arena. 'He's a very, very funny guy. He's very normal, too. It's not like he really tries to be funny,' said Murray, who was invited to watch Connolly's show.

Murray is certainly no luvvie, but the opportunity to meet the actor Kevin Spacey during the 2012 US Open was not one he was going to pass on. 'That was cool seeing him, because *The Usual Suspects* is one of my favourite films. I hadn't really met that many movie stars before,' Murray recalled. Spacey had been concerned that Murray would regard him as 'a twat famous person'. 'To be honest, I just really didn't want to bother him. Here's a guy who is a top athlete, who just wants to stay focused and stay concentrated and I didn't want to come in the way of that. But he was very kind and said some nice things about the work I have done and that he liked some of my films. I was acutely aware that I didn't want to be annoying and some kind of "twat famous person" that he had to be friendly and chatty with. But Andy and his team were so friendly and generous towards me,' Spacey told *GQ* magazine. 'Nowadays, a lot more people are giving Andy a really good shake, and realising he's not this gloomy person he has been portrayed as. He loves the game as he is passionate about it.'.

Spacey was given the opportunity to hit a few balls with Dani Vallverdu on the Arthur Ashe Stadium. 'So I went on court and remember I was dressed in normal clothes, normal shoes, and I maybe hit five balls, and on the last shot I f****** got it and it was a winner. I said, "That's it, I'm done", I'm in the Arthur Ashe Stadium, I'm quitting on a high, and as I walked to the side of the court feeling very pleased with myself, Lendl looks at me and says: 'Why are you puffing?" F****** Lendl.'

One of the strangest encounters of Murray's life came when he was invited to No. 10 Downing Street, and he ended up playing tennis with Prime Minister David Cameron in the State Dining Room. The room had been cleared of furniture before a reception for all the players who had qualified for the season-ending championships in London in 2010, and Cameron challenged Murray to a game; they came very close to hitting the chandeliers.

'I was scared as I didn't want to break anything. The prime minister was hitting the ball really hard at me,' Murray has recalled. 'I have no idea if everything in there is incredibly expensive but it looked very old-fashioned. There was a chandelier above where the dining table would normally have been. Some of the balls flew dangerously close to it. Mr Cameron definitely looked like he knew what he was doing. He spoke about tennis with a lot of knowledge and said that he tried to play a couple of times a month. He also explained how he'd had to change his grip as he had grown up using a wooden racket. These are strange experiences. When I played Wimbledon for the first time, it was a huge shock to me. But playing tennis at Number Ten Downing Street? That's not something anyone would ever think they would do.'

Murray's meeting with the Queen, on the members' balcony

at the All England Club after a second-round match at the 2010 Wimbledon Championships, was more controlled. In the days leading up to the Queen's visit – which was to be her first to the tournament since Virginia Wade won the ladies' singles in 1977 – there had been some speculation as to whether Murray would bow before her. You got the impression that it was the same people who had attacked Murray for his joke about the England football team who were now hoping that he was going to make a faux-pas, and then they could bash him for being a chippy, Scottish republican. Murray was understandably annoyed, and that probably made him more nervous, affecting his technique – when he watched the slow-motion replays, it confirmed his initial thoughts, which was that his bow had been far from perfect.

Murray has always taken the most pleasure from meeting other athletes, as he has appreciated the chance to talk about training and the demands of other sports. In addition to his friendships and acquaintances with boxers – Ricky Hatton has been his guest at a grand slam – he has also spent some time with Beckham. As early as 2005, Beckham was speaking about Murray's 'exciting talent'. And soon after Murray started his association with XIX Entertainment, he spent the day with Beckham as they promoted the Malaria No More initiative with an appearance at Wembley Stadium and by meeting Gordon Brown, the then prime minister, at Downing Street.

Murray's memories of the day were how normal Brown was, and also that Beckham gave him a pair of football boots, though the tennis player felt as though he had not impressed anyone with the quality of the free-kicks he had taken on the Wembley pitch. One thing is for sure, Murray did not come away from that day hoping to be even half as famous as Beckham. The footballer has since followed Murray closely. There have been times when Beckham has texted members of his management team for real-time updates on Murray's matches at Wimbledon and other grand slams, and when Murray played in his first Wimbledon final, Beckham was there to watch, sitting in the Royal Box with his wife.

Beckham is not the only leading sportsman to have dropped by at the All England Club. Rory McIlroy, the Northern Irish golfer, interrupted one of Murray's training sessions at Wimbledon one summer to say hello, and Lewis Hamilton has also been at Centre Court.

One of the first celebrities to have taken an interest in Murray was Sir Sean Connery, who had watched his fellow Scot play David Nalbandian in the third round of the 2005 Wimbledon Championships. The next day, Connery had phoned Murray. That was a great thrill for Murray, because as a boy he had spent his pocket-money collecting the James Bond films. 'Every December in our electronics store back home, they used to do a two-for-one offer on videos, and they had every single James Bond film. So when you lined them up, you could see the pictures of all the different Bonds,' Murray would tell the *New York Times* during the 2012 US Open. He said that *Goldfinger*, a Connery picture, had been one of his favourite Bond films. And, seven years after becoming a fan, Connery would break into a press conference to pass on his congratulations in person. Murray said afterwards: 'That was cool.'

Discussing money isn't considered vulgar at the All England Club. For all their class and refinement, they're operating in the modern world, and they don't shy away from telling you how much winning the title is worth to the men's and women's singles champions (and also what's on offer for all the rest, plus the doubles players). Every spring there is an annual prize-money press conference to announce the compensation for that summer's Championships, and in 2013 there was plenty to say, with a huge increase in the total pot to £22.6 million, a jump of £6.5 million from the year before. And – just look at the noughts on those cheques! – the men's and women's singles champions would each receive £1.6 million, which was a rise of £450,000 from the £1.15 million in the summer of 2012 (so if Murray won Wimbledon he would take his total career prize-money to approximately £20 million, but don't imagine for a moment that he was thinking about any of these numbers as he dashed about the grass).

In the middle of what was supposed to be an economic downturn, this was quite astonishing; clearly, austerity stopped at the iron gates of the All England Club. Or perhaps it wasn't extraordinary at all, the counter-argument being that the players were still being grossly under-paid – that they were being fobbed off at below market-value, that £1.6 million each wouldn't be adequate compensation when you looked at what the champions brought to the tournament over a fortnight. In which case, this was a move in the right direction, but it didn't go far enough; they deserved a bigger rise.

The background to Wimbledon's large increase in funds was that the locker-room militants had been making the case that they deserved more. However, this was a debate which mostly concerned the B-, C- and D-listers, who even talked about the possibility of boycotting one of the grand slams unless they were paid more for losing in the early rounds, claiming that they had been unable to make much of a profit because of the costs of touring. Boycotting one of the slams would have been a guaranteed public relations disaster for the locker-room as, whatever the reality, the perception would have been of multi-millionaire tennis players striking in the middle of a recession. The A-list were doing just fine, even if a few of the sport's most recognisable faces kept looking with envy at the money golfers were making.

When *Forbes* magazine – the publication for the super-rich and the super-envious – produced a list not long before the tournament of the top 100 highest-earning athletes in the world, with six tennis players among that group, it was bound to generate debate. Even if no one should have been that surprised that Roger Federer was the highest tennis player on the list – and was second overall, behind only the golfer Tiger Woods – with an estimated annual income of £47.1 million.

Clearly, being 'boring' wasn't hurting Federer – during the French Open, a Latvian player called Ernests Gulbis accused all of the Big Four in men's tennis of being dull in interviews, and, worst of all, that Federer was the Prince of Bland, inspiring the generation below that boring was best (there was some truth to this – Murray wasn't the only one who was stripping some of the colour and personality out of his media exchanges to avoid controversy). But sponsors clearly liked what they were seeing with the Swiss, described by *Forbes* as being 'as bankable as they come – the next stop for Federer could be the *Forbes* billionaires list'. And that wasn't hyperbole; they calculated that Federer has earned close to a quarter of a billion dollars. (About the only way that Federer could possibly have made more money would have been if he had been born American, as that would have allowed him to have best exploited the American market, but that is debatable as being Swiss is also a commercial advantage; no one is ever offended when Federer says he's from neutral Switzerland.)

Next on the *Forbes* list was Maria Sharapova on £19 million, followed by Novak Djokovic (£17.7 million), Rafa Nadal (£17.4 million), Serena Williams (£13.5 million) and Li Na (£12 million). Murray, who at the time of the list's publication was the Olympic and US Open champion, wasn't in that top 100 (*Forbes* had produced a list before the 2012 US Open of the highest-earning tennis players, in which they calculated that, in the period between July 2011 and July 2012, he had made £7.9 million).

For the elite, prize-money was just the start. The breakdown of the headline figures in the *Forbes* list confirmed that most of their income was not from prize-money, but from endorsement contracts, appearance fees and playing exhibition matches. Tennis is an attractive sport for companies wanting to reach an affluent demographic, and especially an affluent female audience. Murray's figure was broken down into £3.3 million in prize-money and £4.6 million in other earnings. Around £3.9 million of that second number was estimated to have come from sponsors and £700,000 from appearances and exhibitions. Going into Wimbledon 2013, Murray had four major partners – with clothing manufacturers Adidas, the Royal Bank of Scotland, Swiss watch-makers Rado, and Head rackets.

According to the 2013 *Sunday Times* Rich List, which had appeared a few months before Wimbledon, Murray was, for want of a much better word, 'worth' £32 million, which was an increase of £8 million from the year before, and wasn't bad for someone in their mid-twenties and only halfway through their career. Tim Henman, by contrast, was said to have amassed 'only' £17 million. About the only people in their twenties on that money list who had earned comparable amounts to Murray either played football or had acted in the Harry Potter films.

A tennis player's most lucrative contract tends to be with his clothing and shoe sponsor, and Murray didn't appear to have broken that industry rule. In 2010, he began a five-year association with Adidas that was believed to pay him around £3 million a year. It was a good bit of business for Murray and XIX Entertainment as he had previously been operating at a much lower level – he had worn Fred Perry clothes, and had not even had a shoe sponsor, just wearing whatever trainers suited him and sometimes swapping from one brand to

A disappointed Murray is unable to repeat his success over Novak Djokovic in the first grand slam of 2013, losing 6-7, 7-6, 6-3, 6-2 in Melbourne. As Murray's hero Andre Agassi said: 'He's coming into his own now.'

Murray takes on London Mayor Boris Johnson just eight days before Wimbledon to support his friend Ross Hutchins's 'Rally Against Cancer' charity event at Queen's Club.

A third trophy at Queen's for Murray was the perfect warm-up for Wimbledon, as he beat Marin Cilic after going a set down.

The scoreboard tells the story, as Murray falls to the ground after winning the Wimbledon title.

Murray kisses the Wimbledon trophy – it was, he said, 'the pinnacle of tennis'.

For the third successive slam they had both contested, Murray and Djokovic posed together holding the winner's and runner-up trophies.

Murray celebrates. In 2013 he had finally won over the crowd to his side.

The day after. Murray checks up on the newspapers to make sure his dream really had come true.

Seventy-seven years since the previous British player, Fred Perry, had won Wimbledon, Murray poses in front of the statue of his forerunner.

A Downing Street reception for Murray from tennis fan David Cameron was part of a whirlwind of post-Wimbledon celebrations.

another when he changed surfaces. It was extremely unlikely that Nike, the American sportswear giant, would have signed Murray, as they already had Federer and Nadal as their male ambassadors, with Sharapova and Serena Williams endorsing their women's lines; the Scot was not going to do better than Adidas.

As part of the deal, Murray would have access to the travelling team of coaches and consultants paid for by Adidas; it was a facility that he would make use of when he was between Miles Maclagan and Ivan Lendl. And while Federer and Nadal's contracts with Nike stipulated that they had to have 'clean' shirts, in other words with no other sponsors' logos anywhere, Murray was permitted by Adidas to have a couple of patches on his sleeves. That advertising space on Murray's arms was an important part of any negotiations with other companies (more about that later).

There was considerable doubt among the tennis industry, though, whether it had been a smart move by Adidas executives to have ended their association with Djokovic so that they could start a new one with Murray. When the decision was made, Djokovic already had one grand slam title, which he had won at the 2008 Australian Open, and Murray was of course still without a major. At that stage, both Murray and Djokovic were trailing Federer and Nadal, and no one, certainly not any of the executives at Adidas, could have foreseen what would happen during the 2011 season when the Serbian won three of the four grand slams, with only the French Open eluding him.

For so long, he had been the third man of tennis, but no one in the Open era had ever had such a brilliant season, not even Federer at his peak. Djokovic's success continued into 2012, when he won the Australian Open for his fifth grand slam title, and at that year's French Open he came within one match of becoming the first man since Rod Laver in 1969 to hold all four major titles simultaneously; only Nadal stood in the way. One respected industry figure was of the opinion that Adidas's decision to drop Djokovic and hire Murray was starting to look like 'a colossal mistake'.

Djokovic was having so much success that Sergio Tacchini, the Italian company which had sponsored him after he was ditched by Adidas, had to wriggle out of the contract because they could no longer afford to pay all the win bonuses and other fees due to him (he would start a new commercial relationship with a Japanese company, Uniqlo). There would have been some relief at Adidas, one has to imagine, when Murray won the Olympics and then his first grand slam title at the 2012 US Open. During his time wearing the three stripes, he had previously lost three grand slam finals – at the 2010 and 2011 Australian Opens, and at the 2012 Wimbledon Championships – with the middle one of those defeats coming against Djokovic. The Serbian had also beaten Murray in the semi-finals of the 2012 Australian Open. Murray's Olympic–New York double had shown that Adidas had been right to have had such confidence in him.

Murray's relationship with the Royal Bank of Scotland, which had started when he was a teenager, was not without controversy. After the bank was bailed out by the taxpayer, there was a close examination of some of the sponsorship deals which had been signed off during the boom years, and Murray came under considerable pressure, from newspapers' City diaries and elsewhere, to volunteer for a significant reduction in his annual fee from RBS.

An important moment in Murray's commercial life was the announcement at the start of the 2012 grass-court season that he would be sponsored by Rado. Federer was a Rolex ambassador and Nadal wore a £250,000 Richard Mille watch which, at a time of Spanish financial crisis, seemed to some almost to border on the obscene; and now Murray had his own watch-deal. Murray's association with Rado did, however, lead to some strange moments just after Murray had beaten Djokovic in the final of the US Open.

Indeed, Murray's first minutes as a grand slam champion brought confusion and panic. Federer is so used to slipping on a Rolex for the trophy presentation after a grand slam final that he probably doesn't even realise he is doing it, but at the time wearing a watch for a prize-giving ceremony was still very new for Murray, having only recently become an ambassador for Rado. Murray was even more anxious in New York as he had forgotten to put the watch on after the 2012 Wimbledon final; he was in danger of standing there after another slam final with a bare wrist. 'I don't have it, I don't have it,' Murray called out to his entourage, and he then hobbled over to ask: 'Do you have my watch? I don't have it.'

The stadium disc jockey had his carefully chosen party

tunes, 'Start Me Up' by the Rolling Stones, and 'Chariots of Fire', but Murray wasn't about to dance – he was fretting about his wristwatch. It was Kim Sears who told him to have another fish around in his bag; the crisis was averted and he could prepare for holding up the trophy. Murray didn't have the same panic after the 2013 Australian Open final – he calmly put his watch on before making his runner-up's speech – and if he could beat Jerzy Janowicz he would certainly pack his Rado before the final.

There was no getting away from the fact that Murray was a long way from earning anything like the money which Federer and Nadal did from off-court deals. Federer and Nadal each had around double Murray's number of sponsors. When the Wimbledon Championships began, Murray wasn't quite as attractive to sponsors as some of his colleagues were – even though he had won the Olympics and the US Open. While Murray's nationality was worth a few million pounds a year, because of Wimbledon and the British tennis market, he did not have the same international appeal as Federer, Nadal or female players such as Sharapova or Serena Williams.

Murray certainly wasn't in the position to have even attempted what Sharapova had done, launching her own range of candy that she was calling – don't laugh – Sugarpova. Those tennis fans who didn't like Sharapova's sweets could instead buy some shoes she had designed, or eat a Federer-branded chocolate truffle or purchase some underwear from Caroline Wozniacki's range of lingerie. Some, such as Serena Williams, have been extremely proactive about using their brand to make money, with the Californian regularly making personal appearances on a home shopping network to push her own designs of clothes and jewellery. Those sort of commercial opportunities – whether Murray wanted them or not – were not yet available to him.

There were suggestions that Murray should have been doing better off-court business. But was that because of Murray's own reluctance to cash in? The suspicion was that Murray himself was not as keen as others to chase every endorsement pound, dollar or euro as, with every deal he made with a sponsor, he would have to sign away a certain number of days per year and that would cut into his time for training, tournaments and recovery. It would be naïve in the extreme to believe that Murray never had a thought in his head about hard cash, as almost every tennis player has a good sense of their own worth. In Murray's head, there was no question that sportsmen were overpaid, 'but it's a short career, and you try to maximise it as best you can'. Murray has certainly never been greedy, or risked compromising his tennis with his commercial activities. When he set out in professional tennis, great wealth wasn't the lure, and he had never stood on a tennis court thinking about the money that was potentially going to flow from his strings. Murray is many things, but he never has been, nor ever will be, the Scottish Anna Kournikova.

Murray's reluctance to stray too far from tennis, and to push himself as a celebrity, also must have counted against him, with one analyst arguing that he needed 'more exposure outside tennis'. One observer thought that, 'Murray has at times driven his agents to distraction through his obsessive focus on the task at hand, refusing to sign up for anything he is not comfortable with or that might compromise his routine – he has turned down a string of lucrative deals either because they make him uncomfortable or because they do not fit in with his schedule'.

The counter argument, expressed by one marketing executive, was that Murray 'not seeking the limelight or acting up to the cameras would, in many ways, make him more bankable from a sponsorship perspective. He's all about credibility and raw emotion. Those two attributes are everything that almost every brand wants.' Plus, Murray's tears at Wimbledon in 2012 had endeared him to American as well as British fans, and he had introduced himself to general sports fans in the States by winning in New York.

The constant plucking of figures from the air during his career, usually accompanied by a 'Murray Minted' headline, had raised expectations of what is possible. Murray's former agent, Patricio Apey of Ace Group, did the player no great favours when they were working together by saying, 'Sixty million pounds, eighty million pounds, these figures could be dwarfed if things work out for the guy.' Apey also once said of Murray, when the player was in his teens: 'He doesn't do commercial smiles. He's as genuine as you get. And that's what companies are attracted to.' Michael Henderson countered Apey's observations in the *Guardian*: 'Where does one start to rebuff this guff. First, "genuine". What is "genuine" about behaving in such a churlish, ill-mannered way that you put off people who, in normal circumstances, would be happy to see him prevail. A grumpy teenager is not, nor ever will be, a thing of beauty.' He went on to deconstruct the rest of Apey's comment before concluding with: 'Then, "that's what companies are attracted to". Some of them might be, now, in Britain, but the McBrat act will not play well in all the lands.'

Within the industry, there was speculation that Murray would ditch XIX Entertainment once the contract expired at the end of 2012. Would Murray look elsewhere for representation? Surely, some were saying, XIX should have found Murray another sponsor – perhaps even a couple – after his success at the US Open? Surely they should have been making more money for him? But perhaps expectations were unrealistic – maybe winning the US Open, a long way from the strawberry fields of Wimbledon, hadn't given Murray the clout that many had believed it would.

'In individual sports, the financial spoils from product endorsements truly go to the largest winners,' *Forbes* magazine had noted. 'And the only way anyone else is going to get a large share of the endorsement pie is to knock off one of the greats – Federer, Nadal or Djokovic – in an epic slam final.' Still, as the same publication had noted, it would have been naïve for anyone to think that Murray winning his first slam, however historic for British tennis, was going to propel him to the top of tennis's money list. Even with a first slam, Murray didn't have Federer or Nadal's history of success, and he also didn't have their polish. Don't think, *Forbes* had argued, that Murray's victory would allow him to start 'sniffing the

Federer–Nadal stratosphere, as those two have simply been too good for too long and have achieved an iconic status in the sport.' How about a Wimbledon victory, you had to wonder, wouldn't that have Murray sniffing that stratosphere?

In the end, Murray stuck with XIX, though in the spring of 2013 he disclosed he was taking on some outside advisers, one of whom was Mahesh Bhupathi, an Indian doubles player who was to retire at the end of the 2013 season, and who for years had had plenty of business interests, including representing other tennis players – a friend had described him as 'the Donald Trump of the locker room'. Bhupathi, a former doubles world number one, who had won the men's and mixed doubles titles at Wimbledon, had been hired to help bring in endorsements and other deals. Hence Bhupathi's Globosport and XIX had come together to create a new venture called XIX Globosport.

Bhupathi – who had been awarded the Padma Shri, which is the Indian equivalent of the British knighthood or the American Medal of Honor, and whose wife Lara Dutta was a Bollywood actress (and a former Miss Universe) – was hoping to sell Murray to Asia and the Middle East. 'India is a growing entertainment market. We have six hundred million of our population who are under the age of thirty. They want to be entertained and are willing to pay for good entertainment. The potential is vast,' Bhupathi, who described Murray as 'personable and shy', told the *Independent*. 'Tennis is a very big sport in India. Andy is big. But I'm working with Andy on a global basis now. It's not like I'm just focused on the Indian market.

There's money in Asia. There's money in the Far East. There's money in the Middle East. So wherever there is money we're going to try to see if there is a fit for Andy. Andy's got qualities that appeal to certain brands, for sure. He's one of the hardest-working guys out there. He's emotional – we saw that after the 2012 Wimbledon final. So we'll work on his attributes and positive qualities and try to find that connect with some brands.'

Even so, Murray – whose other new adviser was Ugo Colombini, an Italian who for years had worked closely with the Argentine player Juan Martin del Potro – didn't have any new sponsors to announce during the first half of 2013, and one of his sleeves would have been blank during the 2013 Wimbledon Championships if he hadn't offered to wear a patch for the Royal Marsden Cancer Charity. It wouldn't be the first time that Murray hadn't made full commercial use of his cotton billboard at a slam; he played one Australian Open with no patches while XIX renegotiated his contracts with his sponsors.

Still, it was not as if Murray's business team had dozed off, and just because Bhupathi was playing in the doubles tournament at Wimbledon – he and Austria's Julian Knowle reached the quarter-finals, losing to the eventual champions, American twins Bob and Mike Bryan – didn't mean that he had forgotten all about the Murray account. For many years, Bhupathi had found enough hours in the day for his racket and his Blackberry. Murray's team were receiving offers from companies keen to rent that space on his sleeve during the grass-court grand slam and beyond. But they felt that it would be a smarter strategy to wait to see how Wimbledon played out. Winning Wimbledon would give Murray much more power in the marketplace, putting him in an exceptionally strong position in any negotiations, either with new sponsors or with those looking to renew their association. It would also trigger any bonus clauses in his existing contracts. This was a gamble, of course – there was a risk that Murray wouldn't win the title, and that they had turned down money which they could have banked.

If Murray had been reluctant to sell off parts of himself to corporations, he had never had any great problem with accepting large appearance fees, as taking the money wasn't going to do his tennis any harm. The rules of tennis allowed these fees to be paid at all tournaments apart from the grand slams, the Olympics, the Masters-level events and the season-ending championships. Turning up at Queen's Club, for some grass-court matches before Wimbledon, earned him a six-figure sum before he even started to think about prize-money. Of course, it suited Murray just fine playing Queen's before Wimbledon – and it is unlikely that the British public would have been particularly sympathetic if he had disappeared to Germany to play a tournament the same week because of a guarantee – but the tournament director agreed to pay a substantial fee, even if it's not something that anyone really wants to talk about in public. Queen's with Murray is a totally different tournament from Queen's without Murray (when there would be lower domestic television ratings, less interest from the public and from sponsors and companies wanting corporate entertainment).

Murray's largest appearance fees are likely to have been paid by promoters in the Middle East, for his appearances at recognised tournaments in Dubai or Doha, or at the pre-season exhibition in Abu Dhabi. And when Murray has gone to the Far East, to tournaments such as the one in Tokyo, it has to be imagined that his guarantees have made the prize-money almost incidental to that week's financial rewards. Soon after Murray started working with Bhupathi, the Indian formally announced his plans for an International Premier Tennis League in cities across Asia and the Middle East, with the intention to create what has been described as the tennis version of cricket's Indian Premier League. Naturally, Bhupathi wanted Murray to be a part of it, and there was talk of the Scot and others being given an equity stake in the league (the aim was for the competition to be launched in 2014).

One concern for Murray was whether it could disrupt his pre-season plans – as at that time of the year he is usually in Miami – but he said that if he tried it, and it didn't feel right, he wouldn't do it again. Going into Wimbledon, Murray wasn't in the same appearance-money league as Federer and Nadal. Whenever Federer or Nadal competed in the Middle East, each player's guarantee reputedly ran to seven figures. In the spring of 2012, at New York's Madison Square Garden, Federer played an evening of exhibition tennis in exchange for a reported £700,000, and at the end of the year he played a six-match exhibition tour of South America that was said to have earned him more than £9 million. But winning Wimbledon could change that for Murray; promoters would pay big beans for Britain's first champion for 77 years.

In the beginning, money had mattered a great deal to Murray. As a teenager, Murray had always been uncomfortable asking his parents for money. 'Mum and Dad always said, "Make sure you have enough money with you, make sure you take enough money out," but Jamie and I never really did like taking money. Then once I started to make money, I started to appreciate it even more. When you spend your first pay cheque and start being able to pay for things yourself, it's a very nice feeling.' When Murray went to North America in the summer of 2005, one of the motivations for playing so many tournaments appeared to be financial gain, because he no longer wanted to be reliant on his parents. Murray's first pay cheque – which he received at one of those Futures tournaments on the lowest level of professional tennis – was around £100. No one needed to tell him that he was now playing, at the 2013 Wimbledon Championships, for 'ridiculous' amounts of money.

Andy Murray's red Ferrari didn't last long. He didn't sell the car because of the cost of insurance, though that was high, but because he felt like a complete prat in it; he could no longer stand the embarrassment of sitting in the Ferrari at a red light or when parking the vehicle. It was a poseur's car, and he wasn't a poseur. People kept honking him at the lights. 'I'm quite a conservative driver, but when I was driving that I'd get beeped just for getting out of the car.' So Murray bought a more under-stated, elegant car, a gun-metal Aston Martin, and in 2012 he would be seen driving a Jaguar convertible.

But Murray doesn't spend all his time in fast cars. During Wimbledon 2013, for instance, he could have been driven in each day in an official tournament car, with a chauffeur and darkened windows; instead he preferred to travel from his Surrey village to the All England Club in the passenger seat of his five-year-old Volkswagen Polo, with one of his friends at the wheel. 'I've kept the Polo, which is my first car, and which I had when I passed my test at twenty-one. It's a good car to have when you're picking people up from the airport or station, it's done about thirty thousand miles and nobody looks at it.' One spring at the French Open, he decided against taking a car on the way to a dinner in Paris, so he walked into the Metro and got lost beneath the city, and it sounded as though he almost enjoyed the experience.

A decent chunk of Murray's money has gone on properties. He knew he was fortunate when, at the age of 22, he was in a position to buy a house worth around £5 million. He has also bought a couple of apartments in Miami, and it has been said that they are big enough that when his whole entourage are in the city he can give them all a room each. Not long after the 2013 Australian Open, Murray announced that he had invested in a hotel near his home town of Dunblane, called Cromlix House, which was where his brother Jamie had had his wedding ceremony.

On top of an additional cost of around £2 million to

purchase the property, Murray was also spending considerable funds on renovating the place into five-star accommodation, with the hotel to have a restaurant managed by a Michelin-starred chef, Albert Roux, though it was said that the project had been complicated by the discovery of some protected bats in the building. In recent years, Murray had started to become more interested in what to do with his wealth, and every three months or so he meets with his investment adviser, Neil Grainger of Talent Financial. 'There are certain things I like to do and that I'm interested in. So I sit down with Neil three or four times a year,' Murray has said. 'He's been around tennis for a long time and he's helped me a lot.'

Beyond the interest in fast cars, Murray has never been particularly materialistic. When he set out on the tour, he didn't own much apart from his rackets, shoes, clothes, a bag and a PlayStation, and though he can now buy himself pretty much anything he desires, he doesn't feel the need to fill his house with shiny objects. 'I haven't spent shocking amounts on myself because I don't need anything,' said Murray, who has his own go-karting gear, including racing shoes and a helmet with 'The Stig' on the back. If Rado didn't sponsor Murray, you have to wonder whether he would ever wear a watch off court at tournaments. And while he had fun wearing a tuxedo for *Vogue*, clothes don't usually excite him. Spending money on others gives Murray more pleasure; though he once said that he would never buy underwear as a present.

Not all the money that Murray has earned should be seen as profit. Simon Fuller's XIX takes a percentage. And Murray must pay his staff; Ivan Lendl's contract would in all likelihood have entitled him to several hundred thousands pounds a year, plus bonuses. In addition, Murray has to pay for his entourage's travel expenses. But let's not forget that tennis players are extremely well treated at tournaments. When Murray played at the season-ending event in Shanghai in 2008, for instance, the hotel had produced personalised bed linen and robes for him, so he had his name on his pillow and on the back of his dressing-gown. But living on the road is not cheap. So while Murray has not always bought first-class plane and Eurostar tickets, he has been extremely irritated if people have ever invoked the stereotype of the mean Scot.

If Murray was that desperate to hoard his money, he would have joined all number of other tennis players by moving to Monaco (it has always seemed a little odd that Novak Djokovic, the great patriot who led Serbia to victory in the Davis Cup, avoids his country's taxes by retreating to a Monte Carlo apartment between tournaments). Murray doesn't see enough of his friends and family as it is. Moving to the Cote d'Azur, for more money and less time with those he cares about, is not something he has ever considered.

Who was happiest when Andy Murray broke early in the fourth set, the player himself or some of the tournament officials (not that they ever would have let on, not even with the smallest of fist-clenchers, or a little 'C'mon' into a walkie-talkie, for fear of being accused of bias towards the home player)? The tournament referee, Andrew Jarrett, will never make a bigger call than when he asked for the big red button in the sky – the one which closes the roof over Centre Court – to be pressed just after Murray had taken a two sets to one lead.

Murray was on a roll; from 1-4 down in the third set, he had won five consecutive games, and, to his mind, there was plenty of daylight left in which to play another set. After all, wasn't this supposed to be an outdoor tournament, with tennis to be played alfresco whenever possible? You could understand Murray's annoyance at around quarter to nine in the evening, especially as he thought the referee had been influenced by Jerzy Janowicz's persistent lobbying to the umpire to close the roof and put the lights on.

'You can't close it now, man. It's not even dark. I don't understand these rules. There are no rules. It's not fair,' Murray said, ahead of the half-hour delay between sets, as everyone waited for the roof to close, and then for the air-conditioning to kick in. Would closing the roof turn out to be the greatest momentum-killer in the history of the Wimbledon Championships? Had Jarrett just wrecked Murray's – and, by extension, Britain's – Wimbledon? The British tennis public aren't the types to rip up seats, or to fling cups of Pimm's on to the grass, showering the officials in chopped mint, pieces of fruit, and vitriol. But if Murray ended up losing this match, some in Centre Court, and plenty in the shires, were going to blame the All England Club.

While Janowicz was playing in his first grand slam semi-final, he certainly wasn't the sort of person to be intimidated by the situation. He didn't care that Murray was angry that he had been urging officialdom to close the roof. He didn't care when the Centre Court crowd booed him for firing a ball straight at Murray. He didn't care that wagging his finger after winning a big point wasn't to everyone's taste. He was in Murray's face, and he was in Britain's face, too. Janowicz hadn't stepped on court hoping to convince Britain that he was a smashing young fellow from Poland; he was there to win, and during those first three sets he had demonstrated he had some game.

No wonder there were some troubled faces around Centre Court. As Matthew Engel noted in the *Financial Times*, 'A week ago, no one outside Poland, barring tennis obsessives, would have been able to distinguish between Jerzy Janowicz and a Jersey cow. Well, we know now.' Janowicz was capable of serving at 140mph, and he didn't mess around with his forehand either, and the power in his game meant that his drop-shots were even more effective; if Murray was hanging back behind the baseline waiting for another atomic groundstroke to come whizzing through the air, he would have further to travel up to the net to reach a ball that had just been dinked over.

You could see why Janowicz wasn't the most popular man in tennis; it was also plain why John McEnroe regarded him as the 'real deal'. Murray had faced that serve once before, at an indoor tournament in Paris towards the end of the 2012 season, which was the week when Janowicz had announced his talent to the wider tennis world by coming through qualifying and reaching the final of the main draw. Murray had held, and failed to convert, a match point that day in France, so you could say he was partly responsible for creating the 'monster' standing between him and a place in the Wimbledon final. For some time, Murray had been widely regarded as the best returner of serve; this was an occasion to test that theory. And if Murray was to be successful, he had to do as Sir Alex Ferguson had instructed, and maintain his concentration.

For the second slam in succession, the home player in the last four had had to sit and watch in the locker-room for the second of the day's semi-finals, as the one which preceded his became an instant classic. No one likes to be upstaged at his own major, and at Roland Garros Jo-Wilfried Tsonga had had to wait for the conclusion of Rafa Nadal's victory over Novak Djokovic, and then when he eventually had his turn on court, he played a very flat match against David Ferrer. Here in London, Murray's semi-final followed the brutal, brilliant hitting of Djokovic's five-setter against Juan Martin del Potro, which had been the most entertaining match of the Championships as well as – with a running time of almost five hours – the longest ever semi-final at the tournament. The biggest difference between the two slams was how the crowd responded. Many of the Parisians with tickets to Court Philippe Chatrier had taken a break after that first semi-final, and so there were large areas of empty seats when Tsonga walked out for what he had imagined was the biggest event of the day. At Wimbledon, Murray emerged on to an almost-full Centre Court; the crowd were going to be there with him as he attempted to make the final.

Later, as Centre Court waited for the resumption of the match, and the start of the fourth set, there was some uncertainty about whether the new conditions – everything tends to feel a little slower under the roof – would favour the Briton or the Pole. And what would happen to Murray's momentum? Murray used the break to take a shower, to speak with his team, and to let the anger fade. By the time he returned to the court, he was no longer upset about the roof; he just wanted to focus on what he had to do: 'I went back to work.' He broke in the fourth set, and then closed it out, so ensuring that this match didn't go to a decider.

So, after almost a fortnight of chaos on the grass, Murray won 6-7, 6-4, 6-4, 6-3, and we had ended up with what the seedings and the draw-sheet had predicted all along: top seed against second seed, Djokovic versus Murray. For the fourth time in Lendl's career, he would be involved in a Wimbledon final, having twice as a player finished as the runner-up – losing to Boris Becker in the 1986 final and to Pat Cash in the 1987 final – and then coaching Murray in the summer of 2012. Some critics had been spectacularly harsh about Lendl the player at Wimbledon, with one commentator saying that he had about as much chance on grass as a toothless goat, but there certainly wasn't the same despondency or negativity about Murray before he played for the Wimbledon title for a second time (he had reached the final of the last four grand slams he had played in). Almost everyone who passed a microphone or a voice-recorder – from McEnroe to Boris Becker – thought that this would be Murray's year. Was this emotion taking over? Had people not given enough consideration to the fact that Djokovic was the world number one, that he was a former champion, and that he was playing better tennis than when he had won the title in 2011?

That would be something for the Royal Box to consider on the second Sunday of these Championships, as they awaited the arrival of the players on court. Prime Minister David Cameron would be among the guests, as would Ed Miliband, the leader of the opposition, Scotland's First Minister Alex Salmond and Serbian President Tomislav Nikolic, as well as Hollywood's Bradley Cooper and Gerald Butler, the former tennis players Roy Emerson, Rod Laver (still regarded by some as the greatest), Tracy Austin, Manuel Santana, Stan Smith, Jan Kodes, Peter Fleming and Greg Rusedski, plus the golfer Justin Rose, the footballer Wayne Rooney, and the fashion designer Victoria Beckham. The last of those, incidentally, would dress Murray's girlfriend for the final, Kim Sears wearing a mint-green creation designed by David Beckham's wife. What of Murray's two celebrity cheerleaders-in-chief, Ferguson and Corden? Ferguson couldn't make the final as he was booked to go on a cruise up the Scottish coast, and Corden wasn't in the Royal Box for the final, and he also wasn't in Murray's guest-box. But he was convinced that his friend was going to win Wimbledon, 'and all those people who used to say he was grumpy, and Scottish not British, they will all be lining the streets to cheer him'.

7

The First Since Fred

The weirdest of ideas can pop into your head when you're just hours away from playing for the Wimbledon title, and there was some confusion in Andy Murray's mind about who his opponent would be in the final of the 2013 Championships. The night before, Murray's subconscious had been fooling around, with the Scot dreaming that he was to play either Radek Stepanek of the Czech Republic or Denis Kudla of the United States – facing either of those two wouldn't have been far off receiving a bye – and it was only on waking on this Sunday morning that it came back to him: the man standing in his way of a first Wimbledon title would be the world number one, Novak Djokovic. It made you wonder; were millions of Britons even the slightest bit fussed who Murray played? You suspect that a large number of the BBC audience of 17.3 million, who had ignored the call of the beach and the barbecue on what was the hottest day of the year so far, would have been watching even if Murray had been facing someone of Stepanek or Kudla's standing.

For many of those at home in front of their televisions, or those who had paid up to £80,000 for a pair of Centre Court tickets, or who had slept rough for two nights to be on Henman Hill, this was all about seeing whether Murray had it in him to win that prize; they could haven't cared less if the guy on the other side of the net didn't have much of a backhand or a backstory.

But what if all those sofa-bound millions, and those hedge-fund managers and happy campers, had got this wrong? Surely the identity of Murray's opponent mattered, and it mattered a great deal, with the Scot much better served by taking on one of the sport's Hollywood names. Let's not forget that Murray's career had always been about the struggle and the doubt, about the constant quest for self-improvement and finding a way to live with, and then beat, these legends of the game; it was a narrative we were used to. If Murray had had it easy, would we have even known what to think about that? If Murray had beaten some second-rater in the Wimbledon final, Britain would rightly still have put the bunting out. But if we – and Murray – were going to take maximum satisfaction from the day, he would have to walk out on to Centre Court to once again be confronted with the reality that he had been born into the 'Golden Age of Men's Tennis'.

In addition to being the world number one, Djokovic was the top seed and a former champion, and those who had watched his semi-final against Juan Martin del Potro couldn't remember an occasion on the lawns when someone had defended like that over five sets. Rubber-legged Djokovic was capable of ludicrous movement, ludicrous defence, ludicrous attack, and ludicrous mental fortitude. Murray's fanbase should have been thrilled. If Murray was going to win Wimbledon, he would do so by beating the best. Djokovic, remember, was someone the BBC had trailed as 'part man, part supreme being'.

Once again – this had happened in his previous six slam finals, including when he had played for the Wimbledon title the summer before – Murray would play someone who, when his career was over, was destined for a place in the Hall of Fame (how seriously you take that depends on whether you're American or not). Murray just kept running into these players – on the draw-sheets, in the largest tennis stadiums in the world, and in all likelihood in his head, too.

Few would dispute that this was the hardest ever era in which to win grand slam titles. Or that this quartet of Europeans – Roger Federer, Rafa Nadal, Djokovic and Murray – was the most talented generation in the sport's history. In many people's eyes, Federer is the GOAT; to the uninitiated, that sounds like an insult, but is in fact the biggest compliment he can have about his tennis – that he's the Greatest Of All Time. By beating Murray at the 2012 Wimbledon Championships, Federer had extended his collection of titles to a record 17, and he had returned to the top of the rankings to move past Pete Sampras's record of 286 weeks as the world number one.

Of course, by the summer of 2013, Federer was no longer the world number one, and he appeared some way past his prime – his second-round defeat by Ukraine's Sergiy Stakhovsky had confirmed that – but that was no reason to start reassessing his body of work. Meanwhile, the Rafaholics of this tennis world wondered whether, given time and a good run with pain-free knees, Nadal would go on to win more slams than Federer. Indeed, he had added to his total just days before arriving in London with his victory at Roland Garros, where he had become the first man to win the major eight times, taking his overall tally to 12. As with Federer, Nadal's early departure from these Championships – in the Majorcan's case, a first-round defeat to Belgium's Steve Darcis – was not a reason to reconsider everything he had achieved over the years. In fact, their early defeats should have made tennis fans have a renewed respect for those years when tennis had simply been the 'Roger and Rafa Show'.

Some wondered whether the results at Wimbledon were an indication that the cartel – meaning the Big Four – had been busted, but wasn't it a little premature to be talking like that? And though Federer and Nadal had not reached the business-end of these Championships, it was not as if Murray had been left to play a lightweight in the Wimbledon final. At the coin-toss, Djokovic already had six grand slams, three of which had come in 2011 when his dominance of the game had been just a few sets from absolute. And while the Serbian was undoubtedly more of a threat on cement than he was on an English lawn, he had past experience of winning Wimbledon – he had gone to the Champions' Dinner in 2011 – and those who had watched him throughout this tournament thought he was playing the grass-court tennis of his life.

Murray was sharing an era with players who had achieved, or had come extremely close to achieving, near-mythical feats. Only seven men in the sport's history had won all four majors at least once, and two of those were Murray's contemporaries – Federer and Nadal. And, at the 2012 French Open, Djokovic had been within a match of becoming the third man of this generation to complete the career grand slam. Had he beaten Nadal in that Paris final, he also would have become the first man since Rod Laver in 1969 to have held all four slams simultaneously. In 2013, Djokovic had come to Wimbledon after the disappointment of a defeat to Nadal in Paris – this time, they had met a round earlier, in the semi-finals – but the thinking was that he would not be as deflated as he had been in 2012. In fact, he looked as though his defeat in Paris had galvanised him ahead of Wimbledon, that he was determined to come away from the two European slams with a title.

Tennis had never seen anything like this before: Federer, Nadal and Djokovic's domination of tennis was such that from the 2005 French Open until Wimbledon 2013, the trio had won every major apart from two – the 2009 US Open, when Del Potro had finished as the champion, and the 2012 US Open, when Murray made his breakthrough. When these grass-court championships began, Federer, Nadal and Djokovic had some 35 slams between them.

Murray couldn't avoid these people. Whenever he reached a slam final, he looked over the net at a modern great. Three of Murray's first six slam finals had been against Federer – he lost to the Swiss at the 2008 US Open, the 2010 Australian Open and the 2012 Wimbledon Championships – and the other half had been against Djokovic, with the Scot finishing as the runner-up to the Serbian at the 2011 Australian Open, beating him at the 2012 US Open, and coming second at the 2013 Australian Open. There had been some thin, less-than-golden periods in men's tennis, such as when Sampras was winding down and before the full flowering of Federer's talent, and had Murray been around then you can be sure that he wouldn't have had to wait so long to win a slam.

But there wasn't much point in Murray thinking about how life would have been easier at any other time in tennis history, and he certainly never asked for anyone's pity. 'I'm very happy to have been part of this era. Playing against them has made me improve so much. I always said that if I had played in another era, maybe I would have won more, but I wouldn't have been as good a tennis player,' Murray has said. He was where he was, which was sitting in the locker-room at the All England Club, just three sets away from becoming the first British man for 77 years – this was the search for the Holy Grail, just with rackets – to hold the singles trophy on Centre Court. 'I think at the end of your career you should be judged, not just on how much you won, but on the people you were competing against and how good a player you actually were. The guys I've been playing against are some of the best of all time.'

The conclusion of this men's tournament could have been the first all-British final since 1909. Strange to think now, as Novak Djokovic travels the world on a Serbian diplomatic passport, draws tens of thousands of supporters to rallies in Belgrade's Parliament Square, or shaves his head to celebrate his country's Davis Cup victory, that he once had discussions with Britain's Lawn Tennis Association about the possibility of becoming a British citizen. Had he done so, he would have been playing for Great Britain's Davis Cup team instead, and he would have had GBR next to his name on Wimbledon draw-sheets.

Those conversations began around the time that Britain played Serbia in a Davis Cup tie in Glasgow in 2006; this was before Djokovic had become rich from the sport, so it was understandable that he and his family, who had made so many financial sacrifices to get him that far, considered taking some of the LTA's money for what would have been a more comfortable existence. Though the Djokovic family did not have any British ancestry, he could have qualified under the residency rules. The LTA's funding wasn't the only temptation: Djokovic also thought that the sponsorship opportunities would be better as a Briton than as a Serbian. It was a stressful, uncertain time for Djokovic, who was still a teenager and making his way in the sport, and he mulled over what to do.

But then he had a moment of clarity, saying to himself: 'What the heck? I am Serbian, I am proud of being Serbian. If I play for Great Britain, deep inside, I'm never going to feel like I belong.'

If Djokovic had said yes to the switch, that would have had a huge impact on the course of Murray's tennis life. It is highly questionable whether the British public would have ever truly accepted Djokovic as a British tennis player. Greg Rusedski had qualified through his mother, who was born in Yorkshire, and there had been still those who had questioned what he was doing in a Union flag bandanna, and in a Davis Cup team with Tim Henman. The term of abuse for Djokovic would have been 'plastic Brit'; some would doubtless have still called him that after his 2008 Australian Open triumph which, had he defected, would have been Britain's first slam in men's tennis for 72 years. In that parallel universe, Djokovic's victory at Wimbledon in 2011 would have given Britain a first men's singles champion for 75 years; the meter would never have reached 77.

Perhaps, in some ways, having Djokovic as a British tennis player, plastic or otherwise, would have helped Murray as there wouldn't then have been such scrutiny of his efforts to win his first major. But it also would have taken away much of the significance of any slam that Murray won; if it hadn't been so long since a British man last won a slam, there would not have been the same interest and emotional investment in the career of the player from Stirlingshire. In this counter-factual account of modern tennis history, it's also worth thinking whether

Djokovic would have had the season he did in 2011 – winning three grand slams – if he had been British rather than Serbian. One of the factors that propelled Djokovic to such heights had been the pride and confidence he had taken from Serbia winning the Davis Cup for the first time at the end of 2010. Even if Djokovic and Murray had won the competition for Britain, would it have felt so special for someone who had learnt to play the sport halfway up a Serbian mountain?

Even without being international teammates, there was plenty to link Murray and Djokovic. Both were born in May 1987, separated by just a week, with Murray the older. Pretty much ever since they had played as 11-year-olds in a junior tournament in the French town of Tarbes, near the Pyrenees, Murray had been compared and contrasted with Djokovic. While Roger Federer and Rafa Nadal have been the iconic players of this generation, Djokovic has arguably been a more central figure in Murray's competitive life. Nadal is just a year older than Murray and Djokovic, and Nadal had also been a rival in junior tennis, but, on the main tour, the Majorcan had always been ahead of the game, winning his first slam just after turning 19.

Murray won easily that day in Tarbes, at an event known as Les Petits As, beating Djokovic for the loss of just one game (as Djokovic recalled, Murray 'crushed' him). But Murray would never again have such a lop-sided victory against Djokovic, and for long periods since those early days it has seemed as though he has been trying to catch up with the Eastern European. Djokovic was the first to make the top 100, and then he was the first to break into the top 10, and then he had been the first to win a grand slam.

But for three years after that first slam, he could not win another, and he went back to being the third man of tennis, behind Federer and Nadal, with Murray following on as the world number four. During that time, there wasn't much between Djokovic and Murray, since the Scot was making grand slam finals. But then, in 2011, Djokovic did so much more than win another slam; he won three, he dominated, and he ended the Roger-and-Rafa duopoly. Djokovic now had a stronger mind, a stronger body and a stronger game. The quality of Federer and Nadal's tennis had forced Djokovic to become a better tennis player. In 2012, he had won a fifth slam, the Australian Open, and then at the 2013 Australian Open he had added a sixth.

There was also no doubt that Murray had become a better tennis player because of the era he was playing in. Like Djokovic, Murray had had to push himself even harder if he was going to be successful at the slams; indeed, when he finally had that breakthrough at Flushing Meadows, it was difficult to think of anyone who had ever put more into winning a first major. In another age, Murray could have been a worse tennis player and a multiple grand slam champion.

Murray and Djokovic knew all about each other's games. They had been playing against each other since the juniors – though there had been a two-year break during their senior careers when they had not played each other at all because, as third and fourth in the world, they were always on other sides of the draw, and so, with Federer and Nadal around, the chances of them playing a final together were always slim.

The pair had also practised together on a regular basis, as well as occasionally playing doubles. And while they were not as close as they had been as teenagers – as Djokovic said, 'common sense tells you we couldn't hang out' – they still sometimes sent each other text messages when their rival had won a tournament. Or, in Djokovic's case, when he had been on a long weekend in Scotland, he sent a photograph to Murray to prove he hadn't been far from Dunblane. To while away some time at the 2012 US Open, as they waited to play their respective semi-finals, they had sat down together in front of a computer to watch Scotland and Serbia play a score-less draw in a World Cup qualifying match. They sat there in near silence. Before this Wimbledon final, Murray said his relationship with Djokovic, once so pally, had morphed into 'a professional friendship'; this match shouldn't have been sold as two buddies playing for the biggest prize in tennis.

To fully understand what was happening in the heat of Centre Court – the referee's office declared it was touching 50 degrees Celsius in the sun – you had to spool all the way back to that occasion at the 2012 US Open when Andy Murray's career and life had been transformed by going for a pee-stop in the loo below the Arthur Ashe Stadium. The Wimbledon final would be Murray and Novak Djokovic's 19th match as adults; Djokovic had won 11 of their first 18 meetings, including three of their four previous encounters at the slams.

But Murray would have been encouraged and emboldened by a couple of their past meetings. One of those was the semi-final against Djokovic in the 2012 London Olympics; the Briton had turned in one of the finest performances of his career to beat the Eastern European in straight sets (they were playing the shortened, best-of-three, version of the game). That was the only occasion, prior to this final, that Murray and Djokovic had met on grass, and it's a match that is remembered for Murray's aggression. The other meeting, of course, was Murray's five-set victory over Djokovic in New York City.

Had Murray lost that match in America, he would have been facing a much greater challenge here in London – that's the thing with tennis, you can travel all the over the world, continent-hopping from one tournament to another, going from first-class cabin to seven-star hotel to practice court to match court, and then doing it all again the following week, but there are certain matches and memories which follow you wherever you go.

If Murray had lost in the US Open final, after leading by two sets to love, it would have taken some recovering from, as it would have come so soon after that disappointment against Roger Federer at Wimbledon. As it was, Murray had had a peaceful evening at home the night before this Wimbledon final, his mother reporting that they ate 'a quiet and normal dinner of roast chicken, potatoes and vegetables' and that he had been 'as calm as he could have been' as they sat outside having breakfast on the morning of the match. Would Murray have been in that calm state of mind if he had fallen short at Flushing Meadows? You have to wonder.

Murray had never questioned himself as much before a big occasion as he had done before playing Djokovic for the US Open title. For all the confidence he had gained from winning the Olympics earlier that summer, he had never had butterflies like this before any match. Sitting in the locker-room before a ball was struck – in a locker-room that was far too quiet for his liking – he hadn't been able to stop himself from thinking back to his past failures. Murray's disappointments during the 2012 grand slam year – coming so close against Djokovic in their Australian Open semi-final and against Federer in the Wimbledon final – had led him to doubt whether he ever would win a major.

'In some ways, I had been preparing myself mentally for it never to happen, to never win a slam,' Murray has disclosed. 'I would say I could live with it if I didn't, but in some ways that was me preparing for the worst.'

Murray's coach Ivan Lendl had made a runner-up's speech after his first four slam finals, and then turned his career around in his fifth. More than anything, Murray didn't want to become the first man in tennis's professional era to lose his first five slam finals. Had Boris Becker been right when he had suggested that the expectation had started to 'eat into' Murray, with the German saying: 'You get to the point where, instead of enjoying reaching a major final, you become weighed down by nerves and expectations'? Lendl had instructed Murray to enjoy the match, telling him he had worked his entire life to give himself this opportunity. That was part of the problem, Murray countered; how could he have fun out there when he had put so much into this?

And fun wasn't having Djokovic, who had seemed out of the final, come from two sets down to take the match into a decider. There are few better analysts of the game than Mats Wilander, a former world number one who won seven grand slam titles, and as he watched Murray during the third and fourth sets, he was more than a little concerned. Wilander thought Murray was looking as though he wanted to leave the Arthur Ashe Stadium, as if he wanted the experience to be over with. And if Murray went on to lose, Wilander predicted that the Scot would have 'a window of maybe another year of pleasure' and then would start to hate tennis. Just as Murray's idol, Andre Agassi, had come to hate the sport.

Agassi had hated the sport because his father forced it on him; would Murray come to loathe it too, because of the agonies and disappointments it kept inflicting on him? If Wilander was right, Murray wasn't just playing to win a first grand slam championship, and to become Britain's first male champion at the majors since Fred Perry was victorious at the 1936 US Open – he was also playing to stay in love with the sport he had dedicated his life to.

Wilander wasn't the only one who believed that the night would forever define Murray's career. Even before anyone had opened a can of tennis balls, John McEnroe had been suggesting on American television that the final would be 'a crucial moment' in Murray's career. 'Either he turns the corner or it will be a really, really tough one to swallow. And if he wins he will become a whole new player, and he will feel different.'

When Djokovic had forced a fifth set, McEnroe would have been absolutely convinced that Murray's career was going to go one way or the other; there was now the very real possibility that the Scot could lose a grand slam final from two sets to love up. As the *New Yorker* magazine had noted earlier in the season, 'Tennis, more than most, is a sport dominated by psychological battles – or, at least, it is a sport whose observers fancy themselves experts in psychoanalysis.' That was never more true than when this match went to a fifth set. Among the armchair and studio psychologists the consensus seemed to be this: Murray was just a set away from possibly earning close to a million dollars – the runner-up would receive $950,000 – and having his world ripped apart.

It was common knowledge in tennis how Murray had reacted badly to past defeats in slam finals, feeling as though he had not only let himself down, but those around him, too. After losing an Australian Open final, he had said to his mother backstage, 'I'm so sorry, Mum.' (Shocked, she responded by telling him that he had absolutely nothing to apologise for and that she had been proud of his efforts.) And, after defeats in his first two Melbourne finals, to Federer in 2010 and to Djokovic in 2011, he had been so badly affected that for months afterwards he had struggled for motivation. After these matches, Murray has sometimes found himself in a 'why bother?' frame of mind, questioning whether all the effort – and all that time on the practice court, the gym and the track – was really worth it. It's a fallacy that defeat immediately inspires you to work hard; sometimes you find yourself examining whether you had become delusional about your chances.

The Olympics had saved him, after the weepy end to the 2012 Wimbledon Championships; without the Games, Murray could have found himself hosting what Maria Sharapova likes to call 'a pity party'. Having to prepare for another tournament at the All England Club meant that he didn't have the time to sit around festering in his own disappointment. No doubt the public's reaction to the tears, and what Murray called 'reconnecting', also helped. Back in the Arthur Ashe Stadium, this was the first time he had won two sets in a grand slam final. To falter from here would keep the stereotype of the British 'loser' going; of the Brit either not talented enough, or too inclined to choke. And while Fred Stolle, an Australian, had lost his first five slam finals, that had been back when tennis was an amateur and more gentle pursuit.

Murray was a set away from the greatest moment of his life; he was also a set away from the greatest disappointment any modern tennis player had ever had. Lendl could speak from experience about how to come back from losing your first four slam finals. Five? Murray would be on his own. Murray was in danger of breaking new ground. Whatever happened, Murray was going to make history: if the night turned against him, he was going to be confirmed as the unluckiest man in tennis.

Many of Murray's fans in the stadium and across the world, while still hoping and keeping everything crossed, were also preparing themselves for his possible defeat. 'Expect the worst, prepare for the worst, witness the worst – this has been the British way in tennis for years,' noted the *Wall Street Journal*.

If there isn't already a plaque outside the 'bathroom' that Murray used between the fourth and fifth sets, there certainly should be. Murray went into that bathroom and stared at the mirror. He has never been a vain man, and at almost any other moment in his life, he would have laughed at what was, even by his standards, a spectacularly bad hair day (it was a windy night, and a writer for *Sports Illustrated* thought that Murray had been transformed, gust by gust, and tuft by tuft, into a 'tennis pro as drawn by Dr Seuss'). But checking his reflection, or emptying his bladder, wasn't the primary purpose of locking himself in that room; the purpose of the visit was to fill up his head with positive thoughts. To beat Djokovic, Murray had to give everything physically – for the first time during the tournament, he had taken painkillers before a match, which was perhaps why he didn't notice that two toenails turned black and dropped off. He would also have to give everything mentally and emotionally. So he stood there in front of the mirror, his hair on end, and said to himself: 'For one set, just give it everything you've got. You don't want to come off this court with any regrets. Don't get down on yourself. Fight.'

Lendl had personal experience of the physical agonies of trying to win a first grand slam. Lendl put so much into beating John McEnroe in the 1984 French Open final – he came from two sets down to do it – that he was mentally and physically exhausted at the end. So much so that he later couldn't even recall talking to a friend in the locker-room. That match also gave Lendl an insight into how one match, or one set, can change a player's reputation. 'When I won my first grand slam, I went from being the guy who could never come back to being the guy who never gives up, but I knew I didn't deserve either of those descriptions.' Here was Murray's opportunity to transform people's perception of him.

So Murray went to the loo, and came back and won the US Open. If Murray hadn't take that loo break, and he had lost that New York final, how would he have been placed – psychologically – ahead of playing the same opponent on Wimbledon's Centre Court? Going to the bathroom in America would help Murray all over the world.

For Murray, who took that final set of the US Open for the loss of just two games, it had been as much about relief as it was about joy. Winning a first slam also allowed Murray to be more at ease with himself on and off the court – it was unrealistic to think that he would have complete inner peace when he was still competing – and also to feel more comfortable in his dealings with the British tennis public. Tennis's Big Four was just that, not a Big Three and a Half. Suddenly, Murray didn't mind people looking at him, or wanting to talk and engage. Before, he had had his head pushed down into his shoulders, hoping that none of those people looking at him were going to spark up a conversation. The best that could happen was silence. Now he held his head up high, happy to be seen and spoken to. For the first time, he finally seemed okay with this crazy idea that he was a public figure. Murray felt 'a bit more accepted'.

And never again would he be asked 'that stupid question' about whether he could emulate Fred Perry by winning a slam. It was 'a stupid question' that Murray had been asking himself just hours before as he sat in the locker-room waiting for the final to begin. 'It's something I had been asked most weeks of my life since I was twenty-one. It had really started to get to me earlier in the year. It wasn't just the media. It was everyone. A lot of people had been coming up to me saying, "Don't worry, you'll win the next one." That had almost made it worse. I'm just glad I can move on.'

Only up to a point. The British tennis public had seen how Murray had won in New York (well, in truth, most of them had slept through it, since the final hadn't finished until 2am Dunblane time, with a fair few going to bed after the fourth set thinking they would be waking to news of a Djokovic victory). And if he could emulate Perry at the US Open, the public were thinking, was there any reason why he couldn't emulate Perry with victory at the All England Club? Any reason at all?

At the 2013 Australian Open, Murray had come close to being the only first-time grand slam winner of the modern era to follow up that breakthrough victory by immediately winning a second major at the next slam – but he lost the final to Djokovic in four sets, with some wondering whether he had been thrown for a while by the intervention of a seagull's feather which had floated into the Rod Laver Arena.

Had Murray won in Melbourne, it would hardly have changed how the public thought about him. True, he would have demonstrated that he wasn't a one-slam wonder – not that such a dismissive term should ever be used in this era – but many Britons would have thought: 'Yes, yes, but we already knew that you can win a slam outside Wimbledon – now how about winning something on Centre Court?' The four slams are supposedly equal, but most people are agreed that one is more equal than the others. The players think so – most, given a choice, would rather win Wimbledon than one of the other three – while most of the British public still watch tennis through purple-and-green-tinted glasses.

To them, Wimbledon is tennis. 'When Murray won the US Open in New York to become the first British man to win a grand slam title for 76 years, it registered as a momentous triumph to those closely involved with tennis or fanatical about the game,' John Lloyd wrote in his *Mail on Sunday* column on the morning of Murray's Wimbledon final against Djokovic. 'But, let's be honest, there are millions within Britain who only take an interest in the game during Wimbledon. So, if Murray became champion on Centre Court, his accomplishment would dwarf what he achieved in New York.' Britain was never going to be satisfied with Murray being a grand slam champion away from Wimbledon's grass courts.

Shortly after Murray was presented with the US Open trophy, Reuters news agency had declared: 'The nation that invented modern tennis finally has a champion for the new age. The jokes about wooden rackets and men playing tennis in long, white trousers have lost their punchline and Perry can now rest in peace.' On this July afternoon in south-west

London, how premature those two sentences, typed the previous September, now seemed.

The more you thought about it during the changeovers, the more you realised just how important Murray's victory in America had been for his chances of leaving these grass-court championships with a smile on his face. Consider this – if Murray had lost the 2012 US Open, he would now have been facing the possibility of experiencing his seventh defeat from his seven grand slam finals. Just imagine trying not to think about such a statistic as you toss up the ball to serve.

There was a more encouraging number for Murray and his team to consider which was that, after his victories at the Olympics and Queen's, and the six rounds he had played to reach this Wimbledon final, he was on a 17-match winning streak on English lawns, the sport's original surface. Murray had been nothing but dogged and persistent in his pursuit of success at Wimbledon, a tournament he was playing for the eighth time – only one player had needed more attempts to win his first title at the All England Club, and that was Goran Ivanisevic, who had been champion on his 14th visit. As a debutant in 2005, Murray had made the third round; the next summer he advanced into the fourth round; and in 2007 he didn't play because of injury. Murray went out in the quarter-finals in 2008, and then, for three successive years between 2009 and 2011, he was a beaten semi-finalist, before in 2012 he was the runner-up. Each summer, Murray had matched or improved upon the previous year's showing.

*

'If you're going to lose,' Ivan Lendl had once implored Andy Murray, 'go down swinging, don't go with your ass against the back fence.' Certainly, the 26-year-old had no intention of spending the afternoon with his ass against the dark green wall behind the Centre Court baseline – at one end, such a position would have been put him just beneath the Prime Minister's seat in the front row of the Royal Box. One of Lendl's greatest contributions – perhaps even his greatest – had been to stop Murray being so standoffish and passive on the big occasion. Of course, there were times when Murray just couldn't help himself, such as in the early stages of his quarter-final with Fernando Verdasco, but Murray knew that he couldn't hold off against Novak Djokovic if he was going to have any chance of smooching the trophy. Murray couldn't allow Djokovic to dictate the rallies, because if he did he would find himself playing fetch.

In any weather conditions, it is important not to find your-self doing considerably more running than your opponent – during the 2012 US Open final, a tired Murray had called out, 'My legs feel like jelly right now,' a line which sounded as though it had been taken straight out of a children's story-book, and which led to 'jelly' trending on Twitter. But it was even more important not to do too much running when you were competing in the Wimbledon heat (that's not a misprint). A Wimbledon final to be played on a hot day? Whatever next at this tournament of surprises? A Briton holding the trophy?

There are times at the Australian Open when the

The First Since Fred

Melbourne sun is in a sadistic mood, and so they close the roof over the Rod Laver Arena for the players' safety, and a day like this in London was probably about the closest you will ever get to hearing someone seriously suggesting that Wimbledon should introduce a heat rule. Indeed, it was so toasty that Tim Henman, usually seen wearing a suit jacket during the Championships, was in shirtsleeves, and many of those inside the stadium, or out on Henman Hill, would have felt that they were starting to melt. For the first time in living memory, a Wimbledon final was causing Britain to have cold sweats (because of the anxiety) and hot sweats (because of the sunshine). During changeovers, the ball-kids would shelter the players under umbrellas and offer to wrap ice-towels around their necks.

When Murray had previously spoken of the need to train in the heat of Miami, he had said it was because he required his body to experience those temperatures before he headed off to Australia for the opening slam of the year, but from now on he can also say that his time in Florida has helped him to deal with the English summer sun. Murray, despite having grown up in the Stirlingshire drizzle, was more accomplished than most in the heat, a quality he had demonstrated a few months before Wimbledon by winning a Miami final against Spain's David Ferrer.

Here on Wimbledon's Centre Court, it wasn't dissimilar to being in a Bikram yoga studio, and Murray had plenty of experience of being in one of those, as something of a veteran of extreme yoga. It soon became apparent that the sunshine would favour the Celt; while Djokovic has long since passed the stage when he used to look extremely uncomfortable playing tennis on a warm day – he no longer has such problems with his breathing – the weather wasn't exactly helping him after his exertions against Juan Martin del Potro a couple of days earlier.

People are forever saying that Murray and Djokovic have very similar games, and that is largely true, and why the pair often ended up producing such epic rallies, as they are both so consistent off the ground, and so excellent at retrieving balls that others wouldn't even get close to. But, on this occasion, Djokovic was using substantially different tactics from Murray. Doubtless that would have had something to do with the weather.

Djokovic was serve-and-volleying much more than he had done in the first six matches of the tournament. And, as the final went on, he appeared to have developed a drop-shot addiction – he just couldn't stop playing them. Coming into the net after your serve, and dropping the ball short, were both ways of trying to shorten points. They could be smart tactics, with Murray noting that some of Djokovic's drop-shots were of exceptional quality. The difficulty for Djokovic, though, was that Murray was so quick across the grass that he was reaching most of the drop-shots.

Though this match contained some of the long, spectacular rallies we had seen in their past encounters – there was one of those on the first point, and there were other times during the match when you had to remind yourself that you weren't watching a tennis video game – it was clear that Djokovic wasn't as enthusiastic as Murray was about duelling from the baseline. Djokovic, a man who had built a career and a life from retrieving and swinging from the back of the court, was in effect conceding that he couldn't beat Murray with his usual game. So even when Djokovic won a point by serve-and-volleying, or by hitting a drop-shot, Murray should have been encouraged by the Serbian's reluctance to keep on engaging in the usual manner. 'It's interesting to see Djokovic moving forward like this,' Tim Henman said of the world number one's net-rushing tactic, 'but is it for tactical purposes or for physical preservation?' On 52 occasions, Djokovic was at the net, and he won just over half of those points, coming off best 30 times. By way of comparison, Murray was at the net 37 times, and also won just over half.

There were moments when Djokovic didn't feel as though he 'had the gas' and so went for a winner earlier in a rally than he would otherwise have done; it was a risky strategy, and he would hit some 40 unforced errors (and the unforced error count, which is subjective, can be on the low side at the All England Club, with some preventable mistakes put down as forced). Djokovic's number was almost double Murray's.

So Djokovic wasn't at the height of his powers. This was the second time, one might suggest, that Del Potro had 'softened up' Murray's opponent ahead of a final at the All England Club, as at the London Games the previous summer he had taken Roger Federer to the limit a round earlier. Federer, who eventually won the final set 19-17 for a best-of-three-set victory that had taken the best part of four and a half hours, looked tired in the gold-medal match, and Murray walloped him. Once again, Murray should have been thankful for the power of Del Potro's forehand. Djokovic would experience physical and mental pain against Murray on Centre Court. And how much did Murray benefit from his decision to skip the French Open? How much fresher were his legs because he hadn't been in Paris?

Still, even when Djokovic's game is slightly off, as it was here, he is nothing less than a formidable opponent. Andy Roddick, a former finalist, was concerned as he watched the final: 'These guys are killing each other. They won't be able to stand if they play five sets.'

It wasn't as if Murray didn't feel the heat, especially as it was the first time he had played in these conditions all tournament. Plus, Murray wasn't entirely happy with his footwear, and so after a few games his friend Rob Stewart drove back to Murray's house in Surrey to pick up some insoles, and then had them delivered on to court. 'I probably did the journey in record time, but I absolutely swear I wasn't speeding,' Stewart would later say of a sub-plot that sounded as though it belonged in a movie – though in the film version, he would have been stopped by police, and would have had to persuade the officer that Murray's chances simply depended on having those insoles (as it was, by the time Stewart made it back, Murray no longer felt there was such a problem with the shoes, and so the insoles weren't even needed).

*

People are forever bringing decibel-counters to Wimbledon to get a reading of Maria Sharapova's screeching, but never to do anything useful, like measuring how loud it was when Andy Murray had made his entrance. So all we can say with any great certainty is this: it was extremely loud. Murray's near-universal support from the Centre Court crowd was mostly thanks to his surging popularity. But it was also, in part, because he was playing Novak Djokovic.

Had Murray been facing either Roger Federer or Rafa Nadal, a significant part of the crowd would have been cheering for the Swiss or the Spaniard; that's one of the perks of having megastar status in tennis, being able to override some of the crowd's allegiance to the home player. Murray's former coach, Brad Gilbert, considered that more than half of the crowd at the 2012 Wimbledon final – he put the figure at 55 per cent – had favoured Federer over Murray. That may have been overstating it, but if Murray had faced Federer in another Wimbledon final, there would have been a few cries of 'Roger, I love you' mixed in with the chants of 'Andy, Andy'.

Djokovic, for all his accomplishments and his sparky personality, has never been loved as Federer and Nadal have, so, apart from the President of Serbia, and a few Eastern Europeans dotted around the stadium, it was a struggle to find anyone who didn't want to see Murray win. And the crowd had it in them to hurt Djokovic. Watching from the side of the court during Djokovic's semi-final, there had been signs that he really didn't like it when the crowd had warmed to Juan Martin del Potro over the course of the match; once again

Djokovic would have to deal with the noise all around him. With every game that passed, it seemed as though the crowd became more involved, more engaged. Virginia Wade didn't remember the crowd being so lively when she won the women's title in 1977, while playing in front of the Queen. Back then, if you wanted noise, you pierced yourself with a safety-pin and sought out the Sex Pistols; in 2013, you could walk away from a Wimbledon final with your ears ringing.

If this had been played in an empty stadium, or on an Aorangi Park practice court in front of just a handful of people, Djokovic would certainly have felt more comfortable. The Centre Court set weren't being hostile – that's not their style – but Djokovic was aware what the crowd had come to see, and it wasn't him bouncing around on the turf, wrapped in a Serbian flag, and kissing the trophy. 'The atmosphere was incredible for Andy, not so much for me.'

The 15,000 spectators were into this from the off, with Murray getting to 0-40 on Djokovic's serve in the opening game. The All England Club had put together a Royal Box they could be proud of – and there were a few other famous faces around Centre Court, such as Ronnie Wood of the Rolling Stones, and Zara and Mike Tindall of the Royal Family – but this wasn't an occasion to be wasted by celebrity-spotting. Djokovic would hold serve in that first game, and Gilbert would later describe that as the key moment of the match, 'as instead of getting down on himself or stewing over it, Murray persevered'.

When you play Djokovic, you really have to take your

chances, but Murray didn't fret about not breaking in the first game, and he also didn't fret when he couldn't convert the first three breakpoint opportunities he had in his opponent's second service game; he just kept on swinging and broke with his fourth. Boris Becker was among those astounded by how much the players had invested at the start of the match: 'The opening exchanges were so fierce that I felt that, psychologically, whoever won the first set would be a step ahead.' The first three games alone had taken 20 minutes. Though Murray immediately dropped his serve, he would score another break, which was enough for the set. Murray was a third of the way there.

Just how important was the appearance of Murray's baseball cap, which arrived after five games of the second set? As a teenager, Murray used to play every match in a cap, and he rarely does so now, so when he put the hat on it looked – in those initial seconds – as though we had all gone back in time. How was a teenage Murray going to deal with this, a Wimbledon final against the best player in the world? But, of course, all that had changed was that Murray now had protection from some of the heat and the glare – it was particularly tough for the server at one end – and maybe the act of putting on the hat changed something.

Granted, it could just as easily have been a coincidence. But here are the facts. A hatless Murray had trailed 1-4 in the second set, and after putting the cap on, he won eight of the next nine games; by the end of that streak, he was 2-0 up in the third set. Djokovic had raged over a line-call towards the end of the second set; he had run out of Hawk-Eye challenges so the only option left was spewing at the umpire. Still, no one should have expected Djokovic to implode from a break down in the third set, and the top seed went on a run of his own, winning four games in succession for a 4-2 lead. But Murray would counter.

Two breaks of the Djokovic serve later, and Murray found himself leading 5-4; all he had to do now was hold serve and he would become the first British man to win Wimbledon since people used to chop down trees to make rackets. Or, if you prefer, the first British champion wearing a baseball cap.

'One little wobble' was how Andy Murray's father Willie later described the tenth game of the third set, in a wonderful example of understatement. Just listen to Nick Bollettieri, regarded by many as the greatest coach of all time, and someone who has been around the tennis block a few times: 'Holy, holy, holy mackerel, and all the fish in the seas – I have been watching tennis for sixty years, and there has never been a more emotionally draining occasion. Oh, baby that was special.'

Would Bollettieri have said that if Murray had just won Wimbledon by beating Djokovic 6-1, 6-2, 6-1? No, of course not. Along with everyone else, Bollettieri had just witnessed the most chaotic, fraught, bewildering and brilliant passage of play ever seen on Centre Court, eclipsing John McEnroe and Bjorn Borg's tiebreak – the so-called War of 18-16 – in the 1980 final. People had camped for two nights, or paid thousands of pounds, for the privilege of watching a match that would cause them more than three hours of suffering. And they never suffered more than in this 12-minute game.

Even Ivan Lendl, who as a player had been so unemotional that he had sometimes been referred to as 'The Blank Czech', and who as a coach had demonstrated that he was capable of sitting through entire grand slam fortnights while maintaining the same non-expression, had forgotten what it was to be either calm or collected. 'Lendl was actually a bit agitated,' said Boris Becker. 'I had never seen him like that before. So he is human after all.'

Pick up a scorecard for this final, and you can't help but immediately turn to that game, and wonder at how much angst and agony is contained in all those dashes and dots on the umpire's grid, akin to the script of a horror movie being transmitted by Morse Code. Never again will Murray experience a service game like this, or play points like that, or contend with those levels of panic, stress and excitement. How Murray would have loved to have taken a mid-game loo break, to have gone off court for a few minutes to splash some water on his face, look himself in the mirror, give himself a pep talk and generally collect himself. But that wasn't an option.

Unlike in American sports, he couldn't form the shape of a 'T' and call a timeout; he just had to stay out there and survive. In all the time that had elapsed since Fred Perry's victory, in all those 77 years, there had never been 12 minutes as excruciating as when Murray served at 5-4. You sensed – and you might have been wrong, but this was how it looked at the time – that whoever won that tenth game of the third set was going to win Wimbledon. Obviously, if Murray won the game, he was already the champion. But if Novak Djokovic broke for 5-5, would Murray have then have been so deflated that he couldn't possibly have been competitive for the remainder of the set and the match? Was the BBC about to find themselves broadcasting The Tennis Apocalypse? And the match itself would just have been the start of it for Murray; he would have had years to relive the time he hadn't converted three Championship points. That's not the sort of experience you're going to get over in a week.

When Murray had served for the US Open's silver trophy, he had thought about Fred Perry, with the Scot giving a few seconds' thought to what he was hopefully about to do for British tennis. Perhaps it had been almost inevitable that Perry would make a guest appearance in Murray's head. After all, Murray had been reminded of him almost every week of his professional life. But that didn't change the fact that Murray was playing primarily for himself, not for Queen and country. And Murray certainly didn't have Perry on his mind as he served for the Wimbledon title; he had more than enough to be processing mentally without giving a moment's thought to Fred.

Or to consider for the umpteenth time that, the year that a British man last won Wimbledon was also the year that the BBC had started broadcasting on television, the British monarchy was going through an abdication crisis, the world's athletes were doing Nazi salutes at the Berlin Olympics, and the book *Gone With The Wind* had just been published.

The First Since Fred

When Perry won the tournament in 1936, did anyone still imagine that, 77 years later, we would still be waiting for the next British male champion on these lawns? The Union flag kept coming out on the day of the final, but only to be draped over the presentation table before some non-Brit lifted the prize.

While Britain waited for another male Wimbledon champion, the Empire disappeared, the Berlin Wall went up, the Berlin Wall came down, man walked on the Moon, the world entered the digital age, and Tim Henman was a tea-time tease. After all that, Perry was still the last champion. To mods, skinheads and the British band Blur, the name 'Fred Perry' meant a brand of their favourite polo-shirts; to anyone in British tennis, and across the sport, his name was forever a reminder of all the years, the decades, that had passed without success (we shouldn't of course forget about Virginia Wade winning the women's title in 1977).

It had been a while since each of the four slams had had a home player win the men's title, but no grand slam nation had waited like the British had. What's two days in the queue, when you've waited three generations for a British champion at Wimbledon? The last home winner at the Australian Open was Mark Edmondson, the champion in 1976, while the last Frenchman to triumph at Roland Garros was Yannick Noah in 1983, and America had hardly been waiting at all since their last winner, which was as recent as Andy Roddick's victory at the 2003 US Open.

No grand slam nation could beat themselves up like Great

Britain could. And Perry, who died in 1996 at the age of 85 after a fall in a hotel bathroom in Melbourne, probably would have quite enjoyed the idea of posthumously tormenting the British tennis establishment. A couple of days before the final, someone wondered what Perry might say to Murray if he had the chance, and the Scot came up with his best line of the summer: 'Why aren't you wearing my kit?' Perry would doubtless have enjoyed that remark, a reference to how Murray had changed kit suppliers from Fred Perry to Adidas.

But would Perry have been smiling down on Murray as the Scot tried to close out a first Wimbledon victory? More likely, given the nature of the match, and Djokovic's reputation for playing himself out of danger, Perry would have been on the edge of some celestial seat (the same part of the seat he would have been on when watching Murray throughout most of the 2012 US Open final).

One tennis modernist once mooted the idea of tennis players wearing heart-rate monitors during matches, with the numbers to be shown live on the video screens inside the stadium and also linked to the television feed – between points, why not also let the crowds listen to the thump-thump-thump. Just imagine if tennis had gone ahead with the idea; there would have been huge concern for Murray's wellbeing as he attempted to serve for the match and then, from being 40-0 up with three Championships points, had found himself breakpoint down. Cardiologists in the crowd would have been making themselves known to the honorary stewards. Could the Victorians have even begun to imagine, during the early years of lawn tennis, what anguish this game would be causing in the 21st century? Anguish not just for the players, but for the spectators, too. Just like everywhere else on Centre Court, the Royal Box was jumping. 'It was just as well there was no sign of the tennis-mad Duchess of Cambridge,' thought Robert Hardman of the *Daily Mail*, 'as this experience could have induced the first royal birth in South London since Elizabeth I came into the world at Greenwich.'

When Murray had sat down at the preceding change of ends, with chants of 'Andy, Andy' all around him, he hadn't felt overwhelmed by what was ahead of him; in fact, he had done just as most coaches and sports psychologists would have recommended if they had had the opportunity, which was to focus on where he was going to serve on the first point. So Murray won the first three points of the game to take the score to 40-0 and to give himself three opportunities, and everything was going as well as anyone could have hoped for. Murray didn't feel that nervous at 40-0, he didn't even feel that anxious at 40-15, but when the scoreboard moved on to 40-30 – rather than what more than 17 million British people were hoping for: game, set and match – tension gripped his body.

By the time Djokovic squared the game at deuce, and then gave himself a point to break serve, Murray was so on edge that he could hardly get air into his lungs. So Murray was playing the biggest game of his life, a game that would define him for the rest of time, and he could hardly breathe and he couldn't think straight. But he was going to have to find a way of getting through this. Somehow, even though his head was now all over the place, he landed a big serve, and Djokovic didn't have the control on his return to put the ball inside the court. Deuce.

But if anyone thought that the panic was over, they were wrong, as on the next point Djokovic's shot struck the tape on top of the net and dribbled over; the Serbian had a second breakpoint. This time, Murray couldn't quickly kill off the danger with a big serve, and a rally broke out. This was an even more impressive save than when he had staved off the first breakpoint, with Murray ending the rally with an angled forehand winner. Deuce again, and Murray and Britain exhaled. Djokovic isn't daft – he would have realised what was going on here. Just break here, Djokovic would have been for-given for thinking, and I can give myself a real chance of winning this match. Still thrusting, Djokovic was, for a third time, a point away from parity in the set.

'When you play Djokovic, we all know it's going to be war out there,' Lendl had said. 'In a final against somebody ranked nine or ten in the world, the match could be a blowout. Against somebody like Novak, it's very unlikely to end up that way. You know at some stage it comes down to who wants it more, who is tougher and who can execute under extreme pressure. I'm not just saying it to sound dramatic – it is war.' That morning, Lendl had reminded Murray to fight for every ball, to give his all in every point, and the Scot had done just that all final. You didn't have to tell Murray that some points were much bigger than others. Think back to the opening stages, and to the tension around the court at the time as a rally had determined whether a server would reach 40-0 or 30-15; here in the tenth game of the third set, these points were worth 50 or 100 times more than those that had once seemed so important.

Murray was aware that the game was 'pretty much taking everything out of me'; with all his emotional energy going into trying to hold serve, how could he possibly cope if he was broken and the match continued? There was a voice in Murray's head asking, 'If this goes the other way, what's going to happen?'

He didn't have the answer to that. What he did have an answer to, in this moment in time, was dealing with Djokovic's game and he saved the Serbian's third breakpoint with a volley winner. Deuce again. Boris Becker thought the Briton was showing his 'heart and soul' in these moments, that he was being 'courageous and bold', and the second seed won a pulsating rally, one he could easily have lost, to give himself another Championship point, his fourth. Murray would later say that he couldn't recall much of the game; that those 12 minutes had just become a blur in his mind. He would later have to watch several replays of the game before he could even begin to appreciate what had happened – figuring out why it had happened was beyond him. What was propelling Murray here? Was it the fact he had always been such a competitive bastard? Or was it instinct? Muscle memory? The crowd?

Or perhaps it really was down to lucky number seven? As most had observed, this was the seventh day of the seventh month, with Murray attempting to become Britain's first male champion for 77 years, and to become the first British singles champion of either sex since Virginia Wade in 1977. And that, on the occasion of Murray's seventh appearance in a slam final, he would be trying to prevent Djokovic winning a seventh major. Some of the nerdier spectators in the crowd would also have picked up on the fact that Murray and Djokovic had been born just seven days apart, in 1987.

A few minutes earlier, when Murray had led 40-0, he had calmly thought to himself, 'Andy, you're about to win Wimbledon,' but as he prepared to serve for the fourth championship point, there was no chance of the world number two getting ahead of himself. Murray's attempt to serve out the match had begun at 5.12pm; now the Centre Court clock was showing 5.24pm, and such was the hysteria inside the stadium that there were a few premature cries when Djokovic's backhand service return flew through the air, the spectators imagining that his shot would bounce long. Murray had known that the ball would be in, so he was already in position to play his next shot, a forehand directed at Djokovic's backhand. It was the last shot that Murray played all afternoon, as Djokovic's response never made it over.

There was a Slazenger in the net, and history had been made at the All England Club. Lendl smiled. The edges of Victoria Beckham's mouth appeared to be turned upwards. And, for the first time since the summer of 1936, since Fred Perry won this competition in trousers, Britain had a men's singles champion. In the time the umpire said, 'Game, set and match, Mr Murray,' half of Centre Court had started to cry, though none so spectacularly as Judy Murray, who was happily weeping.

With the exception of Perry, who would mark victories with a signature leap over the net, just to show his vanquished opponent that he still had much more to give, no tennis player has ever known how he will react after winning a grand slam. They would have rehearsed the moment a thousand times in their head, imagining what it would feel like to win that championship point, but still they would have had no real idea what they would do.

A few Americans had complained after Murray's US Open victory that he hadn't emoted enough, that he hadn't provided the tears, the dosey doe or the big embrace, the Big Fat Emotional Response that the news channels could put on a loop. 'The ending was poor television,' the *New Yorker* magazine noted. 'When it was over it was as if the sensational play on the court had sapped away whatever energy there might be around it. Djokovic did not seem all that dejected, and Murray did not seem at all that excited.'

In America, Murray had just crouched down and put his hand over his mouth. There were a few tears, but most didn't notice them, because he didn't sob again. He was sorry, he later said, if he didn't look that happy on the outside, because he was very happy on the inside. And he wasn't about to change his behaviour, and turn up the dial from looking 'shocked and pleased' to 'ecstatic' just because that's what New York was expecting of him. In a way, there was something quite appealing about Murray's understated reaction, and in the next issue of *Private Eye*, a British satirical magazine, they published a small item on 'The Many Faces of Andy Murray'. The same image was repeated four times, with four different captions: defeat, disappointment, frustration, triumph.

So Murray's Wimbledon celebrations would be natural and spontaneous; he certainly wouldn't be doing anything for effect.

When Djokovic's backhand smacked into the net, Murray turned towards the corner of the court – he had dropped his racket, and his cap had also fallen off – and with both fists raised and pumping, and while letting out a triumphal roar, he stared intently at the media seats. But Murray's first act as a Wimbledon champion shouldn't be interpreted as a rebuke towards the journalists, though the relationship between the champion and those who covered him had not been without its tricky moments over the years.

'Understand: Murray was not declaring payback,' observed S.L.Price of *Sports Illustrated* magazine. 'His life with the British press has never played out like the Athlete vs Media dynamic seen in America; the British press were his prime cheerleaders. And there's the rub. Once Murray broke out in 2005 as their next great hope, the tabs and the broadsheets only served as the bright exposed nerve-end of a deep national need. It wasn't really the faces that he showed his fists on Sunday. It was that need.'

There's another theory – and this one is equally compelling – that Murray's first move, had he been at the same end of the court as his guests-box, would have been to turn and face his 'corner'. But he wasn't, and so after spinning around in that first moment, his eyes locked on faces he recognised. After embracing Djokovic, Murray dropped to his knees on the grass, and then bowed his head. Once he was back on his feet, he was walking around slapping hands with spectators in the front row, and he was floating about, not quite sure what to do with himself. All this was being broadcast to the largest British TV audience of the year to date, and it was a long way from being poor telly.

This had been nothing less than epic. It had been an unexpected end to an unexpected fortnight; while the great majority of the sport's former champions had predicted that Murray would win, had anyone imagined that he would beat the world number one in straight sets? And had there ever been a less straightforward straight-setter? Some past five-setters at the All England Club suddenly seemed a little unremarkable when put next to Murray's excruciating 6-4, 7-5, 6-4 victory. 'If you saw the scores,' noted a past winner, Richard Krajicek, 'you'd think, "Oh, that must have been a boring final," but that was one of the most exciting finals I've ever seen.' It was the product of some three hours and ten minutes of uninterrupted stress. How different this had been from Perry's victory over a German aristocrat, Gottfried von Cramm, in the 1936 final. That truly had been a straightforward and lop-sided straight-setter, with Perry winning 6-1, 6-1, 6-0 after von Cramm injured himself in the opening minutes and tore all the drama out of the day.

Andy Murray: Wimbledon Champion

The first player to have climbed up into the stands after winning Wimbledon was Pat Cash, who did so after his victory over Lendl in 1987. Did the Australian ask anyone's permission before he did that? You would imagine not. But Murray checked first before going mountaineering around Centre Court, asking the tournament referee Andrew Jarrett whether he had time to go to say hello before the presentation ceremony began. 'Yes, if you're quick,' Jarrett replied, and so off Murray went, shaking John McEnroe's hand as he passed the ESPN commentary booth during his climb.

So he hugged and kissed them all – Lendl, his girlfriend Kim Sears, all the important people in his life both on and off the court, all the people who had enabled him to realise his ambition of winning Wimbledon. Murray knew that for Lendl, who as a player had failed in his quest to win the tournament, this victory would be the next best thing to actually being there on the court holding up the trophy himself. 'I am glad I could be part of it,' Lendl would later say. In fact, Murray had hugged and kissed all of them apart from one – he had forgotten his mother, who was seated just behind his guests-box. As the champion would later tell it, he heard his mother 'squealing' behind him and he had to do an about-turn.

On Henman Hill, meanwhile, it was still raining beer, Pimm's and champagne. (As a footnote, let's allow Tim Henman to keep his Hill, as a reminder of all those years of hope, frustration and despair, rather than rushing to rename it Murray Mound.)

Watching Murray hug his mother made Martina Navratilova cry for the second time that afternoon – there had also been tears when he had closed out that game. 'It's amazing for one man to be in a position where he can give millions and millions of people that much pleasure,' she would write in *The Times*. 'And I admit it, I cried. I know what Murray went through to win Wimbledon and then there was the emotion of him hugging everyone and I was saying: "You forgot your mom." I think he didn't know where she was sitting.'

Murray's parents, along with every other one of his guests, later assembled on the competitors' lawn where they drank glasses of champagne and tried to make sense of it all. For Judy, watching her son play at Wimbledon is rarely better than a mixture of 'nausea and heart-attack', but it had never been as extreme as this. 'It's the best feeling ever to see your son winning Wimbledon. This is what he talked about winning since he was a little boy, and it's a dream that has become a reality now,' she said. 'I have been shaking for the last three hours. I was an emotional wreck. I can't remember exactly what happened in that last game. He gutsed it out. There were some outrageous points.' For Willie Murray, the experience had been 'terrific, fantastic, absolutely wonderful, a spectacle, great fun and a bit surreal'. 'I might be biased but I truly do think that this might be the best achievement by a British sportsman ever. It's not bad for a gangly boy from Dunblane, is it?'

Now both Murray brothers were Wimbledon champions, with Andy's victory coming six years after Jamie won the mixed doubles with Serbia's Jelena Jankovic. 'What an incredible day, so proud of my little brother,' said Jamie, who had known before a ball was struck that watching Andy would be 'agony'. Sir Chris Hoy, an Olympic cycling champion, said it had been an honour to have been among Murray's guests.

That morning in Dunblane Cathedral, the minister had said at the morning service: 'There is a certain tennis match going on today. Of course, God doesn't have favourites. But we do. Good luck, Andy.' Murray's paternal grandmother, Ellen Murray, had been too nervous to watch, and so sat in the summer seat by the window of their house in Kilsyth, reliant on Murray's grandfather Gordon for updates.

'It was marvellous. He did it,' she said. 'To see that big smile across his face was lovely.' For the first time in years, Murray's maternal grandparents, Roy and Shirley Erskine, hadn't travelled to Wimbledon as she was recovering from a broken leg. Back in Dunblane, Roy did a little dance. Not long after the match was over, Murray would call. 'How are you doing, Gran?' he enquired, as interested in her wellbeing as he was in telling her what he had been up to on Centre Court. Shirley knew that, for days or even weeks to come, Roy simply wouldn't be able to just 'pop to the shops', that going to the High Street would take a minimum of two hours with locals wanting to talk tennis.

Djokovic could hardly have been more generous and gracious in defeat. 'You threw everything you had at him,' Sue Barker said to him during the on-court debrief, to which he replied, smiling as he said it: 'It still wasn't enough.' During the build-up, had Djokovic felt as though this would be just another grand slam final? Perhaps. But he knew this was no ordinary day in the life of his opponent. Djokovic told the crowd he appreciated how much the result meant to Murray and to the British public, and that he had felt honoured to have been a part of it. Djokovic would also acknowledge that Murray had been the better player at the big moments.

Djokovic's coach, Marian Vajda, is a decent man, and he would also have some kind words to say about Scotland's first Wimbledon singles champion since Harold Mahony in 1896. Navratilova was thrilled when she saw Djokovic's mother Dijana give Judy Murray a congratulatory hug. 'There is such fabulous camaraderie between the two camps, and I didn't want the drama to arise from two personalities not liking each other. I wanted the drama to come from great tennis,' said Navratilova, a winner of a record nine Wimbledon women's singles titles. Around the grounds, everyone was hugging everyone else. Welcome to British tennis's summer of love. The mood at the All England Club was such that Alex Salmond, Scotland's First Minister, was just about forgiven for pulling a Saltire from his wife's handbag and waving it around the Royal Box.

The trophy that the Duke of Kent presented to Murray didn't have his name on it, which threw him at first. 'When I looked at the Wimbledon trophy and my name wasn't on it, there was a moment when I thought, "What's going on?" To hold that unique, historic trophy on Centre Court was an incredible feeling, but when I was looking down the names of the past winners, I couldn't find my own,' Murray disclosed in a column on the BBC website. 'But it turns out they've run out of space over the years and my name is on the base, so I didn't actually get to see my name when I was handed the trophy, but I can confirm that it's on the one I have at home.'

There was no gushing from Murray, no tears either. Murray's on-court interview began with Barker saying to him: 'I don't know if you realise what you've just done.' (She also informed him that watching that last game had been torturous, to which he replied: 'Just imagine playing it.') Becker thought there would be a moment when Murray would suddenly think to himself, 'Wow, what have I done?'

That moment didn't come as Murray strolled around the lawn cuddling his trophy. And it also didn't come when he left Centre Court and was shown the board of champions – there was space left for him there – or when he was taken to a balcony out the back to show off his prize and to pump his fist at his public below, many of the crowds on Henman Hill having made their way across the grounds to see the champion in the flesh. No, something approaching a wow moment came almost an hour after the final, when Murray plonked himself on a chair just before peeing into a sample bottle for the dope testers. 'I sat down. I was waiting to do the drugs test and it just hit me. I got so tired and everything started to sink in.' Note the 'started' in that sentence; he almost certainly still didn't fully comprehend what he had achieved. The comment that best summed up Murray's thinking was this one: 'Wimbledon is the pinnacle of tennis. Winning Wimbledon,

I still can't believe it, can't get my head around it.' Murray was happy, and he was bewildered.

After every Wimbledon final, the two players return to the same locker-room; Murray was very aware of how Djokovic would have been feeling, and so didn't want to upset his 'professional friend' by dancing on the benches, or leaping about the place. Celebrating in an opponent's face has never been Murray's style. Murray probably thinks braggadocio is cold meat, and, anyway, he didn't have the energy. Still, Murray's backstage celebrations wouldn't have been complete without someone hosing him down with a bottle of champagne. Murray covered his face with a towel to stop the bubbles getting in his eyes, emerging a few seconds later to take a swig, which he hated, not enjoying the burn on his throat.

It had been the best day of Murray's life, and it wasn't over yet, as he was off to the ball. Well, actually he wasn't, as the All England Club's post-tournament black-tie function is a dinner rather than a ball, and the men's champion doesn't dance with the women's champion – still, no one would have stopped Murray or Marion Bartoli if they had felt like doing the Can-Can as they made their entrances at a Park Lane hotel.

Wimbledon is the only one of the four grand slams to hold such a dinner for the champions. After winning the US Open, Murray and his team made their own fun at a Chinese restaurant in midtown Manhattan – though Lendl skipped it, saying he was too tired, to which Murray responded: 'Tired? He just sat there. I'm the one who has played for five hours.' The formal part of Murray's New York celebrations had come the following day when a reception was held in his honour at the British Consul-General's residence on East 51st Street, with a piper playing 'Scotland the Brave' as he arrived. For all the guests, there were sausage rolls, cucumber sandwiches, balloons and mini-flags. For Murray, there was a hamper full of British junk-food: Hob-Nobs, salt and vinegar Hula Hoops, winegums and Maltesers. Murray reached first for a bottle of Irn-Bru, the bright orange fizzy drink.

There could be no doubt that dressing up in a tuxedo added to the sense of occasion after Murray's triumph at the All England Club. You don't win Wimbledon and then disappear into the night. After arriving around midnight, Murray was fed – he sat down to a dinner of sea trout, crab and seared scallop, followed by halibut, then flourless chocolate cake, and finishing off with coffee and petits fours. He was also feted, with the guests giving him a standing ovation. It was during the dinner, incidentally, that Murray was reminded of the £1.6 million he had won for his efforts over the fortnight; until then, he hadn't given a moment's thought to the money. One guest reported that he had never seen Lendl smile so much in such a short period of time (he hadn't ducked out this time). Murray left the party at 2am, accompanied by his girlfriend, walking beside him in bare feet.

Andy Murray was whacked – 'subconsciously, everything that goes with Wimbledon, the pressure, the tension, the questions and the build-up, not just now but for years, took their toll' – yet he had slept for just an hour and a half. And it wouldn't have been the best hour and a half of sleep he had ever had, as he and Kim Sears had allowed their dogs, Maggie May and Rusty, into the bed. Still, given the peculiar dreams that Murray sometimes has after big occasions – after the 2012 Wimbledon final, for instance, his mind had tricked him into believing he had actually beaten Roger Federer – it was probably for the best that there hadn't been much time to snooze and to dream.

'You don't want to go to sleep in case you wake up and it didn't actually happen,' Murray would later disclose, so he lay in bed sending text messages to his friends (throughout the Wimbledon fortnight, he hadn't checked his phone as often as he normally would have done, just as he had avoided newspapers and the internet, which was an 'unnatural but necessary' way to try to protect himself, though he had still found that he 'literally couldn't escape').

After climbing out of bed around 6am, and feeding and walking the Border Terriers, Murray went to have a look at his trophy, then showered and pulled on a pair of blue jeans and a grey tracksuit top in readiness for his 'media blitz'. It was the morning after what Murray's manager, Simon Fuller, regarded as the greatest occasion in British sport since England won the football World Cup in 1966 – 'everyone's in heaven,' he had exclaimed – and Britain's first Wimbledon champion for 77 years returned to the All England Club for several hours of interviews.

Perry would have been horrified by Murray's media obligations. Long gone were the days when the champion could escape after one press conference and a couple of broadcast interviews, all of which would have been completed on the day of the final. One journalist who saw him that morning – Christopher Clarey of the *New York Times* – thought that Murray 'looked good' for someone who had only had an hour and a half's kip, and 'his voice always sounds like he has had ninety minutes of sleep'.

There were a few yawns along the way but Murray, who had felt 'beaten up' on waking, was deliriously happy and running on adrenaline. 'You're ours now, you belong to us,' Holly Willoughby, a presenter on ITV's *This Morning*, gushed at Murray, and she also wanted to talk to him about his love life: 'I'm trying to think what your next challenge will be. You've had the US Open, the Olympics, now Wimbledon, could it be popping the question?' To which Murray politely replied: 'I only met you ten minutes ago, so I wouldn't be telling you first.' There was a sometimes surreal interview on BBC Radio Four's *Today* programme, with the presenter John Humphrys asking Murray whether he liked smooth or fluffy tennis balls, and whether he would prefer to be the prime minister or Wimbledon champion. 'Er,' Murray said, 'I don't know a great deal about politics.'

Murray relived that 'crazy' final game. 'When Novak had breakpoints, it was panic time,' Murray wrote in his column on the BBC website. 'I must admit that if I'd lost that game, I don't know whether I'd have recovered. To come through was such a relief, and I can't imagine I'll ever feel pressure like that again.' Murray also said: 'When I came off court I had no recollection of that game. It was just a crazy way to finish the match and I didn't think it would have happened for me any other way. For everyone watching, it needed to be like that to make it even more special.'

As Murray flicked through that morning's British newspapers – there was a whole coffee table covered with front-page images of himself – he would have gained more understanding of what he has accomplished. 'Seventy-seven years. That really is an awfully long time,' Simon Barnes wrote on the front page of *The Times*. 'The world has changed beyond recognition – in society, in politics, in population, in wealth, in technology, in destruction. It seemed that the only constant was the British failure to win their own championship.'

On the cover of the *Daily Telegraph*, Paul Hayward declared that 'the most painful wait in sport is over'. 'The shame has passed. Frustration has been banished. Wimbledon fortnight is no longer a ritual of hope and despair.' But perhaps, for Murray to truly appreciate the significance of his achievement, he should have sought out some of the international press coverage. The outsiders – the international press – had some interesting takes, with the *New York Times* wondering: 'Whatever will the British talk about at Wimbledon next year? For 77 years they had Fred Perry and the noble yet clearly star-crossed search for his successor as a conversation starter in early summer days at the All England Club. But now, in a flurry of booming serves and full-stretch forehand winners, Andy Murray has given them the privilege of moving on.'

The Spanish title *Marca* noted that Murray had 'chased

away the ghosts of the past', while the French sports newspaper *L'Equipe* observed: 'The best things are often those you have to wait a long time for. After 77 years of waiting and disappointments, Great Britain has been able to scream out its delight. When Djokovic's backhand found the net you had to understand the collective monster cry from the crowds on Centre Court that were on the verge of a nervous breakdown, then look at the incredulous face of Murray after the match point. You had to see the champion submerged by emotion.' Some of the kindest words were in the Serbian press, with *Blic* thinking it wouldn't have been a surprise if Britain had marked Murray's victory with Big Ben striking 77 times, 'once for each year without a Wimbledon champion. If it happens, we shouldn't blame them, as they had long desired a king on the throne.'

One of the most memorable images of the day was of Murray posing in front of Perry's statue. It was almost as if, now Murray had the Wimbledon trophy, he was finally able to linger by the bronze of Perry. Maybe word had reached Murray of how Perry's children were happy for him. 'I am thrilled that a British man has finally won Wimbledon again,' said Perry's son, David. 'I think my father would have said, "Do you know what, it's time for somebody else to have that title."'

Perry's daughter Penny suggested that her father would have 'absolutely been in hysterical mode because we have a British champion, and he was patriotic, but it also would have been bittersweet. It's the same when anyone breaks your record. He was human after all. And you're not human if an element of you isn't saying, "Goddamnit". I can't believe Andy played that way. I'm absolutely stunned. I need a cup of tea.'

Bud Collins, the most experienced American tennis commentator of them all, told Murray of the conversations he had had with Perry each summer. 'Every year I'd come to Wimbledon and I'd say to Fred, "Is this the year?" He'd say, "I don't think so." It went on like that for several years and finally Fred couldn't make it any more. Anyway, he kept hoping this day would happen, and I'm glad to report it has.' Murray, who was pleased to hear what Collins had to say, thought it was a shame that he had never had the chance to meet Perry and to talk shop.

Murray's return visit to the All England Club also gave him the opportunity to stroll around an empty Centre Court to chat with some of the groundsmen. But he couldn't hang around, as his was a carefully choreographed day, including an event for Adidas in Kennington in London where he played 100 mini-matches against amateurs. In an indication of Murray's new status, Prime Minister David Cameron, Deputy Prime Minister Nick Clegg, Leader of the Opposition Ed Miliband and the SNP's Westminster leader Angus Robertson had all cleared time in their diaries for an afternoon reception held in his honour in Downing Street.

The *Guardian* thought Murray, who had worn a suit for the occasion, 'was the coolest dude in the Rose Garden, alongside the guffawing PM, his normally morose sidekick Clegg and

Miliband, who could do with a good laugh'. Earlier in the day, Cameron had suggested that Murray deserved a knighthood (though he did stress that the process was independent). It wasn't the first time that a knighthood had been mooted, but Murray's stance appeared to have changed. After his US Open victory, Murray thought it would be premature for him to graduate from Mister to Sir, saying that no one should be knighted for just one good tournament, but now he sounded as though he embraced the idea a bit more.

It was inevitable, after Cameron's remarks, and also the images of Murray at Downing Street, that Westminster's commentators and cartoonists would tease politicians for thinking there were votes in being associated with a Wimbledon champion. A cartoon in *The Times* recreated the moment when Murray had let the racket fall to the ground, only now he had several politicians desperately clinging to the bottom of his shirt. The truth is, the politicians were damned either way; if they have a drinks party, they're accused of trying to hijack Murray, and if they don't they will be charged with ignoring Britain's best tennis player since the 1930s. Here was a thought, though: for the first time, people were being accused of trying to buy, borrow or steal some of the public's warmth and goodwill for Andy Murray.

There was one awkward moment for Murray at the end of his first full day as Wimbledon champion, which came as he was leaving Nobu restaurant after a dinner with friends. He wouldn't have enjoyed the paparazzi's sodium-white flashes very much; but what he would have liked even less was being poked in the eye with a programme by an autograph-hunter wanting it signed. As Murray was driven off, he rubbed at his eye. But thankfully for Murray, and for the fan, the Scot was fine and didn't have to spend the next week wearing an eye-patch.

Walking from the restaurant door to the car door couldn't have taken longer than a minute or so, but that had been long enough for Murray to have had it confirmed in his mind that there was much about fame he still didn't like. Djokovic hadn't slunk away. Across town, he was hosting a charity function for his own foundation, with Kate Hudson, Goldie Hawn, Marion Bartoli, Sarah Ferguson and Boris Becker among the guests. That was never going to be a downbeat occasion – Djokovic doesn't need to be told, when raising money for disadvantaged children, that worse things can happen to you in life than losing a Wimbledon final – but that could have been a very different party if the Serbian had broken Murray in that tenth game of the third set.

In the days that followed, there was a partial return to normality – Murray went to the dentist – but also much happened that was a long way from the ordinary. The Royal Mail announced plans for a commemorative set of stamps, while the Royal Horticultural Society announced that they had named a flower – a dark-stemmed dahlia with a golden flower – after him. His victory was referenced in an episode of *EastEnders*. He processed the fact that the Queen had sent him a private message, and that David Beckham had called to say well done. But he was just as pleased, if not more so, that tennis players and coaches had sent him notes of congratulations, as he had always sought the respect of the industry.

News filtered through of a yachtsman off the Isle of Wight having to be rescued by a lifeboat after dislocating his shoulder as he jumped into the water to celebrate Murray's victory. A few days before the tournament had started, Murray had been talking to his team about having a good look around the Wimbledon Museum; now the curators were asking for the clothes he had worn for his victory, and he was happy to help them with the request. Some bookmakers were already paying out on Murray winning the BBC's Sports Personality of The Year award. The sun was out – there was a post-Wimbledon heatwave – and Britain had a champion. In short, life was good.

So Murray took a short break with Kim Sears in the Bahamas (paparazzi shots would show them playing with bats and a ball in the surf), leaving others to speculate about what he would do next on a tennis court. Lendl appeared to suggest, regardless of what the ranking computer said – it stated quite clearly and accurately that Djokovic was the world number one – that Murray was the best player in the world. After all, Lendl said, on leaving the All England Club, Murray was now in possession of two grand slam titles, in addition to the Olympic gold, while Djokovic and Nadal had one slam each.

Could Murray go on to become Britain's first world number one? He would certainly have every chance, but he was more interested in winning grand slam titles than in reaching the top of the list. Obviously, one tends to follow the other, but, given a choice between the ranking and bagging more slams, Murray would always pick the majors. As Lendl put it, you remember how many slams you win; you don't recall how many weeks you spend at the top of the rankings.

For Lendl and Murray, this certainly wasn't the culmination of their project. In the hours after Murray's victory, Lendl was probably already thinking how the Briton could better himself. In their first year and a half together, Murray had won three of the biggest prizes in tennis – one gold medal and two majors – but he was aware that Lendl wouldn't have been completely satisfied with that, with his coach thinking that he could have also finished as 2013 Australian Open champion. But the future looked good. Winning Wimbledon doesn't mean you will never experience self-doubt again, but it was fair to assume that Murray would spend the rest of his tennis life just that bit freer.

John McEnroe was of the opinion that Murray could go on to win as many as six grand slam titles, while Richard Krajicek thought the Scot could score up to nine, and Mats Wilander was the boldest when he said double figures was possible: 'I think Andy can win six, seven, eight, nine, ten majors.' At any other time in Murray's career, people would have heard those comments and wondered whether McEnroe, Krajicek and Wilander had been hitting the champagne bars. And it's true that a lot of bold predictions and projections are made in the immediate aftermath of every grand slam final. But that Sunday afternoon at Wimbledon had changed people's perception of Murray, the young man from 'The Worst Tennis

Nation in the World'. As Murray's manager Simon Fuller had said (and no one had accused him of hyperbole): 'Anything is possible.'

Whatever happened to Murray in the rest of his tennis life, he already knew that he would never have a greater day than that sunny Sunday when he won Wimbledon. 'I'll never top that. Anything I do now, I'll never have the same pressure, that same expectation, that same release, after the match,' Murray has said. 'I hope I don't lose that hunger and my plan is to use this experience as motivation. I know what it is like to lose a Wimbledon final and to win one – and it's a lot better winning than losing.'

Acknowledgements

I'm indebted to my fellow tennis writers for their help with this project, and in particular to Simon Cambers of The Tennis Space, the *Independent*'s Paul Newman, and Stuart Fraser. My thanks to Ian Marshall, Kyle McEnery and the rest of the brilliant team at Simon & Schuster, and to David Luxton of David Luxton Associates.

Andy Murray's Career Record

Grand slam record

2005 Wimbledon:
- First round: Beat George Bastl (Switzerland) in straight sets
- Second round: Beat Radek Stepanek (Czech Republic) in straight sets
- Third round: Lost to David Nalbandian (Argentina) in five sets

2005 US Open:
- Murray won three rounds of qualifying to reach the main draw
- First round: Beat Andrei Pavel (Romania) in five sets
- Second round: Lost to Arnaud Clement (France) in five sets

2006 Australian Open:
- First round: Lost to Juan Ignacio Chela (Argentina) in straight sets

2006 French Open:
- First round: Lost to Gael Monfils (France) in straight sets

2006 Wimbledon:
- First round: Beat Nicolas Massu (Chile) in straight sets
- Second round: Beat Julien Benneteau (France) in four sets
- Third round: Beat Andy Roddick (USA) in straight sets
- Fourth round: Lost to Marcos Baghdatis (Cyprus) in three sets

2006 US Open:
- First round: Beat Robert Kendrick (USA) in four sets
- Second round: Beat Alessio Di Mauro (Italy) in straight sets
- Third round: Beat Fernando Gonzalez (Chile) in five sets
- Fourth round: Lost to Nikolay Davydenko (Russia) in four sets

2007 Australian Open:
- First round: Beat Alberto Martin (Spain) in straight sets
- Second round: Beat Fernando Verdasco (Spain) in straight sets
- Third round: Beat Juan Ignacio Chela (Argentina) in straight sets
- Fourth round: Lost to Rafa Nadal (Spain) in five sets

Murray missed the 2007 French Open and Wimbledon because of a wrist injury.

Andy Murray's Career Record

2007 US Open:
- First round: Beat Pablo Cuevas (Uruguay) in straight sets
- Second round: Beat Jonas Bjorkman (Sweden) in five sets
- Third round: Lost to Hyung-Taik Lee (Korea) in four sets

2008 Australian Open:
- First round: Lost to Jo-Wilfried Tsonga (France) in four sets

2008 French Open:
- First round: Beat Jonathan Eysseric (France) in five sets
- Second round: Beat Jose Acasuso (Argentina) in straight sets
- Third round: Lost to Nicolas Almagro (Spain) in four sets

2008 Wimbledon:
- First round: Beat Fabrice Santoro (France) in straight sets
- Second round: Beat Xavier Malisse (Belgium) in straight sets
- Third round: Beat Tommy Haas (Germany) in four sets
- Fourth round: Beat Richard Gasquet (France) in five sets
- Quarter-final: Lost to Rafa Nadal (Spain) in straight sets

2008 US Open:
- First round: Beat Sergio Roitman (Argentina) in straight sets
- Second round: Beat Michael Llodra (France) in four sets
- Third round: Beat Jurgen Melzer (Austria) in five sets
- Fourth round: Beat Stanislas Wawrinka (Switzerland) in straight sets
- Quarter-final: Beat Juan Martin del Potro (Argentina) in four sets

- Semi-final: Beat Rafa Nadal (Spain) in four sets
- Final: Lost to Roger Federer (Switzerland) in straight sets

2009 Australian Open:
- First round: Beat Andrei Pavel (Romania) after a retirement in the second set
- Second round: Beat Marcel Granollers (Spain) in straight sets
- Third round: Beat Jurgen Melzer (Austria) in straight sets
- Fourth round: Lost to Fernando Verdasco (Spain) in five sets

2009 French Open:
- First round: Beat Juan Ignacio Chela (Argentina) in straight sets
- Second round: Beat Potito Starace (Italy) in four sets
- Third round: Beat Janko Tipsarevic (Serbia) after a retirement in the second set
- Fourth round: Beat Marin Cilic (Croatia) in straight sets
- Quarter-final: Lost to Fernando Gonzalez (Chile) in four sets

2009 Wimbledon:
- First round: Beat Robert Kendrick (USA) in four sets
- Second round: Beat Ernests Gulbis (Latvia) in straight sets
- Third round: Beat Viktor Troicki (Serbia) in straight sets
- Fourth round: Beat Stanislas Wawrinka (Switzerland) in five sets
- Quarter-final: Beat Juan Carlos Ferrero (Spain) in straight sets
- Semi-final: Lost to Andy Roddick (USA) in four sets

Andy Murray's Career Record

2009 US Open:
- First round: Beat Ernests Gulbis (Latvia) in straight sets
- Second round: Beat Paul Capdeville (Chile) in four sets
- Third round: Beat Taylor Dent (USA) in straight sets
- Fourth round: Lost to Marin Cilic (Croatia) in straight sets

2010 Australian Open:
- First round: Beat Kevin Anderson (South Africa) in straight sets
- Second round: Beat Marc Gicquel (France) in straight sets
- Third round: Beat Florent Serra (France) in straight sets
- Fourth round: Beat John Isner (USA) in straight sets
- Quarter-final: Beat Rafa Nadal (Spain) after a retirement in the third set
- Semi-final: Beat Marin Cilic (Croatia) in four sets
- Final: Lost to Roger Federer (Switzerland) in straight sets

2010 French Open:
- First round: Beat Richard Gasquet (France) in five sets
- Second round: Beat Juan Ignacio Chela (Argentina) in four sets
- Third round: Beat Marcos Baghdatis (Cyprus) in four sets
- Fourth round: Lost to Tomas Berdych (Czech Republic) in straight sets

2010 Wimbledon:
- First round: Beat Jan Hajek (Czech Republic) in straight sets
- Second round: Beat Jarkko Nieminen (Finland) in straight sets

- Third round: Beat Gilles Simon (France) in straight sets
- Fourth round: Beat Sam Querrey (USA) in straight sets
- Quarter-final: Beat Jo-Wilfried Tsonga (France) in four sets
- Semi-final: Lost to Rafa Nadal (Spain) in straight sets

2010 US Open:
- First round: Beat Lukas Lacko (Slovakia) in straight sets
- Second round: Beat Dustin Brown (Germany) in straight sets
- Third round: Lost to Stanislas Wawrinka (Switzerland) in four sets

2011 Australian Open:
- First round: Beat Karol Beck (Slovakia) after a retirement in the third set
- Second round: Beat Illya Marchenko (Ukraine) in straight sets
- Third round: Beat Guillermo Garcia-Lopez (Spain) in straight sets
- Fourth round: Beat Jurgen Melzer (Austria) in straight sets
- Quarter-final: Beat Alexandr Dolgopolov (Ukraine) in four sets
- Semi-final: Beat David Ferrer (Spain) in four sets
- Final: Lost to Novak Djokovic (Serbia) in straight sets

2011 French Open:
- First round: Beat Eric Prodon (France) in straight sets
- Second round: Beat Simone Bolelli (Italy) in straight sets

- Third round: Beat Michael Berrer (Germany) in straight sets
- Fourth round: Beat Viktor Troicki (Serbia) in five sets
- Quarter-final: Beat Juan Ignacio Chela (Argentina) in straight sets
- Semi-final: Lost to Rafa Nadal (Spain) in straight sets

2011 Wimbledon:
- First round: Beat Daniel Gimeno-Traver (Spain) in four sets
- Second round: Beat Tobias Kamke (Germany) in straight sets
- Third round: Beat Ivan Ljubicic (Croatia) in four sets
- Fourth round: Beat Richard Gasquet (France) in straight sets
- Quarter-final: Beat Feliciano Lopez (Spain) in straight sets
- Semi-final: Lost to Rafa Nadal (Spain) in four sets

2011 US Open:
- First round: Beat Somdev Devvarman (India) in straight sets
- Second round: Beat Robin Haase (Netherlands) in five sets
- Third round: Beat Feliciano Lopez (Spain) in straight sets
- Fourth round: Beat Donald Young (USA) in straight sets
- Quarter-final: Beat John Isner (USA) in four sets
- Semi-final: Lost to Rafa Nadal (Spain) in four sets

2012 Australian Open:
- First round: Beat Ryan Harrison (USA) in four sets
- Second round: Beat Edouard Roger-Vasselin (France) in straight sets
- Third round: Beat Michael Llodra (France) in straight sets

- Fourth round: Beat Mikhail Kukushkin (Kazakhstan) after a retirement in the third set
- Quarter-final: Beat Kei Nishikori (Japan) in straight sets
- Semi-final: Lost to Novak Djokovic (Serbia) in five sets

2012 French Open:
- First round: Beat Tatsuma Ito (Japan) in straight sets
- Second round: Beat Jarkko Nieminen (Finland) in four sets
- Third round: Beat Santiago Giraldo (Colombia) in straight sets
- Fourth round: Beat Richard Gasquet (France) in four sets
- Quarter-final: Lost to David Ferrer (Spain) in four sets

2012 Wimbledon:
- First round: Beat Nikolay Davydenko (Russia) in straight sets
- Second round: Beat Ivo Karlovic (Croatia) in four sets
- Third round: Beat Marcos Baghdatis (Cyprus) in four sets
- Fourth round: Beat Marin Cilic (Croatia) in straight sets
- Quarter-final: Beat David Ferrer (Spain) in four sets
- Semi-final: Beat Jo-Wilfried Tsonga (France) in four sets
- Final: Lost to Roger Federer (Switzerland) in four sets

2012 US Open:
- First round: Beat Alex Bogomolov Junior (Russia) in straight sets
- Second round: Beat Ivan Dodig (Croatia) in straight sets
- Third round: Beat Feliciano Lopez (Spain) in four sets
- Fourth round: Beat Milos Raonic (Canada) in straight sets

- Quarter-final: Beat Marin Cilic (Croatia) in four sets
- Semi-final: Beat Tomas Berdych (Czech Republic) in four sets
- Final: Beat Novak Djokovic (Serbia) in five sets

2013 Australian Open
- First round: Beat Robin Haase (Netherlands) in straight sets
- Second round: Beat Joao Sousa (Portugal) in straight sets
- Third round: Beat Ricardas Berankis (Lithuania) in straight sets
- Fourth round: Beat Gilles Simon (France) in straight sets
- Quarter-final: Beat Jeremy Chardy (France) in straight sets
- Semi-final: Beat Roger Federer (Switzerland) in five sets
- Final: Lost to Novak Djokovic (Serbia) in four sets

Murray did not play the 2013 French Open because of a back injury.

2013 Wimbledon:
- First round: Beat Benjamin Becker (Germany) in straight sets.
- Second round: Beat Yen-Hsun Lu (Chinese Taipei) in straight sets.
- Third round: Beat Tommy Robredo (Spain) in straight sets.
- Fourth round: Beat Mikhail Youzhny (Russia) in straight sets.
- Quarter-final: Beat Fernando Verdasco (Spain) in five sets.
- Semi-final: Beat Jerzy Janowicz (Poland) in four sets.
- Final: Beat Novak Djokovic (Serbia) in straight sets.

Other career highlights

First final on the ATP Tour:
In Bangkok in 2005

First title on the ATP Tour:
In San Jose in 2006

Year-end ranking:
2003: 546
2004: 51
2005: 64
2006: 17
2007: 11
2008: 4
2009: 4
2010: 4
2011: 4
2012: 3

****

2012 Olympic Games singles (best of three sets apart from the final, which was the best of five sets):
- First round: Beat Stanislas Wawrinka (Switzerland) in straight sets
- Second round: Beat Jarkko Nieminen (Finland) in straight sets

Andy Murray's Career Record

- Third round: Beat Marcos Baghdatis (Cyprus) in three sets
- Quarter-final: Beat Nicolas Almagro (Spain) in straight sets
- Semi-final: Beat Novak Djokovic (Serbia) in straight sets
- Final: Beat Roger Federer (Switzerland) in straight sets

Murray also won a silver medal in the Olympic mixed doubles tournament, with Laura Robson.